D0915716

THE CONCEPT OF REALITY

By the same author

Ironie als Daseinsform bei Soeren Kierkegaard
Husserl and Phenomenology
Von Husserl zu Sartre
Phenomenology and Philosophical Understanding (ed.)

THE CONCEPT OF REALITY

Edo Pivčević

St. Martin's Press   New York

© 1986 by Edo Pivčević

First published in the United States of America in 1986

ISBN 0-312-16007-0

Library of Congress Cataloging in Publication Data

Pivčević, Edo
    The concept of reality.

    Bibliography: p.
    Includes index.
    1. Philosophy—Addresses, essays, lectures.
    2. Reality—Addresses, essays, lectures. I. Title.
    B29.P57   1985   110   85-19578
    ISBN 0-312-16007-0

Printed and bound in Great Britain by
Redwood Burn Limited, Trowbridge, Wiltshire

Contents

Truth is no harlot who throws her arms round the neck of him who does not desire her; on the contrary, she is so coy a beauty that even the man who sacrifices everything to her can still not be certain of her favours.

A. Schopenhauer, *The World as Will and Representation*

Preface

All philosophical problems are interconnected, but the connections are often complex and hard to detect. Yet unless some method can be found of discovering these connections, there is little chance of gaining sufficient clarity about the range and significance of any such problems, let alone solving them. What is needed is an insight into the structure of the context of which such problems form part, and this requires an approach on a broad front. This is not to underrate the value of a piecemeal micro-analytical effort designed to clear the undergrowth of ambiguity and error surrounding individual issues. But unless such an effort forms part of a wider strategy that transcends parochial boundaries, its results are likely to remain meagre.

Consider an issue which has recently once again occupied the centre stage of philosophical debate. It concerns the conflict between what might be called the 'mentalist' and the 'anti-mentalist' interpretation of experiences. From Descartes onwards this conflict has increasingly come to be connected with the problem of how to deal with the sceptic's attack on the common sense belief in the existence of an 'external world'. In general, those who (with Descartes) take the view that the sceptic's arguments are important and should be taken seriously, tend to argue that the only safe way to begin is to concentrate on what is accessible to immediate experience, and moreover that experiences are such as can be accurately described, in the final analysis, only from the experiencer's own point of view; whereas those who reject the sceptical assault on common sense as incoherent tend to argue that the content of experiences, such as can be communicated in words, depends more on external matters of fact than on what is going on 'inside our heads', and hence that there is a sense in which all 'mental contents' can be said to be *publicly accessible*.

All such arguments, I shall maintain, are fruitless and do not advance our understanding of the nature of reality one whit. If the sceptic's argument is incoherent, and hence (as is claimed) cannot be used to justify an 'internalist' approach to experiences, the anti-sceptical argument, if closely examined, can be seen to be circular, and hence cannot be plausibly employed to underpin an 'externalist' style of reasoning. Neither side is able to present a convincing case for the simple reason that they both underestimate the complexity of the issues involved.

In an effort to counter such defective moves it is sometimes urged that the internal/external distinction, and indeed all other cognitive categories, should be treated as social constructs. The concepts in terms of which we try to make sense of what we experience, it is argued, all have a social history; therefore a description of the world should appropriately begin with an investigation into the nature of 'social praxis'. But this approach clearly cannot provide a satisfactory solution either, for in addition to involving an a priori commitment to the existence of other selves, it leads to obvious difficulties, inasmuch as it tends to obscure the distinction between the historical and the logical conditions of meaning and knowledge.

So the question is, how should we approach the task of making the world intelligible to ourselves? Indeed what exactly is meant by 'the world'?

The view that I shall defend in the following pages is that an answer to this, so far as an adequate answer can be given at all, should be sought by subjecting the basic philosophical categories to a comprehensive contextual analysis. The world, I shall argue, can be appropriately described only in terms of *structure*. The world is not an entity nor a collection of entities or species of entities, be they physical or non-physical. The concept of an entity is not a logically primary concept. Nor, for that matter, does this status belong to the concept of an event, if, that is, events are conceived in a purely naturalistic sense. Perhaps the first major philosopher of the modern age radically to challenge the post-Renaissance science-inspired metaphysics of entities, or naturalistically conceived events, was Hegel. In fact, the kind of approach that I shall be advocating has a certain degree of affinity with Hegel's own project, although unlike him, I do not think that clear sense can be made of the idea that the structure which is the world represents part of a self-displaying activity of a cosmic agent. The structure has no core, no metaphysical centre.

In some chapters I have made use of the material that I have previously published in the form of articles. I am grateful to the Editors of *Mind*, the *Review of Metaphysics* and *Sociology*, respectively, for allowing me to use this material. Although I am now severely critical of some of the theses and arguments put forward in those articles, they contain a quantity of what still seems to me to be a valid and useful analysis.

This book has benefited over the long period of its gestation from the many discussions I have had with friends and colleagues about the various theses and arguments advanced in it. I am particularly grateful to John Cleave for his helpful comments and constant encouragement. I have also greatly profited from comments by Sir Peter Strawson, Rom Harré and Michael Dummett, all of whom have read earlier drafts of various chapters. Last but not least, I am indebted to Stephan Körner, a colleague and friend of long standing, who has always taken an active and sympathetic interest in my work. It is to him that this book is dedicated.

Bristol 1985   F. P.

1. The Problem of Reality

There is nothing easier to understand, it seems, than what facts are; and yet there is nothing that is more elusive. We distinguish between fact and fiction but there is, it would seem, precious little that we can say about this distinction beyond asserting it. Facts are simply facts, the opposite of fiction. Everyone is confident he knows what this means. We feel sure we understand this distinction just as we feel sure we understand the distinction between truth and falsehood, or the distinction between good and evil. It is when we make an attempt to clarify it that the confidence begins to desert us in the face of difficulties.

For what reply could we give if asked to explain the meaning of 'fact'? In a sense, it is not unlike being asked to define the quality red. In either case there is, it seems, little that we could do except give examples. Thus we might look around and point to something red and say 'This is coloured red'; and then, perhaps, in order to forestall any tendency to mistake the word for the name of a particular shade of red, gesture towards another thing of a similar but not quite the same hue, and add 'And that is red too'. Analogously one might say 'that the Earth is round is a fact', 'that Ruritania does not exist is a fact'. Facts are whatever it is that is expressed by true propositions, and 'The Earth is round' and 'Ruritania does not exist' both happen to be true.

But this explains nothing at all. Examples do not define, they illustrate; and they are illustrative only to those who are capable of grasping the general concept that underlies them and represents their 'species-identity'. The concept is their governing rule, their principle of unity. Yet what 'rule' do the above examples come under? The red thing A is colour-similar – as distinct from shape-similar or size-similar, although it can be all of these – to the red thing B. But their colour cannot be defined in terms of their colour-similarity. To say that A and B are colour-similar is not to say *what* colour they are. Their colour-similarity is a necessary condition of their belonging to

1

the same colour species, not a definition of their colour.

So how should one define that which both 'The Earth is round' and 'Ruritania does not exist' have in common? They both express facts, we have said; but this reveals little. What is required is an explication of the principle under which they both can be classified under the same species of item. If, being true, they both portray certain aspects of reality, just what is meant by 'reality'?

That the question is not an idle one can be seen if one looks a little more closely at the second of our two examples. On the face of it, in asserting that Ruritania does not exist we seem to be asserting something about Ruritania. But if the asserted proposition is about Ruritania, then surely it must be false, for in that case the subject term has a reference, i.e. there is something for the proposition to be true *about*. If, on the other hand, the proposition is true, then by the same token it cannot be about Ruritania, for Ruritania does not exist; it is fiction. This ancient puzzle has prompted some philosophers to draw a distinction between 'being' and actual existence, and to claim that what is being talked about in such cases has being, even though it does not exist in reality. Others have criticised such a view on the grounds that it introduces an undesirable ambiguity into the concept of existence, and have argued that propositions of this kind should not be taken at their face value but should be paraphrased in such a way as to prevent spurious names from usurping the role of subjects.

Inevitably this raises a question about the logical structure of existential propositions in general. Such propositions act as vehicles of explicit ontological claims and are as a rule informative, synthetic propositions (some, like Kant, would argue that they are *necessarily* synthetic) which, if true, widen our knowledge. Yet even on the most charitable view of facts, one can hardly treat propositions like 'Ruritania does not exist' as being on the same logical footing as any other synthetic true singular propositions without throwing into confusion the whole concept of existence. But how, then, should such propositions be interpreted? What is their logical grammar? What kind of facts do they express?

The predicate 'exists' and the verb 'to be'

An answer to these questions, if a satisfactory answer is to be possible at all, cannot be given except as part of a theory of reality, and my purpose in the following pages will be to sketch out the fundamentals of just such a theory. However, I propose to begin by first exploring what might be called the 'reductivist strategy'. As often, when one is confronted with what appears an intractable philosophical problem, there is an overwhelming temptation to try to argue it out of existence by showing that the linguistic expressions with which it is linked can be modified or paraphrased into other, less problematic, expressions without any loss of truth or philosophically relevant meaning. Might it be possible to make such a method work in the case of existential propositions?

Consider, to begin with, the words 'existence' and 'exist(s)'. Notoriously these words have crept into ordinary usage from mediaeval philosophical Latin. The Scholastics employed them as technical terms in a deliberate effort to separate the 'existential' sense of *to be* from its 'copulative' sense, i.e. its function as an auxiliary to predication. Yet in Greek philosophy, it appears, these two senses of *to be* were not always very clearly distinguished from each other, and sometimes moreover there was a strong tendency to amalgamate them in a single concept.[1] From a reductivist standpoint, certainly, there is no justification for keeping these two senses strictly apart. Whether or not the Scholastics misinterpreted the Ancients on this point, their insistence on separating the 'existential' from the 'copulative' sense of *to be*, a reductivist might argue, has had large and undesirable philosophical repercussions, in particular by encouraging treatment of existence as a property of objects, or a 'first-level predicate', and by inspiring faulty metaphysical arguments for the existence of God. But the function of

[1] Plato seems to be taking this line in the *Sophist*. (Cf. G.E.L. Owen, *Plato on Not-being*, in G. Vlastos (ed.), *Plato*, Vol. I, 1971; also Richard S. Bluck, *Plato's Sophist*, 1975.) According to some commentators, Aristotle's writings too provide evidence of this, although the interpretation placed on his texts by the Scholastics tends to obscure the fact. Thus A.C. Graham (see *'Being' in Linguistics and Philosophy: A Preliminary Inquiry*, in *The Verb 'Be' and its Synonyms*, Part 5, ed. John W.M. Verhaar, Dordrecht-Holland), argues that the Scholastics were most probably influenced by the mediaeval Arab translators of Aristotle who owing to the peculiarity of the Arabic language were unable to reproduce the Greek verb *einai* with a single word, combing its copulative with its existential sense. 'In place of the single verb *einai*, Arabs found in Aristotle a set of abstract nouns, each rooted in either the existential verb or the copulative sentence patterns. This deformation often obscured Aristotle's meaning, a fact that some of the Arabs discerned.' (ib. p. 228).

to be, surely, is not to supply logically independent existence predicates, but to help turn other words into predicates. It is a mere auxiliary verb, a syntactical instrument enabling us to specify what philosophers sometimes used to call the 'essence' or 'quiddity' of a thing; the verb *esse*, to be, acting in such cases literally as a pointer towards *essentia*.

If this is true, it follows of course that the use of inflected forms of *to be* in predicate places (as, for example, in 'I think, therefore I am') must be rejected as ungrammatical; and similarly for the verb *exist*, especially in singular propositions. '*X* exists' evidently cannot be treated on a par with '*x* is green', or 'is fat', or 'runs', for all their surface similarity. Something may be green, or fat, or it may be running, and it may have all these properties or none without ceasing to exist. But if it does not exist, it does not exist; it does not have the 'property' of non-existence. And if non-existence is not a property, neither is existence.

Expressed in another way, in attributing existence to an entity one is not saying anything about that entity that has not already been said by naming it. The predicate 'exists' in such a case plays no useful role and can be safely axed. If 'Jones' is a proper name, then 'Jones exists' is tautological and 'Jones' does not exist' self-defeating. What can be asserted meaningfully and non-trivially, at best, is 'Men exist' and 'Dragons are fictional'. Which only goes to show (so it is said) that existential propositions are *general* propositions, or else they do not qualify as genuine propositions at all.

This, incidentally, at the same time seems to dispose of the view that existential propositions might be interpreted as involving an ascription of the property of existence to certain objects of thought. For what object of thought is one referring to when one is asserting the existence of men? Is any specific individual intended? Manifestly not. One is saying something about men in the plural, but no specific *group* of men is intended either. What is more, there would be no need to change the statement if it turned out that only one man existed. But, then, what might the intended object be in such a case? What object of thought is the 'property' of existence being ascribed to; a property that – one assumes – such an object may but need not possess? (I shall revert to the topic of objects of thought later on.)

In fact, even propositions like 'Men exist' and 'Dragons are fictional', despite their obvious generality, are viewed as a rule with a considerable amount of suspicion. Their surface syntax, it is argued, involving as it does the use of 'existence predicates', tends to obfuscate their true 'logical grammar'. For a closer analysis shows that what is really being talked about in such propositions is not men or dragons, but the *concept* man and the *concept* dragon, and what is being said is that certain things fall under the former concept, whereas the latter concept is empty. A more accurate way of conveying the thought that men exist or that dragons are fictional would be by saying 'For some (at least one) x, x is a man' and 'Nothing is a dragon'; employing expressions, that is, that correspond to what logicians call, 'quantifiers', and enable us to dispel any lingering illusion that existential propositions might have a subject/predicate structure. None of them do.

The doctrine of quantification and the reductivist strategy

The replacement of 'existence predicates' with quantifiers along the lines indicated above represents a vital opening manoeuvre in a reductivist strategy. The intention behind it is to help unmask the metaphysical problems surrounding the 'existence predicates' as essentially sham problems. But the manoeuvre, I shall argue, fails.

The doctrine that existential assertions, in effect, reduce to certain claims about relevant concepts and the doctrine of quantification both go back to Frege. The influence of these doctrines on modern analytical thought has been profound and lasting, and so, alas, have been the philosophical misconceptions which these doctrines tended to engender. Some of the reasons for these misconceptions will become apparent in a moment. First, let us take a brief look at Frege's theory of concepts.

According to Frege, concepts represent a sub-class of functions; more specifically, a concept is a function 'whose value is always a truth-value'. Frege, it should be stressed at once, interprets functions basically by analogy with machines, i.e. he sees a function as a kind of logical mechanism, such that if certain numerical constants or 'arguments' are 'fed' into it, it will produce certain values. Concepts, in his view, behave in very much the same manner. Briefly, they represent a sort of propositional machine, such that if 'arguments' of the appropriate type are 'inserted' into them – the term 'argument' now to be understood in the sense of *any* object-naming symbol – they yield significant, true or false, *propositions*.

Fundamental to Frege's whole approach is the assumption that there exists an unbridgeable logical gulf between concepts and objects. Like functions, he claims, concepts are intrinsically incomplete or 'unsaturated'. In a sentential context, they are represented by syntactically incomplete predicative expressions. By contrast, 'arguments', or object-naming expressions, are possessed of a certain inherent completeness. Unlike predicates, they have no 'gaps' as part of their logical structure and are therefore naturally fitted to play the role of subjects. Nevertheless object-words or names, on their own, despite their intrinsic 'completeness', are strictly void of significance, and it is only in combination with certain predicative symbols – viz. certain one-place, or more-than-one-place, predicables, as the case may be – that they produce meaningful wholes. Thus the propositional schema 'x is a man' can be appropriately filled in by inserting a proper name, say 'Jones', in the place occupied by the variable, yielding a meaningful proposition whose truth-value happens to be true. Which, at the same time, provides supporting evidence for the proposition that the concept man is not empty, viz. that (Ex) x is a man, or 'For some x, x is a man'.

But does such an analysis of concepts enable us to gain a a clearer insight into the meaning of existential propositions? There is one problem that immediately crops up here, and may be stated as follows. If 'Jones is a man' is true, then, of course, it necessarily follows that something falls under the concept man, i.e. 'For some x, x is a man' is true also. Any meaningful singular proposition licences an 'existential generalisation' of this sort, and if the former is true, so inevitably is the latter. The existential proposition here merely expresses in a general form what we know to be the case in a particular instance, i.e. that the concept man does indeed have an application. But suppose we don't know of any particular instances. Suppose we begin with an existential *hypothesis*, without being able to point to any confirming evidence. What makes such a hypothesis meaningful? Should we assume that the meaningfulness of such a hypothesis necessarily depends on the possibility (in principle, at least) of turning the relevant propositional schema into a meaningful *singular* proposition, viz. by replacing the 'bound' variable (the variable governed by the 'existential quantifier') with an appropriate name, or a naming phrase?

We are here already in deep waters, for what needs to be decided is just what sort of existential claims can be significantly made. If the proposition we start out with is simply that men exist – which, we are told, should be more appropriately expressed as (Ex) x is a man – then no doubt sooner or later we shall run into Jones and will be able to proclaim the happy discovery. But if we begin with the assumption, say, that there is at least one star in the heavens that never has been, or ever will be, discovered or talked about, then evidently no meaningful let alone true singular proposition can be produced in support of such an assumption, for no such object can be named.

So the question arises, how should the 'existential quantifier' be interpreted? What kind of claim, precisely, does it serve to convey? Evidently it is not much use replacing existential propositions with their properly quantified 'canonical' paraphrases, if the concept of existential quantification itself gives rise to obscurities and cannot be made sufficiently precise.

As a matter of fact, I do not believe that existential propositions, in particular those intended to transmit ontological claims, can be satisfactorily replaced by the relevant quantified paraphrases, in the manner suggested. In order to see why such a replacement is not possible, consider the distinction, now widely accepted among logicians, between the 'objectual' (or 'referential') and the 'substitutional' reading of the quantifiers. On the 'objectual' interpretation, the quantifiers are seen as ranging over the objects within a specified domain of discourse and generally as vehicles for rendering the 'ontological commitment' underlying the statements of a theory explicit. On the 'substitutional' interpretation, they are seen simply as relating to certain *terms* which if substituted for variables in the relevant propositional schemata yield (contextually) true propositions, irrespective of whether or not such terms stand for actually existing objects. Unlike the objectual interpretation, the substitutional interpretation of quantifiers is ontologically non-commital (unless terms are counted as ontological items). To illustrate this with an example, on the objectual interpretation '(Ex) x is a three-headed dog guarding the entrance to Hades' is false, because there is no such entity; but on the substitutional interpretation a replacement of x in 'x is a three-headed dog guarding the entrance to Hades' with 'Cerberus' yields a true proposition; which, if we are talking about Greek mythology, is of course as it should be.

This distinction has a direct bearing upon the problem under discussion; for if, as is suggested, the quantifiers can be read in two different ways, then surely we shall not be able to get rid of 'existence predicates'. Briefly, if it is possible to interpret (Ex) Fx substitutionally as well as referentially, then it won't be superfluous to say that F's actually exist, for on a substitutional interpretation they *need not do so*. To return to our earlier example, a conseqence of this is that it will not be possible to claim on valid grounds that 'Men exist' or rather 'actually exist', reduces to, and can be replaced *tout court* by '(Ex) x is a man'.

Some further attempts to eliminate existence predicates

Nevertheless, it might be argued that this merely exposes certain limitations of quantification as a logical device, but does not show that existence predicates are not eliminable. Not only are such predicates eliminable, it might be argued, but conceivably it might be possible to devise a method of paraphrase which would enable us to dispense with quantifiers as well; and if the latter can be achieved, then the myth of the 'logical independence' of existential propositions will have been exploded once and for all. Existential propositions are not really necessary – logically necessary – for a complete description of the world. If it were possible to compile a complete list of the basic propositions needed to say everything that essentially needs to be said about the world, existential propositions would not be among them. But if so; if there are no 'irreducibly existential' propositions, then there are no 'irreducibly existential' facts; and hence no metaphysical problem of 'being qua being' either.

The reductivist argument might take three different forms, which I shall label 'ontological', 'epistemological' and 'syntactical' respectively. The ontological version of the argument involves the claim that existential propositions, in the final analysis, can all be shown to be about certain concrete ontological items and attributes of such items. It envisages, that is, the possibility of a description of the world in which all subject terms refer to actual existents, and all explicit existential assertions give way to 'existential presuppositions'. The epistemological version involves an assumption that all significant existential claims can be translated into claims about potential knowledge. Finally, the 'syntactical' version of the argument involves an attempt to circumvent the need for any direct ontological or epistemological commitment by showing that what is being primarily 'talked about' in existential propositions are syntactical properties of certain *linguistic expressions*. The argument, I shall maintain, is unsuccessful in all its versions. Nevertheless there are important factors that give a strong impetus to a reductivist reasoning.

Let us consider the ontological version first. The world, the reductivist might argue, consists of certain entities and their properties and relations, and all facts, including 'negative' facts, are *literally* facts about such entities. The notion of fact is apt to cause difficulties only if facts are treated as some special species of existences. But there are no such existences. That the cat is on the mat is unquestionably a fact, but the expression 'That the cat is on the mat' does not denote an entity as 'the cat' denotes a cat. What it denotes, if anything, is the proposition 'The cat is on the mat'. Propositions, if true, 'express' facts; they don't name them. There is, then, no danger of investing fiction with some kind of existence by asserting a negative existential proposition, or any negative proposition for that matter, and the ambiguities allegedly inherent in the concept of fact are more imaginary than real.

The starting premiss here coincides with what is basically the common sense belief, viz. that things or entities constitute the hard core of reality. It is assumed, in addition, that all significant propositions, irrespective of their truth or falsity, must in principle be explicable in terms of propositions about such entities as a *condition of their significance*. It follows that fictional things cannot function as genuine subjects of predication, and in the strict sense cannot be 'talked about' at all. If propositions purporting to be about fictional things are to be accepted as meaningful, then it is only on condition that they can be paraphrased into propositions about non-fictional things; for example, into propositions about persons who are thinking, alleging, claiming, etc. something fictional.

The scene is thus set for large-scale reductivist paraphrases, which in different ontological theories take on different forms, depending upon what kind of entities are regarded as basic. A central feature of all such theories is the distinction between that which exists in a fundamental sense, i.e. the basic entities (I should emphasise that I am here using the term 'entity' in the broadest possible sense) and that which is regarded as existing in a secondary, derivative, or parasitic sort of way. Only the basic entities are said to qualify as genuine ontological objects; all other objects are merely *quasi-objects*, i.e. they are explicable as logical constructions from ontologically fundamental items, and can be treated as a sort of convenient logical artefacts. In general, anything that is not a basic entity is either a feature of such an entity or in some way depends upon such entities for its own existence. This, it is claimed, provides at the same time a clue as to the meaning of fiction; for fiction really is the result of treating that which can exist only derivatively, or 'parasitically', as if it existed in its own right.

The immediate practical problem that confronts such an approach is how to determine what items do exist in an ontologically fundamental sense; or, to phrase it differently, what objects do qualify as 'genuine' ontological objects? A quick glance at any history of philosophy reveals a multitude of mutually competing ontological theories, each postulating different basic entities and wielding different arguments, and there is no obvious clue as to how, if at all, their differences could be resolved from an 'impartial' point of view.

However, I shall leave this problem to one side for the moment and concentrate instead on pursuing the general line of reductivist strategy, which remains unaffected by the choice of basic entities. Thus it might be argued that the basic premises of an entity-oriented ontology alone, if conceded, provide a sufficient justification for maintaining that existential propositions in particular are logically dispensable.

It should be emphasised that what is meant here is not just 'contextually' dispensable but 'universally' dispensable. The relevant argument might be presented as follows. To claim that things of a certain sort exist, it might be said, is no different, truth-functionally at least, from claiming that a certain disjunction of singular propositions about entities of which the world happens to consist is true. Thus given that the world is made up of $a,b,c \ldots n$ objects, 'Men exist', or more precisely 'For some x, x is a man', is coextensive with 'Either a is a man or b is a man or c is a man or $\ldots n$ is a man'. Every affirmative existential proposition can thus, theoretically, be replaced by a disjunction of positive singular propositions. Similarly, negative existential propositions can be reproduced in terms of, and are theoretically interchangeable with, certain conjunctions of negative singular propositions. For to say that entities of a certain sort do not exist is to say, in effect, that not a single entity in the world has the indicated property, or properties; or, expressed differently, that the relevant concept cannot be correctly applied to anything.

Such a reductivist analysis, however, is vulnerable to two immediate objections. First, its underlying assumption is that the number of entities that the world consists of is finite. For if it were infinite, it would be logically impossible to complete the analysis of any existential proposition along the lines suggested, and hence there would be no valid grounds for claiming the equivalence between such propositions and the corresponding disjunctions (or conjunctions). But the thesis that the set of basic entities is finite, while not altogether implausible, needs to be argued for, and as yet must be regarded as unproved. Secondly (as was pointed out by Russell, among others), even if it were true that the number of basic entities was finite, the proposed analysis still would not yield the desired result. For suppose 'Men exist' was rendered 'Either a is a man or b is a man or c is a man or ... n is a man', with $\{a \dots n\}$ being a finite set. Then having completed the disjunction, one would have to indicate this by saying 'And there are no more entities left in the world', or words to this effect. But this would mean asserting another existential proposition, and moreover one that patently cannot be analysed in the same way; so the problem of sorting out the significance of existence claims would still remain unresolved.

But let us suppose the reductivist took the epistemological option. He might concede that it is indeed absurd to pretend that in asserting an existential proposition we are in effect talking about all the things in the world. We are doing nothing of the sort. All we are saying in claiming the existence of men, he might argue, is that 'x is a man', given an appropriate substitution for x, can yield a knowable proposition. Conversely, to deny the existence of dragons is to deny that 'x is a dragon' can be converted into a knowable proposition (unless, of course, 'dragon' was used metaphorically, as in 'Mrs Thatcher is a dragon'). In other words, what is really being 'talked about' in existential propositions he might say, are not – not primarily, anyhow – any ontological objects and attributes of such objects, but knowledge, and the possibility of knowledge, of certain propositions.

But the objection here might be that the suggested paraphrase merely involves a surreptitious quantification over propositions. What is being said, in effect, it might be argued, is that there exist certain propositions which can be known to be true, and if so, existential propositions will not have been 'eliminated'; only the values of the variables of quantification will have been changed, with propositions taking the place of ontological objects.

In any case, if one insists on talking about knowledge, the question that will have to be answered sooner or later is what does constitute genuine knowledge, and if it should turn out, as it well might, that in defining the conditions of knowledge one has to make use of existential propositions of one sort or another, then the suggested reductivist paraphrase will not have achieved its purpose.

Let us now consider the third version of the argument. There is no need, the reductivist might argue, to involve ourselves in any extra-linguistic considerations. Existential propositions can be treated simply as metalinguistic reports concerning syntactical properties of certain 'object-language' expressions. Existence claims, after all, involve certain claims about concepts, and concepts are represented by predicative expressions. Surely, then, we can confine ourselves to exploring the syntactical properties of such expressions and leave the ontological and epistemological issues, temporarily at least, to one side? If we manage to sort out the syntactical problems, we might find that in the end the other issues will get sorted out of themselves.

But just how does this work in actual practice? Take again 'Men exist', or rather its 'logically regimented' paraphrase '(Ex) x is a man', or perhaps '(Ex) x is human'. The main problem here is what to do with the existential quantifier. Now it is of course always possible to substitute $\sim (x) \sim Fx$ for (Ex) Fx, replacing the existential quantifier, that is, with a universal quantifier plus negation, but there is nothing much to be gained by such a swap, for to paraphrase the proposition that something is human by saying that it is not the case that everything is non-human is merely to beg the question. Everything and something and nothing are all logically interlinked and none of them makes clear sense without the others. A rather more promising approach might be to treat the existential quantifier itself as a kind of predicate – a second-level predicate to be precise – which, in our example above, says something about the 'first-level' predicate 'is human', namely that the latter can be completed to produce a true proposition. The emphasis here is thus transferred from a straightforward assertion of the (ontological) existence of a certain type of things to an assertion to the effect that a given predicate can generate a true proposition. This interpretation, in a sense, represents a further refinement on the 'substitutional' interpretation of the quantifiers, and suggests the possibility of a complete elimination of quantifiers in favour of some appropriate operators on predicates.[2]

---

[2] A logician's dream is to construct a language in which all the facts there

But this flight from objects into the land of predicates really solves nothing, for the problem of 'ontological commitment' soon reappears in a new guise. To revert to our example, we shall have to account for the fact that the predicate *human*, or rather the predicable ' – is human', unlike the predicable '– is a dragon', has the capacity of being turned into a true proposition, and in order to do this, we shall have to make use of our original proposition, viz. that men do actually exist (in the full-blooded sense of 'exist'), and if so, nothing of any substance will have been accomplished by the attempted 'reduction'.

What can the reductivist say in reply to this? The only possibility left to him of safeguarding his own position, it seems, is to deny not only that 'Men exist' but '(Ex) x is human' too can be treated as genuine propositions. Similarly he might reject both 'Dragons do not exist' and '$\sim$ (Ex) x is a dragon' as ill-formed. The kind of unqualified quantification illustrated by such examples, he might argue, does not really make clear sense. Existential claims are more naturally expressed within the context of a specific domain of discourse. Thus a more natural way of asserting the existence of men would be by saying 'Some living creatures are men', or something along these lines; employing, that is, a proposition of the 'Some S are P' type. If, however, an existential claim is expressed in such a manner, then it can be paraphrased in terms of valid inference. Thus to assert 'Some living creatures are men', or to phrase it in a 'canonical' form, 'For some x, x is both a living creature and a man', is equivalent to the

are could be expressed exclusively in terms of predicates and operators on predicates. A version of such a language, involving a modification of some ideas first put forward by Schönfinkel and Curry, is sketched out by Quine in his paper 'Variables explained away' (*Selected Logic Papers*, New York 1966). Quine's model involves the use of only six operators on predicates. These operators, he claims, enable us to eliminate 'existence prefixes and variables altogether'. The main operator is called 'derelativization operator' or DER, and its function is to transform an n-place predicate into an (n-1)-predicate; which, in the case of a one-place predicate, yields us a nought-place predicate or a complete sentence. Thus if we have a one-place predicate such as 'human' and wish to assert (Ex) x is human, i.e. that there are men, it is sufficient to write DER(human), and correspondingly for dragons NEG DER(dragon). But this is clearly just a notational device. Suppose I invented an operator on predicates, say 'HOOKED', and used it in the same way, viz. HOOKED(human), NEG HOOKED(dragon), etc. No one would be any the wiser unless I explained what I meant by 'HOOKED', and at some stage in my explanation I would have to use an existential sentence.

denial that the inference from the proposition of the form '*x* is a living creature' to the proposition of the form '*x* is not a man' is valid. The concept of existence is thus shown to be essentially the same as that of valid inference.[3]

The conclusion that follows from this is obvious. If it is possible to show that existential propositions are equivalent to denials of the validity of inferences of a certain kind, then instead of talking about existence we can confine ourselves to talking about the validity of inference. Existential propositions, contextually indispensable though they might be, are not logically essential for a complete description of the world. They should be treated as place-holders for other propositions, rather than as representing a logically independent class of propositions of their own. But if there are no logically independent existential propositions, then obviously there can be no 'irreducibly existential' facts (and hence no irreducibly *negative* existential facts either). In other words, there is no need to rack one's brains about the problem of 'being qua being'.

The eliminability of predicates 'true' and 'real'

Before commenting on these moves, it might be useful to consider briefly an extension of the reductivist argument. The quantifiers, as we saw, can be interpreted in two ways: 'objectually' and 'substitutionally'. The 'substitutional' interpretation involves a transfer of emphasis from existence to truth. Whereas under the 'objectual' interpretation the central issue is that of 'ontological commitment', under the 'substitutional' interpretation the focal problem is what 'substitution instances' of the propositional schema controlled by the quantifier can be regarded as true.

The spotlight is thus trained on truth; in particular on the conditions under which a given 'substitution instance' can be legitimately described as 'true'. But this merely raises the problem of a definition of 'truth conditions' and it is difficult to see how such a definition can steer clear of the question of 'ontological commitment'. The ghosts conjured up by the concept of existence thus reappear to haunt us. If the reductivist is to be consistent, he will have to say not only that explicit existence claims are not a necessary constituent feature of a complete description of the world, but that

---

[3] For an elaborate version of the reductivist argument along these lines see C.J.F. Williams, *What is Existence?*, Oxford 1981.

explicit truth claims aren't either. We can hardly deny that 'existence predicates' carry a logically independent descriptive content without being prepared to say the same of 'truth-predicates'. If there is no separate philosophical 'problem of existence', neither is there a separate philosophical 'problem of truth'.

Willy-nilly one is thus forced to extend the reductivist argument and adopt the position of what has become known as the 'redundancy theory of truth'. The central thesis of the 'redundancy theory', which goes back to F.P.Ramsey, is that the predicate 'true' and locutions such as 'It is true that ...', 'It is a fact that ...' are all logically dispensable. 'It is true that *p*' is semantically equivalent with '*p*'. To say that Socrates is mortal is true is not to say anything that cannot be said by asserting that Socrates is mortal. Truth is not a 'property' that a proposition may but need not possess; nor does truth represent a 'relation' between a proposition and an 'external' fact. Truth is literally what a true proposition *expresses*. As for the word 'true', this word is used merely 'for emphasis or for stylistic reasons'. We say 'true', 'correct', 'so it is', etc., but we could just as well reiterate the proposition concerned. Similarly to call a proposition 'false' is not to provide any essential factual information about the proposition in question that cannot be provided by asserting its negation. A possible difficulty might be thought to arise when a proposition is obliquely referred to rather than explicitly stated. Thus one might say 'What A says (i.e. the proposition A states) is true', which, on the face of it, seems to represent a clear case of property ascription. In fact – it is argued – any such statement can be perfectly adequately re-phrased as 'A says that *p*, and *p*', without using the word 'true'. It follows that technically it is possible to dispense with 'truth-talk' altogether, and if so, the alleged puzzles surrounding the concept of truth are shown to be more artificial than real. Or, to quote Ramsey: '... there is really no separate problem of truth but merely a linguistic muddle.'[4]

How does this bear upon the concept of reality? Evidently if the above theory is correct, there can be no question of explaining truth in terms of the 'correspondence with (external) facts' The exponents of the theory, not unnaturally, tend to equate facts with true propositions. It follows that if 'true' is logically dispensable, so is

---

[4] F.P. Ramsey, 'Facts and propositions', in *The Philosophy of Mathematics*, London 1931, p.142.

'fact'. If 'truth-talk' can be avoided, so can 'reality-talk'. Neither 'fact' nor 'fiction' are essential for a complete description of the world. And the same, inevitably, applies to the word 'real'. If 'real' is used in the sense of 'actual' or 'actually existent', rather than in the sense of 'genuine', say, then (to re-state the familiar view) it can be paraphrased out of the relevant context without any great difficulty, and it makes no difference whether we speak of God or the table in this room. To say that this table 'actually exists' is to say no more and no less than that this is a table; or, if preferred, that it is 'tabling' in this particular spatial region. If the word 'real' in the sense of 'actual' or 'actually existent' has any discernible function at all, then it is only to indicate in a roundabout way that a certain proposition, or propositions, are true[5]; and 'true', as we have just seen, is itself eliminable as a propositional predicate. But if so, then the difficulties involved in an attempt to 'define' the concept of truth, or the concept of reality, for that matter, need not detain us any longer. A general definition – apart from a perfectly trivial nominal definition, such that truth is whatever is the case, or whatever true propositions

---

[5] There are plenty of indications of the close semantic links between 'real' and 'true'. When we ask 'Really?' we wish to know whether a truth claim has in fact been made, or whether what has been said is true. 'Really?', 'Zbilja?', 'Wirklich?', 'C'est vrai?', 'Davvero?', 'Pravda?', all ask the same question, although the first three are based on the adjective 'real' and the last three on 'true'. In addition, of course, 'real', like 'true', is often used in the sense of 'genuine'. Thus if someone is a 'real' friend, he is a 'true' or 'genuine' friend. However, the concept of genuinness has other distinctive characteristics of its own, and the overlap in meaning is partial rather than total. 'Genuine' is related to 'original' and 'authentic' and is opposed to 'spurious', 'counterfeit' and 'phoney'. To describe something as a 'genuine article' is to say that it is exactly what it shows itself to be; that it does not involve deception or an intention to deceive. It is because counterfeit objects or simulated actions are intended to mislead us into attributing to them certain properties which they do not in fact possess, and consequently into making false reality assumptions, that we associate 'genuine' with 'real'. Nevertheless the counterfeit coin is no less part of the actual world than the genuine one; the only difference being that the counterfeit coin does not have all the properties that a genuine coin is expected to have. As to which objects are to be regarded as genuine and which as counterfeit, this is largely a matter of convention and depends upon the context. It is not inconceivable, for example, that someone who had seen only artificial flowers would regard a natural flower, if he suddenly came across one, as an all too imperfect imitation.

express – cannot be provided; nor, strictly speaking, is it needed. All that one can profitably do is concentrate on weeding out the propositions with faulty grammar and those that contextually give rise to paradoxes.[6]

Criticism of the reductivist argument

What reply might be given to all this? The first thing to note is a certain confusion of words with concepts underlying the reductivist reasoning. Thus the tendency is to concentrate an analysis of the concept of existence or that of truth around the use of predicates such as 'exists (exist)' and 'true', and their cognates; the idea being that if it can be shown that such predicates can be paraphrased out of the relevant contexts by employing a different type of idiom, then there is little that remains to be said about the concepts. But neither do such concepts reduce to the corresponding predicates, nor indeed are such predicates entirely dispensable.

Take the predicate 'true'. It is clear, to begin with, that the thought that p is true is not identical with the thought that p. I can entertain a thought that p without thinking of p as true. How else would I be able to think of states of affairs that are merely possible? I might conceivably be interested merely in a hypothetical situation,

---

[6] It was precisely the difficulty of making sense of truth and falsehood as properties of propositions that prompted Frege to treat them as *unanalysable objects* (*das Wahre* and *das Falsche*, as he called them) and to argue, accordingly, that truth-predicates were dispensable in a logically purified language. Tarski's account of truth, on the other hand, involves a retention of truth-predicates, but at a strictly meta-linguistic level. Tarski draws a distinction between an object language and a correlated semantic metalanguage, and treats 'true' as a metalinguistic predicate of the sentences of the object language. This yields the well-known formula 'The sentence "S" is true if, and only if, S'. A definition of truth (which Tarski couches in terms of the semantic concept of 'satisfaction') is regarded as 'materially adequate', if it entails all exemplifying instances of this formula. This has been hailed (e.g. by K. Popper; cf. his *Objective Knowledge*, 1973, p. 319ff.) as a rehabilitation of the classical correspondence theory of truth. But Tarski's is not so much a definition of 'truth' as a definition of the metalinguistic technical term 'true in (a formally specified language) L'. I shall discuss truth in Chapter 14.

trying to decide, say, what consequences would follow if *p* were true, without wishing to commit myself one way or the other (although, as will be shown later on, one cannot coherently posit the possibility of *p* being true except with regard to possible *truth claims* that might be made in respect of it). In addition, we ordinarily assume that what is stated on one occasion may be identical with what is stated on a different occasion, even though its truth-value might change. But this is incompatible with the 'redundancy theory'. So either we shall have to disallow such a possibility and decree that nothing qualifies as a genuine proposition unless its truth-value is fixed for all time, i.e. that all propositions are what is sometimes called 'eternal' propositions, or we shall have to accept that truth-value is not an integral part of the objective propositional content. If we take the former option, i.e. if we lay down that only 'eternal' propositions shall be genuine propositions, then this threatens to blur the distinction between contingent and necessary truth. For if *p* is true, then necessarily *p*, whatever *p* might be. If it is true that Socrates (during the relevant period of his life) is bald, then to say that this could have been false is a contradiction in terms. A proposition cannot change its truth-value without in effect becoming a different proposition. If, on the other hand, we accept that the truth-value is not an integral part of the propositional content, then of course the predicate 'true' and 'false' will not be redundant.

But consider now a somewhat different version of the 'redundancy thesis'. There is no need, it might be argued, to make far-reaching metaphysical assumptions about the nature of propositions in order to justify the thesis that truth-predicates are logically redundant. It is sufficient to consider the manner in which truth-claims may be communicated. Thus it is clear that 'true' or 'false' neither add nor detract from what is actually asserted on a given occasion. They are redundant, but not because the world can be described in terms of 'eternal' propositions which are true or false in virtue of being the propositions they are, but because they advertise certain claims which can equally successfully be conveyed *implicitly*, viz. by asserting the proposition or its negation, as the case may be. In short, rather than worrying about 'eternal' propositions we should focus on implicit-versus-explicit truth-*claims*. This latter version of the 'redundancy thesis' certainly looks the more plausible of the two. The transference of emphasis upon truth-claims, in particular, seems to be a move in the right direction. Truth, as I shall argue later on (see Chapter 14) does not reduce to 'true propositions' but demands an exploration of truth-claims. But of course it is not enough to point out that such claims can be made implicitly. Whether they are made implicitly or explicitly, the problem still remains of clarifying their *meaning*. A mere elimination of explicit truth-claims – assuming such a thing was possible – would not in itself contribute anything towards clarifying the concept of truth. As it happens, explicit truth claims are not entirely dispensable. Take again our earlier example 'What A says is true'. The suggestion was that this should be paraphrased as 'A says that *p*, and *p*'. But conceivably I might be particularly anxious to emphasise that A is not stating a falsehood; that he is a reliable witness, say, which might be important in certain circumstances. Or suppose I wished to challenge what A said. I might tell him 'What you say is false'. How will he reply to this charge? He might say 'Things are exactly as I said they are'. But suppose I insisted that he was uttering a falsehood. Then the only defence left to him is to answer 'No, what I say is the truth'. There is no way in which he could emphasise the veracity of his testimony except by literally asserting it.

Let us now return to the topic of 'existence predicates'. The reductivist position, as we saw, was that such predicates were not only eliminable, but that moreover their elimination was a philosophical desideratum and a vital step towards a logically purified language. Sentences like 'Jones exists' were dismissed as cases of bad grammar on the grounds that the use of the proper name already dispensed with any services that the predicate 'exists' might provide. Even sentences such as 'Men exist' and 'Dragons are fictional' were said to offend against certain logical proprieties and were replaced by suitably quantified paraphrases. Finally, an attempt was made to show that, theoretically at least, quantifiers themselves could be got rid of too.

I have distinguished between three different versions of the reductivist argument. The 'ontological' version, as we saw, involves an assumption that existential propositions, in the final analysis, can be reproduced in terms of propositions that do not explicitly assert but rather presuppose the existence of certain ontological objects. In other words, the possibility is posited of a description of the world in which all subject terms refer to actual existents and all existential propositions are analysed out and replaced by 'existential presuppositions'. But this was shown to be an unattainable goal for the simple reason that the meaning of an existential proposition cannot be made fully clear without making use of some existential proposition or other as part of the explanans. Moreover the ontological reductivist cannot state his own philosophical position coherently. For in order to explain the reasons for own reductivist beliefs he will have to make certain claims that are impervious to his own analysis. Thus he will have to say: There is nothing except objects and their properties and relations (or places and qualities, or whatever). But this means that he will have to concede that at least some propositions are 'irreducibly' existential, and if he does, he will have disavowed his own argument.

But the 'epistemological' version of reductivism is just as defective. The main idea here is that existential propositions can be paraphrased in terms of propositions about knowledge. Thus the claim that there are F-things is said to reduce to the claim that 'x is an F' can be converted into a knowable proposition by substituting an appropriate object-term for x. But a moment's reflection is sufficient to show that no such reduction is possible. This does not mean, incidentally, that we have to accept that $(Ex)Fx$ can be meaningfully claimed to be true *irrespective* of the possibility of knowledge. We might very well take the view that 'x is an F' must in principle be convertible into a knowable proposition, without thereby implicitly accepting that '$(Ex)Fx$' and " 'x is an F' is convertible into a knowable proposition" are equisignificant. They clearly are not.

Lastly, the reductivist argument fails in its 'syntactical' version too. The strategy employed here, to begin with, is to insist that all existential propositions of the natural language be replaced by properly quantified paraphrases; next, propositions involving un-qualified or unrestricted quantification are proscribed on the grounds that they are 'obscure' and are replaced by propositions involving a qualified quantification into a specified domain (corresponding to ordinary language propositions of the 'Some S are P' type); finally, a paraphrase is attempted of the qualified quantification in terms of the validity of inference. On the surface, it looks a bold and attractive programme. In fact, if inspected more closely, it shows itself to be a rickety structure of ad hoc contrivance and ill-founded reductivist moves. Thus there are no compelling philosophical reasons for proscribing unqualified quantification other than the fact that such a quantification resists a reductivist analysis. Propositions like 'Men exist (or actually exist)', it is claimed, look odd and mysterious, and their quantified 'canonical' paraphrases, while admittedly helping to remove any suggestion that such propositions might have a subject/predicate structure, do not quite suceed in alleviating the mystery. They should be replaced by propositions such as 'Some living creatures are men'. But the difficulty, of course, is that any such replacement involves a radical change of content. To say that men exist, or rather 'actually exist', strictly, is not to say anything either about living creatures or the nature of men. That men are living creatures is a contingent fact. Conceivably they might not be. Equally conceivably I might not be aware that they are. I might not even know what 'living creature' means. 'Men actually exist' reveals nothing about who or what men are; all it says is that men are not fictional, that they are part of the actual world.

In point of fact, even if a replacement of unqualified with qualified quantification could be justified, this would still not ensure the success of the reductivist enterprise. The main thesis, as we saw, was that existential propositions involving a qualified quantification into a specified domain can be replaced by propositions about the validity of certain inferences. But the validity, or otherwise, of such inferences will depend upon considerations of certain *matters of fact*. To take again the above example, the proposition 'Some living creatures are men' carries an existential commitment, and the validity of any inference that might act as its replacement, evidently, will depend on the assumption that the respective classes of objects are non-empty. In short, such propositions are not susceptible to a kind of analysis that might be applied, for example, to universal propositions which have no existential import. If living creatures, or men, do not exist, then 'Some living creatures are men' is false, and if so, then any corresponding inference will be invalid. But if we have to make an explicit assumption that living creatures, or men, do actually exist in order to make an inferential paraphrase work, then a reductivist analysis fails to achieve its purpose and we are back exactly where we began.

The problem is even more acute than it appears, for singular existential propositions too resist a reductivist treatment and cannot be simply brushed off as 'ungrammatical'. Whether, in a given context, the use of 'existence predicates' might be avoided, this will depend upon whether it is clear what kind of claims are being made and whether there exists a consensus about those claims. Thus, given the way the word 'I' is used, there is no startlingly new information to be derived from a person's statement 'I actually exist' If 'Socrates is eating an apple' is true, then clearly there is nothing that can usefully be added to this statement by saying that the apple Socrates is eating is not fictional. To say 'The chair I am sitting on actually exists' is similarly uninformative, since the chair I am sitting on already implies that a chair is there. The predicate 'actually exists' here performs no useful function and can be left out altogether.

However, this need not *always* be the case. Conceivably I might be misreporting the whole situation. It is possible that I am not sitting on a chair at all, but lying on a sofa. In any case, it is perfectly intelligible to say in reply to someone's persistent talk about 'this chair': Look here, that chair exists only in your imagination. But if such a retort is both meaningful and non-trivial, then surely so is the statement (that might be made, for example, in reply to a request for information from a third person) that 'the chair' being talked about – the 'posited chair' – is not fictional, i.e. that it actually exists, even though those who take this statement on trust might find out otherwise to their cost.

It seems, then, that in some cases at least 'exists', or rather 'actually (or really) exists' does have some useful work to do in a subject/predicate context and cannot be dismissed out of hand as a 'spurious' predicate. To illustrate this with some further examples, there is surely nothing odd or unintelligible in statements such as that Dickens's Micawber was a real life character, i.e. actually existed, that Napoleon actually existed, that Carthage once existed but no longer does, etc. Unlike 'I actually exist' such statements are non-tautologous and can be significantly denied. But even 'I actually exist', it might be argued, though trivially true *as I speak it*, is not entirely uninformative, for I might never have existed.[7]

---

[7] Although I exist, I am not a 'necessary' existent (unlike mathematical objects). The reductivist, however, would have us believe that the statement 'I might never have existed' is not really about me at all but rather about certain *properties* which, as a matter of empirical fact, are exclusive to me but which conceivably no one (myself included) might have had, i.e. which might not have been instantiated at all. But this surely is a fallacy. The above statement cannot be about properties if only because there is no single property that individuates me in an *absolute sense*. As Leibniz already realised, nothing short of the totality of properties would do. And even he did not simply *equate* the numerically unique substance with the totality of its properties. See Chapter 3.

Existential facts: an existentialist interpretation

The reductivist enterprise thus inevitably comes to grief, and it is not altogether surprising that it does. It would indeed be difficult to imagine a language that would do all the work that our ordinary language does but would not include any 'existence predicates'. Quantification evidently cannot help 'eliminate' such predicates. It is not only that quantification cannot help eliminate such predicates, but often we have to make use of such predicates in order to make clear that the given quantified sentence does indeed convey an ontological claim. Existence predicates are prime instruments for making such claims explicit. But this merely brings us face to face with our old problem again. If such claims cannot be 'explained away'; if they do not reduce to ascriptions of certain attributes to certain entities; if furthermore they cannot be paraphrased simply in terms of knowledge, or translated into claims about the syntactical properties of certain expressions, the question is, how exactly should they be interpreted? What is it that makes them intelligible? What kind of *facts* do the propositions communicating such claims express?

One well-known and well-publicised attempt in recent philosophy to address this problem in a 'non-reductivist' spirit has gone under the name of Existentialism, and I shall now comment briefly on what I take to be the main features of the existentialist approach before outlining my own position.

The main thesis of the existentialist approach is that in order to elucidate the full significance of ontological claims conveyed by existential propositions we ought to begin by focusing attention upon the one for whom the 'problem of existence' presents itself in the first instance as a problem of *his own* existence. The 'subject of knowledge', it is argued, should turn his attention to himself as a historical individual, and explore the essential aspects of his own manner-to-be. In other words, an inquiry into the meaning of existence should begin as an 'existential phenomenology'; with the existential *self-knowledge* being the primary objective. This pursuit of existential self-knowledge, however, does not yield the knowledge of a substantival self. Rather the opposite, it helps to show why the self cannot be known as an object. It also helps to show that more fundamental than any knowledge of objects are certain feelings, needs and desires, and that it is upon a phenomenological elucidation of such feelings, needs and desires that an ontological description of the world must be based.

The main result that emerges from such an existential self-analysis is that man owes his understanding of the meaning of being to the fact that he exists in an object-transcending manner, and is therefore able to conceive of the possibility of nothingness, i.e. of the world *not existing at all*. It is precisely in virtue of his capacity to grasp this possibility that man is 'ontologically fundamental'. He is fundamental, that is, not as a privileged object in a world of objects, but as an existential subject; someone who can 'transcend' the world of objects, and is able to understand the difference between being and not-being.

However, there are at least two problems that immediately confront such an approach. First, the idea of an existent capable of 'transcending' the world of objects implies that there can be no criteria whereby such an existent might be 'externally' identified in respect of its characteristic 'mode of being'. That an 'external' identification strictly is not possible is due to the fact that such an existent in respect of its characteristic mode of being is not object-like. The point, in short, is that such an existent is typically someone who knows and refers to himself as 'I myself', and that all reports that identify this existent in an *essential* way will have to be phrased in the first person singular. Not surprisingly, what an existentialist account of existence does not provide is a clarification of the conditions of *objectivity*.[8]

Secondly, and in conjunction with the above, the old spectre of reductivism seems to enter the scene again. Consider what is being claimed. It is claimed that the meaning of existential assertions can be fully clarified only by clarifying the mode of being of the one who makes, and understands, such assertions. In order to be able to explain what is involved in saying that something actually exists, it is necessary first to clarify the characteristic features of man's own

---

[8] Some so-called 'philosophers of existence', like Heidegger, for example, affect to abhor all 'subjectivism', and even reject the label of 'existentialism' for their philosophy. Nevertheless the fact remains that by virtue of their approach they are incapable of supplying a satisfactory account of the conditions of objectivity. Heidegger's philosophy is based on a phenomenology of *Dasein*, i.e. an existent 'like myself', and the *being* of such an existent, as he says, necessarily presents itself in each case as 'my own being'; it is *je meines*. (Cf. *Sein und Zeit*, Part One, Ch. 1.) In other words, one has no option but to begin in the first person singular.

manner of existing. This is the task of what Heidegger calls the 'fundamental ontology'. But what does such a 'fundamental ontology' reveal? It reveals that man is essentially cast in the mode of being-in-the-world, and moreover that the world itself can be made sense of only in the context of man's own 'projects'. It follows that the meaning of ontological claims becomes fully transparent only if such claims are seen in the context of certain life-modalities of those who make such claims; in effect, all such claims become interpretable as forms of man's own self-understanding.

And here, of course, lies the rub. For if all ontological claims are to be understood as forms of man's own self-understanding, rather than conveying, successfully or otherwise, certain objective 'existential facts', then existentialism itself turns out to be a form of reductivism. The point is that the objectivity conditions for ontological claims are not provided, nor, strictly, can they be. The 'fundamental ontology' essentially paints a picture of the world from my own point of view. I am the ultimate source of meaning of all 'existential facts'; all such facts, in the final analysis, turn out to be explicable in terms of facts about my own existence. Everything relating to an 'external' world, including the existence of 'others', is subsumed under the general aspect of my own manner-of-being. An existentialist analysis, consistently pursued, thus yields in effect a subject-oriented description of the world, with peculiar reductivist implications of its own. As a theory of existence it is implausible and defective, and must be rejected.

A structuralist approach to an analysis of 'existential facts'

The only rational alternative, I shall argue, is to adopt a structuralist approach. Ontological claims as made explicit in existential propositions, I shall maintain, involve certain claims about the world as a whole, and the world is not just a horizon of my 'existential projects'; nor is it a substance, or an aggregate of substances of this or that sort. Rather it represents a configuration of several different and mutually interlocking strands, in which substances appear as objects in an intersubjective context. It is a structure, and moreover a structure that 'talks about itself'; with existential propositions being a principal instrument of its self-reference.

Of course, not all existential propositions are intended to carry ontological claims. 'There are zebras in Africa' is on a different footing from 'There is gold in El Dorado' or 'There are flying monkeys in the land of Oz', although all these propositions are true. Whether 'existence' means 'existence in reality', or 'in fairy-tale', or 'in mythology', will depend on when, how and in what context the relevant proposition is asserted. An assertion made on a stage in the context of a play will be judged by different standards from those it would be judged by if it is made in daily life. Even an indexical phrase like 'This chair' does not transmit an 'ontological commitment' on each occasion of its use. Such a phrase may feature as part of a quotation, or a paraphrase, as in indirect speech; or it may be used in respect of an object which we know to be fictional, for example in the context of a story or a fairy tale. If, on the other hand, I point to an object in my immediate surroundings and say 'this chair', then, unless I am deliberately lying or trying to mislead, I indicate an implicit assumption on my part that there is something out there, something external to my act of pointing, which I take to be a chair.

This assumption can be made explicit by making literal use of an 'existence predicate', and sometimes any residual doubts about what is assumed on a particular occasion can be resolved only by a repeated and emphatic use of such predicates; but, as is clear from what has been said so far, the use of such predicates is not analogous to acts of property ascription, especially if 'properties' are understood in the sense of 'accidental properties'. Existence is not an 'accidental' property of anything.

It is clearly not a property of ontological objects, despite the fact that singular existential propositions can make perfectly good sense. Nor can it be treated as a property of objects of thought. That the latter view is untenable becomes apparent as soon as we consider statements such as 'Men (actually) exist'. In making such a statement, evidently, one is not addressing oneself in thought to any specific individual or group of individuals; although, as will be shown later (see Chapter 13), one does by implication say something about the class of man-like things, viz. that every single one of its members, no matter how many of them there are, is as a matter of fact man-like.

In fact, the above view cannot be sustained even in cases where the intended reference is strictly to individuals. Thus to claim that Atlantis actually existed, or that Achilles actually existed, is not to ascribe the property of existence to Atlantis or Achilles qua objects of thought, but simply to claim that the world contained Atlantis or Achilles. If tomorrow someone discovered that Atlantis actually existed, he would not be adding a new property to the island state talked about in Plato's *Timaeus*, but dispelling the suspicion that Plato, or someone else before him, invented the legend. That Atlantis was discussed in the *Timaeus* may have been significant, but it was not crucial. Plato, after all, might never have thought of Atlantis; and similarly Homer might never have thought of Achilles; although this does not necessarily mean that if they did exist, they *pre-existed* thought in an absolute sense.

Finally, existence cannot be treated simply as a property of concepts either. This too is evident from our earlier discussion. Frege argued that in asserting an existential proposition one is in effect saying something about the relevant concept, namely that certain things fall under it, or, conversely, that nothing falls under it, i.e. that the concept is empty, as the case may be. However, since concepts, according to Frege, are essentially predicative, this automatically excludes singular existential propositions, and I have argued that such propositions cannot be dismissed as 'ungrammatical'. But even if we subscribe to the view that all genuine existential propositions are by nature 'general' propositions, Frege's theory is not entirely satisfactory. For what remains throughout of central interest and importance are the *ontological claims* expressed in such propositions, and to say that such propositions communicate certain characteristics of relevant concepts does little to explain the meaning of such claims. Thus the statement 'The concept lion is not empty' obviously is not likely to convey the desired information unless it is already clear from the context, or is otherwise indicated, that what is being talked about are actual and not merely imagined or fantasized lions. In other words, an understanding is presupposed of the distinction between the concept *actual lion* and the concept *imagined lion* (a cartoon-film lion, say). Similarly we are expected to understand the distinction between Atlantis *qua* actually existing and the idea of Atlantis as conceived by this, that or other person, writer, scholar. Yet it is precisely the rationale of this distinction that demands an elucidation.

So, ontologically speaking, there is not much enlightenment to be-gained by pursuing this road either. Existence is not a 'property of concepts' (qua functions); although ontological claims in general do entail claims about concepts. The point is that a statement to the effect that a given concept is non-empty *presupposes* an understanding of 'existence' rather than enabling us to grasp its meaning; unless, of course, the concept is such that its non-emptiness *analytically follows* from its meaning, in which case all that is required is to understand the concept. But, then, we shall have to devise a different theory of concepts to accommodate such a possibility.

It follows that there can be no question of the ontological claims expressed in existential proposition being explicable in terms of attribution of certain properties to certain items which may or may not possess such properties. What such claims convey, as I hope my analysis will show, can be more appropriately interpreted in terms of part-whole relation than in terms of 'properties'. In a sense, it is precisely the vain attempts to interpret existence as a 'property' and the difficulties created by such interpretations that have inspired the various reductivist moves in an effort to dispose of the whole problem, by showing that existential propositions are in principle 'eliminable', and hence that there are no 'irreducibly' existential facts. Against this, as we saw, the existentialists argued that rather than making futile attempts to 'eliminate' the problem one should subject it to a different type of treatment that would help place it in a proper philosophical perspective, and this was correct as far as it went. Unfortunately, the treatment offered was itself restrictive and inadequate, with the existentialist analysis proving utterly incapable of providing a satisfactory account of the objectivity aspects of ontological claims.

The only remedy, then, is to dig deeper into the conceptual roots of such claims and subject them to a comprehensive structural analysis. Such an analysis, if vigorously pursued, will show, among other things, that all properties are ultimately functions of certain structures, and that reality in the most fundamental sense of the word is structure *simpliciter*. It is not an 'aggregate' of certain objects and attributes. Rather it 'contains' objects with attributes. It has no 'inner core', no 'hard centre'. If it can be made intelligible, then it is only in terms of certain structural concepts which are all interdependent and mutually complementary, and together make up a logically self-subsistent whole.

The plan of inquiry

My method in what follows will be to begin with an analysis of the concept of an ontological existent and its associated categories of identity, individuality and plurality, and by pursuing the leads that such an analysis yields to their logical conclusion demonstrate that such concepts form part of a complex structure of closely inter-related ideas. A central problem that an analysis of the concept of an ontological existent brings to the surface concerns the distinction between numerical and qualitative identity. We distinguish between species and specimens. Two specimens of the same species, we normally assume, are numerically distinguishable even if they are qualitatively completely alike. Yet what are the grounds for such an assumption? What makes such an assumption *meaningful*? Traditionally, an answer to this problem has been sought by trying to define a 'principle of individuation' for ontological particulars. In Chapter 3 I discuss some of the reasons why this approach must fail and why the idea of individuality cannot be 'defined' in terms of certain criteria whereby ontological particulars are re-identified and distinguished from species. Criteria belong to an explanation of identity claims, but an explanation succeeds only in the context of what can be *understood*. Any attempt to define the criteria for verifying identity claims in respect of individuals already presupposes a degree of intelligibility of the idea of individuality. Yet what makes this intelligibility possible? An attempt to answer this question takes us into the field of a phenomenological epistemology. In order to clarify the conditions of intelligibility of identifying references to ontological existents it is necessary to explore the conditions under which such existents are constituted as target topics of relevant experiences. An ontological existent while being posited in the modus per se is nevertheless an object of thought. In Chapters 5-8 I address myself to the topic of experiences from a phenomenological point of view. I analyse the various types of experiential modalities, and in particular the manner in which objects are targeted, and present themselves as objects to our evidential consciousness. A phenomenological exploration of topic-directional modes of experiencing is essential to a clarification of the structure of reference. In Chapter 8 I analyse the manner in which experiences themselves present themselves to us in a biographical context. This analysis yields the notion of a unity of biographical time as a phenomenological precondition of any meaningful identifying references to ontological individuals.

Another basic problem that emerges from a discussion of the concept of an ontological existent concerns numerical diversity. How does one explain the possibility of numerically diverse particulars? If it is not possible to define the idea of numerical identity in terms of the criteria of re-identification, surely the idea of a plurality of particulars similarly cannot be defined in terms of the criteria under which such particulars are differentiated from each other. But if so, what makes the idea of a pluralistically structured world intelligible? In Chapter 4 I show that an attempt to prove the possibility of pluralism by proving the existence of irreducibly 'external' relations presupposes a distinction between a subjective and an objective order. This distinction, however, is itself analytically linked with the idea of a plurality of selves; and the latter idea, in turn, is inseparable from, and inexplicable independently of, the idea of *error*. I discuss error in Chapter 9. To have a concept of error is to accept that we can be in error on a given occasion even though we do not believe we are, and hence that we can be corrected by others. Nevertheless the belief in our own fallibility is itself an 'incorrigible' belief; i.e. if we *believe* that we are somerimes mistaken, then we are most certainly sometimes mistaken.

The idea of error, however, demands the possibility of public criteria for correcting error, and the concept of public criteria is unintelligible without the possibility of other witnesses, other selves. In fact, I go further than this and argue that if there is to be public criteria, there must *be* other selves. The availability of such criteria depends upon the *existence*, not just the possibility, of a social context. An objective criterion is a typically social construct and presupposes a degree of inter-subjective understanding and cooperation. In Chapter 10 I analyse the inter-subjective conditions of objective validity and the relation between objective validity and truth.

This concludes Part One. Part Two begins with a synoptic review of the basic categories highlighted by the discussion of ontological objects, experiences and objective order in Part One, viz. identity, individuality, unity of biographical time, error and plurality. All these categories form part of the same logical structure and none of them is intrinsically more important, or more fundamental, than any of the others. In Chapter 12 I give additional clarifications about my use of the word 'structure' and try to explain why a structural approach is incompatible with a description of the world in terms of objects and attributes. I then go on to discuss the idea of 'independence of thought' and show why a metaphysical, as distinct from a 'critical', realism cannot be coherently defended. In Chapter 14 I sketch out the fundamentals of a structuralist theory of truth.

Part One

Analytical Basis of Philosophical Reasoning about Reality

A. Ontological Existents

2. Ontological Existents
as Topics of Discourse

Ontological existents are a sub-species of possible topics of discourse, and any topic of discourse, qua topic of discourse, is such that on different occasions it can be referred to as 'the same A'; with 'A' being a descriptive expression of some sort. Either this condition holds or the concept of a topic of discourse is unintelligible; and hence nothing whatever is intelligible. Notice that this condition says nothing about the possibility of *proving* that a topic referred to on a given occasion is the same as the topic referred to on a different occasion. It merely articulates the principle of identity embodied in the concept of a topic of discourse, and any attempt to prove (or disprove, for that matter) the identity of a topic talked about on two separate occasions already presupposes the validity of this principle.

But while all topics are necessarily subject to identity, clearly not all topics qualify as possible existents, and only a miniscule proportion of possible topics actually exist, and herein lies our problem. For what is it that qualifies a given topic as a *possible existent*? What is involved in saying that something exists in its own right, while something else does not? Where and how do we draw a line between ontological existents and fictions?

We refer to things like chairs and tables and trees and houses as 'the same'. We make identifying references to 'the same' persons. We recollect, describe 'the same' experiences. We recognise 'the same' sounds, 'the same' colours. We speak of events, situations, numbers, times, as 'the same'. We expound, analyse, discuss 'the same concept', 'the same proposition', 'the same problem', 'the same theory'. All such topics can be referred to with the help of suitable denoting phrases and used as grammatical subjects in subject/predicate propositions. But this alone does not qualify any of them as possible existents, let alone ensure their existence. They may act as legitimate grammatical subjects, but they are not necessarily also the 'logical' subjects of the propositions concerned, in the sense of representing the genuine basis of predication in the given instance. Before any of them can be significantly claimed to be logical as well as grammatical subjects, and treated as denoting certain objects that exist in their own right rather than merely describing attributes of such objects, or representing something purely fictional, certain additional conditions must be fulfilled. But what are those conditions?

We might try to approach an answer to this question by first looking at some specific features that characterise the identifying references to different kinds of topics of discourse. Taking a very broad view, topics of discourse may be divided into two basic categories: meanings and non-meanings. Consider meanings first.

Identity of meanings as topics of discourse

We use language to talk about the meanings of linguistic expressions as well as about things that are not meanings. When I say 'The oldest tree in the park is an oak', I am referring to the the tall tree of rich foliage standing half-way between the eastern gate and children's playing ground. But if someone asked me what the 'oldest tree in the park' meant, or what 'oak' meant, or what the meaning of the sentence as a whole was, I would have to explain to him the meaning of these expressions with the help of some other expressions which he could understand. Moreover we can discuss the meaning of what is being said even if it so happens that there are no trees in the park, or if all the trees happened to be the same age and none of them was an oak. None of this renders any of the expressions meaningless. Thus I might say to someone 'Let's go and find out which is the oldest tree in the park', without fearing that I may have said something unintelligible just because neither of us is certain what the outcome of our search will be. The content of what I say can be analysed, commented on, communicated to third parties. I can assert of the oldest tree in the park (if there is such a tree) that it is an oak, but I can also say of the sentence 'The oldest tree in the park is an oak' that it means the same, or that it expresses same thought as, say, its French or Chinese translation, irrespective of whether it says anything true.

If by 'meaning' is understood the objective content of linguistic utterances, or what might also be called their 'objective thought-content' (I shall discuss later the 'historical', performative aspects of such utterances), then, on the face of it at least, there seems to be nothing odd or improper in making identifying cross-references to meanings. After all, we do make, and claim to understand, references to 'the same propositions', 'the same descriptions', 'the same arguments'. We say things such as 'I repeat what I said earlier', or 'That is not what I meant', or 'I have heard that argument before'. Admittedly statements of this kind are occasionally challenged. Our hearer may even reject them outright as false. But the point is that it makes sense for him to reject such a statement as false on a given occasion, only if he is prepared to admit that in different circumstances the same statement could be true. As it happens, such statements are very frequently accepted as true.

Some doubts about ascribing identity to meanings

Nevertheless serious misgivings may persist about the wisdom of ascribing identity to meanings.

Surely, it might be said, to interpret identificatory references to meanings in a literal sense is to treat meanings, in effect, on a par with objects. But meanings are not objects. There are no meanings '*per se*', as distinct from meaningful *expressions*; and what an expression means is determined entirely by the use that such an expression may be put to within the particular language game of which it forms a part. Meanings are functions of words; they are not some ghostly essences, capable of subsisting independently of their phenomenal embodiment. To say of two linguistic expressions that they have the 'same meaning', at best, is to say that under the same sort of conditions, they can be used in the same way, to the same effect.

This is not a particularly happy way of phrasing the objection, though, for the question immediately arises what is meant by 'can be used in the same way', 'the same sort of conditions', 'the same effect', etc. If we can understand the identity of the criteria of sameness of use, then we can understand the sameness of meaning.

But the identification of the criteria poses no lesser problems than the identification of what the criteria are for. It might therefore seem that the best, and the only rational, solution is to abandon all references to identity in connection with meaning. If it is true that meaning reduces to use, then surely all mention of 'identity' is inappropriate and can only lead to confusion. For what we are really talking about are merely linguistic symbols and the manner in which such symbols are manipulated within certain contexts, and all that can be detected here are certain similarities. There are no recondite semantic entities over and above such similarities; and if there are no entities, there is no identity either. It follows that, strictly, we cannot justifiably speak of the 'same propositions', or the 'same concepts'. Rather than 'identical concepts', all that is available, and can be significantly referred to, are (in Wittgenstein's famous phrase) 'family resemblances' as between different uses of concept-words.

It is in these terms that an attack is often mounted on the whole idea of synonymy. Since the precise criteria of synonymy cannot be defined, it is argued, there can be no useful work for this concept to do; unless one thinks of synonymy merely as one of 'degree'. Certainly no two expressions in any natural language are ever completely equisignificant. Nor, for that matter, is it possible to circumscribe the meaning of an expression in an absolutely definitive fashion while this expression remains part of the living body of language. On the other hand, an arbitrary rule of substitution whereby two expressions are decreed to be interchangeable for each other within a given context, reveals nothing about the 'sameness of meaning' unless we are in a position to explain the general rule governing such substitutions, which would ensure that the truth-value of the propositions in which such substitutions are carried out remains always and necessarily unaltered. In other words, we need certain criteria of sameness, and no such criteria can be provided. But, then, we should give up the concept of 'identical meanings' and accept that there can be only relative similarities of use, and hence only approximate, pragmatically testable, sub-stitutability of certain expressions within similar contexts.[1]

---

[1] W.V. Quine in his celebrated article on 'Two dogmas of empiricism' (1951) notoriously used the argument against synonymy expounded above in order to expose the vagueness of the notion of analyticity, and thereby to undermine the 'dogma' of the distinction between analytic and synthetic propositions. Analytical propositions are generally said to be true in virtue of

But the fallacious assumption underlying this reasoning is that the idea of identity of meaning makes sense only if the criteria of equisignificance can be clearly defined, whereas the simple fact is that any reference to the criteria of equisignificance already presupposes the notion of sameness of meaning. The chief source of confusion, briefly, is a conflation of the criteria of sameness of meaning with the meaning of 'sameness of meaning'. But although connected, these two concepts are not identical. In fact, any argument directed against the applicability of the idea of identity to meanings is really self-stultifying, for such an argument would imply, among other things, that no topic could be significantly referred to as 'the same' on two separate occasions, with the inevitable consequence that the argument itself could not get off the ground. The point is not only that we do as a matter of fact accept 'the same meaning' and 'a different meaning' as intelligible concepts, but that any attempt to define the criteria of interchangeability of expressions with regard to their meaning *presupposes* their intelligibility.

Meanings are not ontological existents

I should stress again that I am here concerned with meanings qua posited objective thought-contents of linguistic expressions. The egocentric and performative aspects of mental and speech acts by historical individuals who use such expressions to make statements, ask questions, etc., naturally enough, often have a direct bearing on the meaning of what is said on a given occasion, and this points to an area of phenomenological problems that needs to be carefully explored if the complexity of the problem of meaning is to be fully understood. But for the present my principal interest is in meanings qua explicitly posited topics of discourse. The objections that are raised against identity assumptions in respect of meanings in such a context are chiefly motivated by the fear that such assumptions might commit us to accepting meanings as some kind of entities. But this fear seems groundless.

A description, a proposition, an argument can be referred to as 'the

the meanings of their terms. But the analyticity so conceived, he argued, depends on the notion of synonymy, and if the latter is unclear, so is the former, and if so, the analytic/synthetic distinction cannot be given any precise meaning.

same' on different occasions, but only in the sense of the possibility of their being reconstituted as 'the same' description, proposition, argument, etc. in acts of recollection. What is here referred to as 'the same' is not an item, or items, capable of existing *per se*, but rather a mode or species of thought; and a species of thought is necessarily 'reconstitutable' in different thought acts, or else it is not a species. Briefly, in talking about meanings as objective thought-contents we are talking, in effect, about certain species of (reconstitutable, re-thinkable) thought, or thought-modalities.

The concept of equisignificance can now be easily explained, for to say of two symbols that they have the same meaning is merely to say that they both express the same species of thought. Such a statement may or may not be true in a given instance, but its meaningfulness does not depend on the possibility of supplying a foolproof criterion of sameness. Nor are such species of thought or thought-modalities capable of existing independently of individual acts of thinking. They can be objects of thought-acts in reflective consciousness, but they do not qualify as ontological existents.

In a sense, meanings qua species of thought or thought-modalities might be said to represent the principles of 'unity' of certain historical mental acts. What this means might perhaps be made a little clearer with reference to what Kant had to say about his 'Ideas', provided, of course, the comparison is not taken too literally.

Kant notoriously drew a distinction between what he called the 'a priori concepts of the understanding' and the 'a priori concepts of reason'. The former are the categories, which, according to him, underly all objective experience and all knowledge of objects. The latter concepts, which he dubbed 'the Ideas', have merely a regulative function, in the sense that they direct the activity of the understanding towards the ultimate goals of unity and completeness, which however remain forever outside the reach of 'empirical synthesis'. They give a sense of unity and coherence to our cognitive effort, but can never themselves be exhibited in sense experience. The Ideas, Kant says, 'have an excellent, and indeed indispensably necessary, regulative employment, namely, that of directing the understanding towards a certain goal upon which the routes marked out by all its rules converge, as upon their point of intersection'.[2] And he immediately goes on to add: 'This point is indeed a mere idea, a

---

[2] *Critique of Pure Reason*, A644/B672.

focus imaginarius ...' It is not an object in the phenomenal sense, and to regard it as such is to invite a profound metaphysical confusion.

We need not concern ourselves with the details of Kant's theory of Transcendental Ideas. What is relevant to our discussion is only the conception of an Idea as a principle of unity, and the fact that an Idea cannot be a phenomenal object. Both these characteristics are applicable to meanings qua species of thought. Meanings are principles of unity inasmuch as they represent the same basic orientation of thought in different mental acts and different instances of use of language. Like Kant's Ideas they have a regulative function, guiding our actions and our cognitive efforts in a certain direction. And, like Kant's Ideas, meanings are not phenomenal objects. But unlike Kant's Ideas they do not represent ontological existents of a special sort. Not only are meanings not phenomenal objects (in Kant's sense); they are not entities at all.

Non-meanings as topics of discourse

The reasons for this will become obvious if we compare meanings with things other than the species of thought. The latter items, of course, like meanings, are subject to identity; i.e. a non-meaning qua topic of discourse is necessarily such that it must be possible to refer to it on different occasions with the phrase 'the same A', where A is a descriptive expression of some sort. But there is also one further condition that must be fulfilled, and this condition has a crucial bearing upon the distinction between meanings and non-meanings. Briefly, it is this: that if a topic happens to be a non-meaning, then it must be possible, in addition, to refer to it by means of different, non-synonymous descriptive phrases expressing different yet essential features of the non-meaning in question. Or, to put it in another way, there must be at least two non-synonymous descriptive phrases of which it can be said both that they are co-extensive in respect of the given non-meaning and characterise this non-meaning in an essential way. No object of thought that is not capable of being descriptively referred to in such a fashion can be significantly posited as an ontological item existing in the modus 'per se'.

Notice that this condition imposes no limitations on the specific nature of ontological items. It is sufficiently comprehensive to embrace all types of non-meanings regardless of their internal constitution or ontological status. At the same time, it represents a necessary condition that must be fulfilled before any references can be significantly made to non-meanings as ontological existents. It does not, however, represent a sufficient condition of the meaningfulness of such references.

I shall consider presently some examples. But before I do, it is necessary to forestall a possible misunderstanding regarding the applicability of the category of identity to non-meanings.

The idea of non-meanings as identical subjects of predication while implying the possibility of a framework within which references to such items can be contextually checked for truth, is not explicable in terms of any particular criteria of re-identification. It would be useleless to pretend that identity of non-meanings, if it is to make sense, ought to be so explicable and then criticise this idea on the grounds that it cannot be so explained. Yet this is not always clearly understood.

Hume's criticism of identity assumptions

Consider, for example, Hume's argument against identity assumptions. According to Hume, 'the view of any one object is not sufficient to convey the idea of identity'[3] A single object, he argues, conveys the idea of unity, not that of identity. The notion of identity has its source in a 'fiction of the imagination', whereby an object is represented as invariable through a supposed variation of time. But nothing can be shown to remain absolutely invariable over any length of time; so how can we be certain that identity can be legitimately applied to anything?

He continues his argument thus. If we analyse what is involved in acts of 're-identification', we shall find that such acts are based, and depend entirely, on the occurrence of certain similar or similarly connected perceptions. What we in effect register when pronouncing something to be 'the same *x*' are merely certain similarities. All our experience of 'material objects', in the final analysis, reduces to our having series of similar, or similarly connected, perceptions. But this means that there can be no justification for supposing that anything remains identical '*per se*'. If we refer to such objects as 'the same', this is simply because we 'confound the succession with the identity'.[4]

[3] *Treatise* (Oxford 1964), p. 200.
[4] ibid., p. 204.

From Hume's standpoint, it is of course precisely this tendency to mistake succession for identity that is chiefly to blame for the metaphysical doctrine of substance as an enduring and unanalysable substratum behind the observable changes. He believes, therefore, that his criticism of identity at the same time helps to put a stop to this virulent and mystifying doctrine. For, surely, once it is realised that all that we do have and can rely upon are series of perceptions and ideas, it becomes clear that there can be no justification for assuming the existence of any such metaphysical 'substrata', and the whole doctrine of substance falls to the ground.

Hume's argument, however, does not hold water for the simple reason that it assumes that the question of the possibility of significantly ascribing identity to objects as ontological existents can and should be decided via an analysis of the conditions of their identification, whereas the simple fact is that the concept of an entity as a potential topic of discourse is analytically linked with, and hence inseparable from, that of identity. Without identity there can be no meaningful references to anything at all, not even to perceptions and ideas. If Hume's argument proves anything, it is just this: that the assumption of identity cannot be explained in terms of the conditions under which the empirical things of the common sense world are re-identified; in particular, it cannot be explained in terms of similarities between perceptions and ideas. But from this it does not follow either that we can dispense with identity or that identity is not really applicable to objects as ontological existents. Certainly we cannot 'test' the category of identity for meaning by trying to define the criteria for its use in terms of certain relations between perceptions and ideas.

A different view of Hume's argument

It is possible, however, to look at Hume's argument from a different, and in general more acceptable, angle. Thus one might treat it as an argument that is designed not so much to challenge the meaningfulness of applying identity to objects qua ontological existents 'out there' as to expose the difficulties of drawing a clear distinction between the numerical and the qualitative (or species) identity in relation to such objects. If viewed in this light, the argument makes better sense, although of course it acquires an entirely new complexion.

More clearly, Hume's argument might be interpreted as an attack on the assumption that a distinction between numerical and qualitative identity can be reliably and unambiguously drawn on the basis of certain empirical criteria. If all that we can rely on are certain similarities between perceptions and ideas, then surely there is no justification for assuming that existents can be unequivocally differentiated *solo numero*. In other words, his argument might be seen as an attempt to confront the common sense with the disconcerting fact that references to what are assumed to be numerically identical spatio-temporal particulars inhabiting an objective world 'out there' cannot be given a satisfactory justification, and consequently that one cannot claim with certainty that such particulars represent the basic material of which the world is made up. If interpreted in this light, the argument becomes not so much an onslaught on the idea of identity as an attack on the idea of empirical things as basic particulars.

That such an interpretation, even though it deviates in important respects from Hume's own intentions, is much less vulnerable to criticism, will be seen more clearly in the next chapter, when we analyse in greater depth the distinction between numerical and qualitative identity, and its ontological significance.

Non-meanings and possible existents

The preliminary conclusion, then, that emerges from our discussion so far is this: that the concept of a topic of discourse is analytically linked with that of identity and that there can be no question of 'defining' this link in terms of the conditions of re-identification of such topics, whether they be meanings or non-meanings, for the simple reason that without presupposing the identity of the topic in a given case, the question of its 're-identification' cannot even be intelligibly raised.

This is not to undervalue the importance of the conditions of re-identification. A judgment of re-identification in a specific instance is made in the light of certain criteria, and is in principle subject to inter-subjective tests in the light of such criteria. Nevertheless if the judgment happens to be false, it does not automatically become meaningless. Moreover if a topic does not happen to have the ontological status ascribed to it, it is still possible to refer to it identifyingly *qua topic* with the phrase 'the same A'. That a topic of discourse is such that on different occasions it can be referred to as the same is an analytic proposition setting out part of what 'topic of discourse' means. What it says is that it would be self-contradictory to posit something as a topic, while denying the possibility of referring to this something with the phrase 'the same A'. It says nothing about the actual conditions of re-identification of any such topic.

But not all topics of discourse, of course, are legitimate candidates for ontological existents. We saw that meanings fail to qualify. Potential ontological existents are topics that are in principle capable of existing independently of individual acts of thought of which they are objects, and meanings cannot so exist. This leaves non-meanings; but non-meanings are a vast class, comprising logically most diverse elements and including a large sub-class of topics that come under the general heading of 'fiction'. This typewriter on my desk is a non-meaning. But so is the number two. And so ostensibly are the greatest cardinal number and the abominable snowman. What has to be decided is which non-meanings may be significantly regarded as existing 'in their own right', and which cannot be so regarded; what conditions must be fulfilled before a claim that a given topic does so exist can be accepted as meaningful?

Language is sufficiently flexible to allow the construction of an infinite variety of singular terms which do not designate any entity. In particular, through nominalisation almost any expression can be turned into a noun phrase and used in a quasi-referential function. There are no formal restrictions limiting the construction of noun phrases and their employment as subjects in subject/predicate statements other than those implicit in the general conditions of coherence and consistency.

The only antidote to an unbridled proliferation of spurious designators is analysis, and of course we all practice analysis in some form or another, even though not always very radically or systematically. The main aim, usually, is to show that sentences containing what are regarded as bogus designators can be adequately replaced by other sentences which do not contain such designators, and hence that the 'real' topic in the given instance is in fact different to what it appears to be. Such analytic paraphrases are usually conducted from the position of a specific (even though not always openly or clearly stated) ontological bias; and often the assumption is made that all purportive references to 'non-meanings' in factual statements, in the final analysis, can be translated into references to ontological existents of the preferred sort.

But the main point is this: that irrespective of whether an analysis is embarked upon from the position of an openly stated or tacitly assumed ontological bias, or whether, on the contrary, the question of an ultimate choice of basic ontological existents is deliberately left undecided, it is usually taken for granted that the concept of an ontological existent is in general well understood. Yet it is this very concept that is in urgent need of elucidation. An ontological existent, we have said, is an object that exists in the modus '*per se*'. But what precisely is the meaning of '*per se*'? What is involved in assuming that there are ontological objects at all? What makes this assumption intelligible? What exactly are we committing ourselves to by making it? Before any programme for an elimination of 'spurious designators' can be properly evaluated, before its feasibility, and above all its significance, can be properly judged, it is essential that the concept of an ontological existent be clarified and made absolutely precise and this task is the most complex and most difficult of all.

Names and descriptions

Let us begin by taking a closer look at the logical structure of referential symbols. It might seem that the most promising as well as most appropriate way to approach the task of clarifying the concept of ontological existent is to begin by exploring the logical characteristics of proper names. Proper names are paradigm referential symbols, and it seems natural to look to them for clues. How, then, do proper names perform their referential function? Do they necessarily have a meaning as well as reference; and if so, to what extent, if any, is their meaning-content relevant to their designatory function? What is the nature of the relationship between proper names and descriptive referential phrases that happen to designate the same objects?

One familiar view is that nothing qualifies as a genuine proper name unless it singles out its object in an unambiguous fashion, and that this task can be accomplished only by a logically simple symbol. It follows that names cannot be descriptions, for descriptions are invariably complex, and (it is implied) inherently ambiguous, i.e. they do not by themselves ensure the uniqueness of the referential relation in any given case of referring. Any complex referential symbol, or a string of such symbols, theoretically speaking, can apply to any number of individuals, but a proper name picks out one object, and one object only, spanning, as it were, the latter's entire career. The conclusion derived from this is that if an object is such that in principle it cannot be referred to directly and unequivocally with a simple symbol, only described, then it cannot qualify as a fundamental ontological existent. It is by definition a complex object, and all complex objects are explicable as logical constructions out of logically simple elements. They represent, in Russell's colourful phrase, the realm of 'logical fictions', and while the life as we know it obviously would be inconceivable without great many of such 'fictions' (they include, among other things, all the spatio-temporal objects of our everyday experience), there are a large number of others which are neither very useful nor indispensable and should be carefully guarded against if we are not to end up with an ontology crowded with all sorts of phoney entities.

Does this give us the clue we need? Can the distinction, that is, between names, conceived as purely referential simple symbols, and descriptions, enable us to gain a clearer insight into the concept of an ontological existent, i.e. an item existing '*per se*', on the one hand, and the 'constructed' superstructure of – convenient, and not so convenient – 'fictions', on the other?

The first, and most natural, reaction to this is to reject the suggestion that there can be such things as non-descriptive, simple referential symbols. A referential symbol, it might be argued, refers only in virtue of what it means, i.e. it necessarily carries a descriptive content. This does not mean that names are always replaceable in a straightforward fashion by descriptive phrases. 'Shakespeare' and 'the author of *Macbeth*' refer to the same person, but evidently they are not always interchangeable. If they were, 'Shakespeare is the author of *Macbeth*' would be a tautology, not a contingent truth. Nevertheless this does not show that 'Shakespeare' is a purely referential symbol devoid of all descriptive content, only that there is a certain difference in scope as between 'Shakespeare' and 'the author of *Macbeth*'; with 'Shakespeare', in the final analysis, unfolding into a complex series of descriptions that uniquely characterise the individual concerned. If, on the other hand, the condition is that the proper name, if it is to count as a proper name at all, must be non-descriptive, then we shall look in vain for suitable candidates, for there can hardly be an expression that communicates something and yet does not incorporate, or contextually presuppose, a descriptive content.

In a sense, of course, all this is true. It is moreover true that names are often *deliberately* chosen for their descriptive content. Columbus had an excellent reason for naming the island where he first landed after crossing the Atlantic 'San Salvador'. In fact, it is fairly safe to assume that all proper names started their denotative careers as descriptions of one sort or another, although in many cases the link with the original descriptive content subsequently became severed or obscured. What is more, proper names are normally introduced into discourse by means of descriptive phrases. Thus I might say 'The man over there is John'. I might of course only gesture and say 'John', but unless my gesture means, or can be understood to mean, 'the man over there', or something akin to this, 'John' will fail to communicate anything. But if descriptive phrases are necessary to introduce names or things that can be seen and pointed at, they are clearly even more necessary in respect of objects that cannot be seen, or no longer exist. Thus no amount of gesturing will help to explain the references of 'Shakespeare' or 'Julius Caesar' or 'Socrates'.

Yet none of this obliterates the difference between the respective roles of names and descriptions. A proper name is no less a proper name for possessing a descriptive content. Moreover no proper name can fulfil its function as a proper name without certain descriptions that specify the conditions under which the name in question can be significantly applied, but it does not follow for this that names are ultimately 'reducible' to descriptions; i.e. that, in the final analysis, there is no real difference between them at all.

Why does this not follow? One *prima facie* plausible answer is provided by another theory, according to which the specific feature that marks off proper names from descriptions should be sought not in any 'logical simplicity' but rather in the 'rigidity of their designation'. The central idea here is that a proper name qua proper name not only picks out one object only, but unlike a descriptive phrase designates that same object in 'every possible world'; a 'possible world' being understood as representing a possible but unactualised situation, or a series of situations, of which the given object might be a feature. Thus the name 'Shakespeare' rigidly refers to Shakespeare, irrespective of whether we happen to be talking about what Shakespeare did or wrote, or did not do or write but might have done or written, i.e. about his actual or merely possible attributes.

On the other hand, 'the author of *Macbeth*' is a non-rigid designator, because the author of *Macbeth* might not have been Shakespeare. For example, he might have been Bacon.

The referential rigidity is said to be subject to a simple intuitive test. Thus if it does not make sense to suppose that the designatum of 'A' might be different from what it is, then 'A' is a rigid designator, otherwise it is non-rigid. To take again our example, Shakespeare could not have been other than Shakespeare (and, of course, Bacon could not have been other than Bacon), but – theoretically – any number of people might have written *Macbeth*. It follows that, contextual substitutions apart, naming symbols can never be entirely replaced by descriptive phrases, for this would mean substituting non-rigid designators for rigid ones, which might very well result in a change of truth-value of the propositions concerned. Thus 'The author of *Macbeth* was born at Stratford-on-Avon' becomes a falsehood if Bacon (or some other person born elsewhere) wrote the play. The distinction between names and descriptions remains thus of crucial importance. A descriptive expression, it is argued, may help fix the reference of a name via some contingent characteristic of the object in question (as is the case with 'the author of *Macbeth*'), but it cannot provide its 'definition'.[5]

Does this give us the answer we need? There is no doubt, of course, that when a given symbol (irrespective of its 'descriptive content') is accorded the status of a name, it acquires the privileged position of a representative of the biographical identity of the object it names, and by virtue of this very fact it can no longer be equated with any description, or series of descriptions. 'Shakespeare' denotes someone who might have had any number of different characteristics. He happens to be called 'Shakespeare', but this does not make 'Shakespeare' equivalent with 'the man called Shakespeare', for he might not have been called 'Shakespeare' at all. He almost certainly was not thus called by his own father. In fact, he might have been, and very probably was, called a number of different names by different people at various times during his lifetime. And, of course, the man referred to as 'Shakespeare' might have been Bacon, or rather he might have had the attributes associated with Bacon. The point is that 'Shakespeare', used as a name, enables us to express intelligibly *all* such possibilities.

---

[5] Cf. Saul Kripke, *Naming and Necessity*, Oxford 1980, passim.

But given the fact that names in such cases do behave as rigid designators, the question is, does the referential rigidity provide a *sufficient* criterion for distinguishing names from descriptions, and the answer to this clearly must be that it does not. Thus it is not difficult to find descriptions that satisfy the 'intuitive test' of rigidity. 'The first positive even integer' and 'the common logarithm of 100' both 'rigidly', refer to the number two. They could not refer to anything else. Any referential term descriptive of a genuine individuating feature of the object concerned is by definition a 'rigid designator'. I am not suggesting, of course, that such uniquely referring terms are available for any kind of objects whatever. In particular, contingent entities cannot be individuated in an absolute sense by any kind of descriptive phrase. No description of such entities is so precise as to exclude a priori all possibility of an ambiguous reference. But numbers belong in a different category, and here descriptive terms evidently can refer just as 'rigidly' as names can.

It follows that the difference between names and descriptions cannot be defined in terms of 'referential rigidity'. What gives a name as a name its special status is that it represents the 'transcendence' of the object relative to any particular description that might be given of that object. An object can be described from an indefinite number of different perspectives. The function of a name is to designate the common target of such descriptions. The target sometimes may turn out to be fictional. Sometimes, as, for example, in the context of a play or a fairy tale, it is not intended to be anything other than fictional. Yet even in such contexts the semantic difference between names and descriptions is not entirely obliterated, although one can hardly talk here of a rigidity of reference across 'all possible worlds'.

What we have to begin with, then, is the posited transcendence of the object relative to its possible perspectival descriptions. This gives us a key to the difference between naming and describing. The concept of referential rigidity in the sense in which it is used in the above theory, on the other hand, goes beyond this in that it already presupposes the idea of '*per se*' existence. To make use again of our example, the referential rigidity of 'Shakespeare' is explained, in effect, by a reference to the actual existence of Shakespeare. If, however, Shakespeare did actually exist, then he must have possessed certain attributes that made him the kind of existent he was, even though no attributes that he may have had would have been sufficient to individuate him in a metaphysical sense. What this boils down to, briefly, is this: that one cannot treat 'Shakespeare' as a 'rigid designator' without at the same time assuming that some 'essence' attaches to it, and hence that certain descriptions necessarily go with it, although no such description, or set of descriptions, can fully reproduce its 'meaning'. Expressed in a different way, one cannot coherently both use 'Shakespeare' as a name and assume that Shakespeare literally could be 'anything'. If 'Shakespeare' names an existent, it names someone with certain specific attributes, although his numerical identity, in the strict sense, cannot be defined in terms of those attributes. (I shall return to this problem later on.)

Some logical constraints on ontological assumptions

(a) Coherence

It is then not so much the distinction between names and descriptions as the distinction between the *function* of naming and the *function* of describing that gives some indication as to what is involved in positing something as an ontological existent. There is no question of any 'definition' of the latter idea, simply the matter of bringing out some of its central implications.

Nevertheless there are certain minimal logical conditions that must be satisfied before any references to ontological existents can be accepted as meaningful. One such condition is a corollary of the Principle of Contradiction, and may be stated as follows. No object can qualify as a possible ontological existent if its notion gives rise to a contradiction. This does not mean that nothing whatever qualifies that could conceivably take 'contradictory' predicates. An object as a temporally extended existent may very well have the predicate p at time t, and the predicate not-p at time t_1. In fact, most objects that we come into contact with do. But, then, we think of such objects as temporally extended. What is not possible is that something should exist (temporally extended or not) of which no coherent notion can be formed.

The implications of the requirement of coherence can be more easily demonstrated in relation to atemporal objects. Take the familiar mathematical example of the greatest cardinal number. If such a number did exist, it would be the last member of the series of cardinals arranged in the order of magnitude. But the series of cardinals cannot have a last member. This follows from Cantor's proof showing that the number of possible selections from a given set of objects necessarily exceeds the number of the actual members of that set, irrespective of how many members the set happens to have. Thus, given a set with just two members a and b, four different selections are possible: $\{a\}$, $\{b\}$, $\{a,b\}$, and the empty set φ. In general, if a set has n members, there will be 2^n possibilities of selection, or 2^n subsets. This remains valid irrespective of whether n is finite or infinite. It follows that there can be no greatest cardinal number, for such a number, if it did exist, would be 'greater than itself'.

A similar problem is presented by the notorious 'Russell's class'. Like the greatest cardinal number, Russell's class similarly fails to satisfy the requirement of coherence. Classes, Russell reasoned, are normally not members of themselves. The class of apples is not itself an apple. If now we conceive of a class comprising all classes that are not members of themselves, would this class be a member of itself, or would it not be a member of itself? Either supposition leads to a contradiction, and the conclusion must be that such a class cannot exist in any conceivable universe.

We have here two examples not just of non-existents but of impossible existents, and the question immediately arises, how can an 'impossible existent' qualify as a genuine topic of discourse? What, if anything, is here being 'talked about'? We have used the phrases 'Russell's class' and 'The greatest cardinal number', but such phrases not only do not, but *cannot* denote any ontological existent. Should they, then, be branded as spurious designators and banished from rational discourse? Yet if we are not allowed to use them in contextual cross-references, how can we succeed in saying what we wish to say, namely that they do not designate any existent?

Russell's own answer to this kind of problem, as is well known, was to suggest that all descriptive referential expressions without exception should be eliminated and replaced by certain predicates. Such expressions, he argued, cannot perform a genuinely naming function, and, ideally, should not be used at all. But this seems much too drastic. If my analysis of the concept of topic of discourse is correct, then clearly any topic can be descriptively referred to. In the above examples, the topics referred to are certain meanings, and meanings, as we saw, do not qualify as ontological existents in any case. What must be possible, at the very least, is to refer to the given item by means of certain coextensive non-synonymous phrases, which form part of the essential description of that item. But references to meanings are generally based on certain accidental characteristics that act as contextual code signals in communication, and can hardly be treated as part of the 'essential description' of their referents.

(b) Determinacy

I turn now to another basic logical condition of meaningfulness of describing something as an ontological existent. This condition is a corollary of the principle of Excluded Middle and may be stated as follows. An item cannot be significantly posited as existing in an ontological sense, without at the same time assuming that from any given point of view, at any given time, out of every pair of contradictory predicates, one, and only one such predicate can be correctly ascribed to it. Expressed differently, for any given existent, in any context in which this existent may be 'talked about', there is a non-arbitrary set of predicates attributable to that existent. Yet more clearly, perhaps, by describing something as an ontological existent we are in effect committed to accepting that this something, at any given time, can be rightfully claimed to belong to one, and only one, out of each pair of mutually exclusive classes in any universe of discourse in which this existent features as a topic.

This may not be immediately obvious, and in some cases it may even appear to be contrary to what one would normally regard as 'common sense'. Surely, it will be said, it is necessary to draw a distinction between predicates which within a given context at a given time can be appropriately ascribed to a given existent, and those predicates which under the same conditions cannot be appropriately ascribed to that existent. Only of the former can it be meaningfully said that either they or their contradictories are true of the existent in question. If Jones has never heard of Tolstoy or read any of his books, it is meaningless to assert that Jones either likes Tolstoy as a writer or does not like Tolstoy as a writer. The question of his liking or disliking Tolstoy simply does not arise.

However, this argument depends too much on the conventions governing ordinary usage. It does indeed sound odd to say, in Jones's case, that he either likes Tolstoy or does not like Tostoy. Yet no great effort of imagination is required to describe Jones meaningfully and accurately as either being like those who are Tolstoy-liking or not being like those who are Tolstoy-liking. As a matter of fact, Jones is not like those who are Tolstoy-liking (i.e. he lacks their Tolstoy-liking views and attitudes). He is of course also not like those who are Tolstoy-*disliking*. Both these statements make perfectly good sense. Moreover they remain meaningful irrespective of whether Jones has read or even heard of Tolstoy.

To sum up, in positing an item as an ontological existent we are at the same time by implication positing this item as a potential subject of a non-arbitrary subset of predicates from among an indefinite number of meaningful predicates, and hence as completely determinate with regard to possible descriptions that may be given of it at any given time.

Notice that we have said nothing yet about the possibility of actually deciding, in a given instance, which of the two mutually exclusive classes the posited existent belongs to. We have merely argued that such an existent necessarily belongs to only one such class, i.e. that it necessarily takes only one out of each pair of contradictory predicates. This is part of what is meant by an ontological existent (qua item existing in the modus '*per se*'). In a sense, this represents the most general and at the same time the most fundamental 'principle of individuation' for such items. But does this enable us actually to decide in each case which predicates do and which don't apply to the item concerned? It seems fairly obvious that often such a decision will not be possible either because no clear decision procedures are available, or because of certain fundamental difficulties involved in applying such procedures. Yet while it may not be possible, in a given case, to come to a clear decision one way or the other, it cannot, I shall argue, be coherently assumed that a decision is logically impossible and at the same time insisted that the object in question exists in an ontological sense. In other words, I shall dispute that ontological existents can be coherently treated in an uncritical metaphysical fashion as 'things (existing unconditionally) in themselves'.

Numerical and species identity of ontological existents

Evidently unless both conditions discussed above are met no references to ontological existents can make clear sense. But although essential, these conditions are not sufficient to explain the full significance of such references. There are at least two other central issues that must be discussed before we can obtain a clearer insight into what is involved in regarding something as an ontological existent. One of them concerns the possibility of a distinction between numerical and species identity, i.e. the problem of individuation of ontological particulars. The other concerns what, by contrast, might be called the 'problem of differentiation', viz. how to explain the possibility of there being a plurality of ontological existents rather than just one. These will be the topics of the next two chapters.

3. The Principle of Individuation

Ontological existents as a sub-species of topics of discourse, it has been emphasised, are inseparable from identity, i.e. it must be possible in respect of any such existent to use the phrase 'the same A', with A being a descriptive expression of some sort. However, apart from some desultory comments about spurious denoting phrases, no attempt has been made to discuss the nature of such identifying references in any great detail. Yet depending upon what A is, the phrase in question can be used to assert the numerical identity of a particular or the qualitative identity of a *species*. We say 'the same man' and mean numerically the same human person; and we say 'the same colour' and mean a quality that can be possessed or exemplified by different individuals.

Obviously to say that an ontological existent qua possible topic of discourse is such that on different occasions it can be referred to as 'the same A' is not to say a great deal unless a clarification is given of the distinction and the relationship between these two kinds of sameness. In the last chapter I have discussed briefly the 'most general principle of individuation', based on the principle of Excluded Middle. But this principle on account of its very generality cannot throw light on the above distinction, and as a result the concept of individuality remains ambiguous and obscure. It is essential but not enough to postulate that an object-topic, if it is to qualify as existing in the modus *per se*, i.e. in its own right and not just as an object of thought, must be a subject, at any given time, of a non-arbitrary set of predicates. It is necessary, in addition, to explain the significance and the implications of the distinction between particularity and specificity involved in references to such topics. What makes it possible to ask meaningfully in respect of a given existent not only in what way it qualitatively differs from any other type of existent, but what makes it numerically, existentially unique? Where does the distinction between particularity and specificity have its roots?

In the following, I shall argue that while this distinction is a vital conceptual ingredient in any meaningful references to object-topics qua ontological existents, it cannot be 'explained' in terms of the criteria under which such existents are numerically and qualitatively re-identified and distinguished from one another. By this I do not mean that the question of criteria is unimportant, or that the distinction remains meaningful even if there are no ontological objects at all to which it might be applied. On the contrary, I shall maintain that this distinction demands the existence of such objects, and that moreover its applicability to such objects presupposes the possibility of certain criteria. But no criteria are sufficient actually to explain this distinction, and in order to elucidate its meaning it is necessary to consider it in connection with certain modes of experiencing with which it forms a structural unity.

Numerical and qualitative identity

Let us begin by examining some traditional views about particular-identity.

Usually one, or both, of the following conditions are said to hold:

(a) No particular can be in two places at once. Two particulars simultaneously occupying two different places are in virtue of this very fact two different particulars. By contrast, universals can be simultaneously exemplified by different particulars in different places.

(b) Particulars exist in time. By their very nature they are temporal entities. They come and go out of existence. Universals are timeless.

Consider (a) first. The idea of particularity is here linked with the idea of place – 'place' being taken in its physical sense of 'spatial location'. It is assumed that a particular's individuality, its numerical distinctness from any other existent, is ensured by the spatial location it happens to occupy at any given time. (The insistence on spatial location as a criterion, it should be noted, means that logical individuals, such as numbers, for example, automatically fail the particularity test.) Universals, in contrast to particulars, are said to be merely 'exemplified' or 'illustrated' at various places. This is often used as an argument in support of the view that universals (as well as logical individuals) cannot be ontological existents.

All this accords well with common sense. Thus the tendency, normally, is to take the view that a condition of significantly claiming x to be actually existent is that it should be possible to ask 'Where is x?'. But it clearly is not meaningful to ask 'Where is the concept house?' or 'Where is the quality green?' What can be asked meaningfully is: 'Where is A's house?' and 'Where is the green hat?' In the latter two cases the objects concerned can be given spatial co-ordinates and thereby unequivocally distinguished from any other particulars of the similar sort.

However, this view soon runs into difficulties. First, there is the problem of change of place. A particular, one normally assumes, can change its place without ceasing to be numerically the same particular. Yet if spatial position is the only criterion of particularity, how can we be certain that a given particular in a different place is still numerically the same particular? Secondly, it is necessary to explain whence and how its co-ordinates are to be assigned. If place is to be defined in terms of co-ordinates, the assumption that no particular can be in two places at once presupposes the (logical) possibility of a unique designation by means of co-ordinates of every single position in space, i.e. the possibility, in principle, of setting up an all-embracing co-ordinate system; making it possible to differentiate unambiguously every point in space from any other from a given origin. But what individuates the origin? We might try to define the origin in terms of some other frame of reference. But this will only raise the problem of a new origin, and so with every other system that we might adopt.

It follows that there can be no individuation, in an absolute sense, of any origin, and hence of any place. Spatial determination by means of co-ordinates, alone, cannot ensure the metaphysical uniqueness of any existent. And if so, we cannot, without qualifications, assert that no particular can be in two places at once. This cannot be asserted as a *metaphysical proposition*; as something, that is, which is true of the world of existents irrespective of the manner in which existents are given in our experience.

Now consider (b). It is maintained that whereas particulars are in time, universals are timeless. Things like pencils and tables and houses and electronic calculators, as well as living beings, are 'temporal' entities in the sense that we can meaningfully speak of their life-span, their 'coming into being' and 'going out of existence' or 'ceasing to be'. If, as is sometimes done, things are assimilated to events, we can speak of particulars as events, and of the latter as being 'temporal' in the sense that every event exhibits a pattern of change in some direction, and can be said to occur simultaneously with, or before, or after, some other event. Concepts, on the other hand, cannot be meaningfully described as 'temporal' in this sense. The desk on which I am writing exists 'in time'; the concept desk does not.

This approach too creates difficulties. But first, a brief general comment about space and time in order to forestall a possible misunderstanding. In distinguishing between (a) and (b) I may have given the impression of wishing to maintain a strict distinction between space and time as against the physical space-time. This distinction may be justified from a limited epistemological standpoint, it might be said, but it does not really make sense in physical terms. Particulars qua ontological existents are not in space and in time; they are slices of physical space-time.

It is not my intention here to question the usefulness of the concept of physical space-time, or any other concept of physics, for that matter. I am merely concerned to point out that a clarification of particular-identity is normally given in terms of our experience with things in perceptual space and perpeptual time. As to whether four-dimensional events rather than perceptual objects should be regarded as ontologically basic particulars, this is a metaphysical decision which need not concern us at the moment. It should be emphasised, however, that epistemologically at least any individuation of such events cannot but begin with an individuation of perceptual things, and consequently that its success or failure will inevitably depend upon the success or failure of the latter.

With regard to 'temporality' (in the sense in which this concept was used above), this cannot be regarded as a sufficient condition of particularity so long as it is not shown that temporality alone (in the indicated sense) ensures numerical identity of particulars; and if we are to be able to justifiably claim that it is a necessary condition of particularity, we must first show that there can be no extra-temporal particulars.[1]

---

[1] I shall argue later on that temporality can help to shed light on the idea of particularity only if it is interpreted as a mode of experiencing, not as a 'property' of objects.

Individuation via demonstrative identification

Nevertheless, it might be argued that the problem of particular-identity, at least as far as perceptual things are concerned, presents no insoluble problems. After all, we demonstrate daily our ability to make inter-subjectively intelligible and successful identifying references to things around us. If this were not possible, inter-subjective communication could not take place. The 'in-dividuating force' of such references depends of course to a large extent upon the context in which they are made. Thus if at this moment someone said something to me about 'that ugly little statue on your fireplace' and accompanied this with an appropriate gesture, I should have little difficulty in identifying the object to which he is referring, but identification may not be so easy if a reference is made to an object that is not accessible to immediate perception, or of which I have no knowledge whatever.

Basically, there are two types of identifying references to particulars: one involving the use of 'demonstratives' (demonstrative pronouns, personal pronouns, adverbs such as 'here', 'there', 'today' etc.); the other relying on descriptions that do not involve the use of demonstratives; one speaker-related, the other 'impersonal'. It is often argued that the latter type of identifying references are really parasitic upon the former. The intelligibility and indeed the success of any identifying references to particulars, it is claimed, depend ultimately upon the intelligibility and the success of demonstrative references to particulars in the context of a speaker-hearer situation. It is the individuation by demonstratives that provides a basis for a unitary system of spatio-temporal relations in which every particular has a unique place and in which we ourselves provide the main point of reference.

By comparison, impersonal descriptive references lack the same individuating force and are frequently ambiguous and misleading. The phrase 'the tallest man in England' will fail to individuate any person if the class of tallest men in England happens to have more than one member. This is not to say that particulars cannot under any circumstances be contextually individuated via 'impersonal' descriptions. In a vast majority of cases such descriptive references are accepted as perfectly adequate. Many particulars cannot be demonstratively identified in any case. But if a particular is to be successfully identified non-demonstratively – it is argued – there must be an individuating fact that relates it uniquely to the 'present situation of reference'. In other words, it must be possible to connect this particular in an unambiguous fashion with certain items that are accessible to direct, or demonstrative, identification.

The basic idea, in short, is that the problem of individuation should be approached from the horizon of ordinary everyday experience. It is hoped that in this way the metaphysical difficulties surrounding this problem will largely melt away. For, it is argued, it makes little sense to worry about the possibility of repetitiveness and reduplication with regard to the world 'in itself' if we can establish the historical uniqueness of particulars in relation to ourselves. There is a system of spatio-temporal relations in which we ourselves have a place and which provides that unified framework within which every particular is uniquely related to every other, and where the distinction between numerical and qualitative identity has a perfectly valid and immediately intelligible application.[2]

Some difficulties of demonstrative identification

But how reliable is demonstrative identification? Consider the following example. Suppose that while shopping in a crowded store I become temporarily separated from a friend and in reply to his anxious call shout back 'I am here'. What with the cacophony of sounds assailing us from all sides and the crowd of shoppers jostling and pressing between and around us, this reply may not give him a very clear indication of where I am standing. But suppose that he proceeds in the general direction from where he assumed my voice came and suddenly found himself face to face with a stranger who looked very similar to myself. In a hurry to find me and too tired to pay attention to detail, he might give him a cursory glance and exclaim, relieved, 'Ah, there you are.' Soon afterwards he may realise his mistake and continue his search. But if the stranger was an exact replica of myself, behaved in exactly the same way, etc., he would obviously find it more difficult to make a correct identification. In fact, he would most probably come to regard the stranger as myself. In order to reassure himself, he might question the stranger about things from my own past, recalling occasions

---

[2] Cf. P.F. Strawson, *Individuals*, London 1964. I shall have to say more about Professor Strawson's theory of particulars later on in this chapter.

which only I could possibly remember and comparing his answers with those that I would be likely to give. But this too might fail to expose the error, for the stranger might simply guess the right answers, or his answers might be so close to those expected of him that even the most scrupulous interrogator would be deceived. Is there anything else that might be done to settle the issue one way or the other?

Suppose my friend turned to other people for help, gathered all the crucial data about myself, consulted everyone who knew me, all my friends and acquaintances. This still might not provide an answer to the problem, if only because he might be deceived by others as well as by the stranger himself. The process of verification of data, theoretically, could go on for ever, always requiring new acts of identification.

But imagine now a slightly different situation. Suppose that my friend was not looking for me at all. He had, in fact, just left me on a bench in a nearby park where we had spent some time together before he decided to go for a stroll. He could then say to the impostor: 'Look here, it is useless to go on pretending. I have just left him in the park. You can't be in two places at once.' If the stranger persisted, he might take him to the park and point at me, which in normal circumstances should be sufficient to settle the matter. But we are now not concerned with what is normally likely to happen, but with what might happen. The stranger might refuse to admit defeat and maintain simply that the person sitting on the bench was not I, that *he* was I, and that it was with him that the man who was now doubting his identity was having a conversation a moment ago. What could my friend reply to this? He might decide to cross-examine both of us in an attempt to detect inconsistencies in our replies, or hope for some slip-up on our part which might enable him to make the correct identification. But if we are both determined to mislead him, he is not likely to make much headway. In desperation, he might appeal to witnesses who had seen me sitting on the bench in the park while he was talking to my double outside. But witnesses too could be mistaken Furthermore, interrogation of witnesses involves another series of identifications which raise similar problems.

In view of all this, he might finally decide that the time had come to give up further arguing and accept what each of us has told him. Thus he might say: 'All right, from now on I shall accept what you say. You now standing on my right are the person I left on the bench, and you on my left are someone else, and neither of you can deceive me any longer.' However, he would have to keep a close eye on our movements from now on, never allowing both of us to disappear from his sight for any length of time. For suppose that he, tired as he must be, closes his eyes for a few moments. Then, on opening them again, he would be confronted with the same problem: which of us is which? If the interval during which he kept his eyes closed was very short, say one second, he could maintain that we could not have exchanged our places in so short a time and invoke the laws of physics in support of his view. But the laws of physics are valid only 'until further notice', i.e. until instances are found that falsify them, and this conceivably might be such an instance.

Now it might be argued that ontologically the decisive factor is that on opening his eyes he found again two distinct individuals. He might not be able to tell with complete certainty which is which, but he can still numerically distinguish them, and, if he so chooses, name them again.

But this clearly is not enough. For the question is, how can he be sure that in observing two similar individuals on two different occasions he is in fact observing the same pair? Furthermore, the fact that he sees them as two distinct individuals does not necessarily mean that they exist as two distinct individuals when they are not perceived. Their perceptual distinguishability, alone, is no proof either of their actual existence or of their distinguishability *per se*. That two such individuals are perceived as two is due simply to their occupying two different positions within the perceiver's own visual field. Thus one might be perceived to the left of the other, or to the right of the other, or above the other. But *left, right, above* conceivably might be merely qualities of the perceiver's own visual field and not at all relations in an objective space. In other words, what is seen, or rather what is *believed* to be seen, as numerically distinct, need not be numerically distinct in reality.

None of these difficulties are likely to trouble us much in daily life, but they remain genuine difficulties none the less and raise issues of fundamental importance; for if there can be no absolutely reliable and unequivocal criteria for deciding whether any given existent remains numerically, and not merely qualitatively, the same from one moment in time to the next, then we cannot hope to be able to 'define' the distinction between numerical and qualitative identity in terms of the criteria of particular-identification. But, then, what, if anything, does justify the assumption that there can be numerically (purely numerically) distinguishable particulars at all?

Four theories of particulars

In what follows, I propose to pursue this question further by considering critically four different philosophical theories of particulars. I shall then briefly outline a structural approach to the problem of the distinction between numerical and qualitative identity.

(a) Kant's theory

Let us begin with Kant. Kant argued that the distinction between numerical and qualitative identity can be meaningfully drawn only in the domain of the phenomenal; i.e. within the context of space and time, which, according to him, are the 'forms of our intuition' and not properties of things in themselves. If space and time were properties of things in themselves, he argued, then if two things had the same properties, there would be no means of telling them apart, and Leibniz's 'principle of indiscernibles' would hold true. But if space and time are merely 'forms of our intuition', then the distinction between numerical and qualitative identity presents no difficulty, for in that case any two things can be numerically distinguished in virtue of their spatial position alone. 'Thus in the case of two drops of water' – he says – 'we can abstract altogether from all internal difference (of quality and quantity), and the mere fact that they have been intuited simultaneously in different spatial positions is sufficient justification for holding them to be numerically different.'[3]

This explanation won't do, of course. It is inadequate, because all it does, in effect, is to transfer the problem from things to spatial positions, or places. Thus the question that immediately arises is, what makes places numerically distinguishable? What justifies the assumption that two qualitatively identical things can occupy simultaneously two different places, or numerically the same place in succession? Above all, what needs to be explained is how we distinguish between places in a phenomenological space and places in

---

[3] Cf. *Critique of Pure Reason*, B319/A263 ff.

an objective space. For it is clearly not enough to say that if two things are observed simultaneously in different spatial positions, then they are two, not one, even though they might be completely alike. This merely amounts to saying that if two things are observed as spatially distinct, then they are not observed as spatially indistinct, which is true enough but hardly illuminating. We need to know something quite different, viz. whether it is possible, and if so, under what conditions, for spatial positions to be an adequate individuating factor in the case of entities which are not, and cannot be, simultaneously perceived.

What is Kant's reply to this? Briefly, his reply is that the key to the individuative power of spatial positions lies in the fact there there is only one all-embracing space, of which particular spaces, or places, are constituent parts (so that every place is almost by definition unique). Not only is space one, but the very notion that there might be different, unconnected, spaces is really unintelligible. The idea of space, he argues, is not obtained by abstraction from particular spatial relations; rather our ability to see things as spatially related already presupposes an idea of a unitary space. Similarly, the idea of time is not extracted from any observation of actual coexistence and succession; on the contrary, any significant references to coexistence and succession already presuppose an idea of time. It follows that neither space nor time can be classified as 'general concepts'. A general concept can be exemplified by any number of particular instances which need not stand in any causal relation with each other. But individual spaces are not exemplifying instances of the concept of space; they are *parts* of space, just as individual times are *parts* of a single universal time.

But this answer is still not satisfactory, for the question remains, why is it necessary for such a unitary space and time to be other than a phenomenological space and time? It is just not good enough to say that a spatial position in a unitary space alone ensures the numerical uniqueness of its occupier. For what guarantee is there that it does so *objectively*? Or, to change the question slightly, if space and time are (as Kant claims) 'pure intuitions', what confers objectivity upon such intuitions?

Kant's argument is of course inspired by his unshakeable belief in the synthetic character and the 'apodeictic certainty' of mathematical propositions. He asks 'How are such propositions possible?', and his answer is that this can be explained only by assuming that space and time are a priori features of our cognitive constitution, not properties of things in themselves. Moreover, the fact that experience of objects is to be had only under the form of space and time ensures the applicability of mathematics to the whole of the phenomenal (and hence physical) world. But Kant's choice of examples is rather unfortunate. Thus that no more than three lines can intersect at right angles in a point; that a line (theoretically) can be extended into infinity; that congruent figures can be superimposed upon each other, while incongruent figures can't (even though they are completely alike in all points) etc.; all of this may be phenomenologically obvious, but why should it be true of an objective world? The question, in short, is, what confers objectivity upon such spatial intuitions? – and the only answer that Kant is able to give to this is: 'The universal validity and necessity of geometrical propositions.' In other words, his argument remains essentially circular.[4]

But even if Kant s idea of a unitary space is granted, it is still not entirely clear how places in such a space can act as a principle of individuation. Places are determined in relation to entities, which means that if places are to perform their individuative function, it is necessary to assume the numerical uniqueness of the entities that act as our frame of reference, and so once again we seem to be caught in a circular argument.[5]

---

[4] Such arguments as he offers elsewhere in the *Critique* (e.g. 'The refutation of idealism') do not help to make it any less so. I shall discuss the problem of objectivity later on.

[5] Some more recent attempts to avoid this circularity by eliminating all references to entities have been just as unsuccessful in dealing with the problem. Thus, according to one view, places should be interpreted as 'four-dimensional space-time positions'. The world, it is claimed, can be fully described in terms of such space-time positions and properties of those positions, both of which can be expressed in appropriate numerical symbols. All sentences in which references are made to substantival entities can in principle be translated into sentences in which all references are exclusively to space-time positions and their properties, and no entities are ever mentioned. (See R. Carnap, *The Logical Syntax of Language*, London 1949, p. 12 and passim.) The role of particulars is thus taken over by space-time positions, which are assigned unique sets of numbers (i.e. spatio-temporal coordinates). But before we can assign unique sets of numbers to such positions, we must identify the place from which the coordinates are to be drawn, and this, in turn, would require a different system of coordinates and a different origin, and the problem would just go on repeating itself.

(b) Leibniz's theory

I turn now to Leibniz. Whereas in Kant's theory, in a sense, there still lingers the common sense conception of space and time as some kind of backcloth against which the positions of phenomenal objects can be uniquely charted and distinguished from each other, Leibniz regarded space and time as properties of entities. It is generally accepted that this theory accords better with the view of modern science and is superior to that of Kant. It certainly seems to escape the circularity inherent in a Kantian attempt to link the particularity of entities with the numerical identity of the places that such entities occupy in a general spatio-temporal framework, which only leads to the problem of having to presuppose the existence of numerically identical entities in order to be able to refer to identical places. Leibniz's view is that the sources of individuation lie within the entities themselves; in other words, entities are regarded as basic, and places are said to be explicable in terms of relations between entities – 'entities' meaning here 'individual substances' or 'monads'.

But what exactly does individuate a monad? What is it that gives it its 'existential uniqueness'? Leibniz's reply to this question is somewhat confusing. He argues that a monad is fully determined by the attributes it has and, what is more, that every monad is qualitatively (not just numerically) different from every other. If two monads coincided in all their attributes, then they would be indistinguishable and one could not properly speak of 'two' monads. This is the gist of his 'principle of indiscernibles', and it might seem that the most natural conclusion for him to draw would be that numerical identity, in the final analysis, reduces to *qualitative* identity and numerical distinguishability to *qualitative* difference.

Yet Leibniz does *not* draw this conclusion. Although he maintains that every monad is distinguished from every other in virtue of the

Ultimately we would have to fall back on some form of 'demonstrative identification', which is precisely the sort of thing the theory was designed to avoid. Nor is this the only difficulty. For if the theory were to be adopted, it would never be possible to say significantly of any two *different* sets of numbers that they designate the same place. Yet we assume that this is possible, and moreover cannot help assuming this, if we want to make assertions about the *world*, not just about the logical properties of certain coordinate systems.

attributes it has, he nevertheless refuses to regard monads as mere 'agglomerations' of attributes – or what might be more appropriately described as groups or 'bundles' of qualities, without a 'substratum'. To him, monads are *substances*, not just bundles of qualities. But the question is, can he both maintain that monads do not reduce to bundles of qualities and continue to adhere to his principle of indiscernibles without being guilty of a serious inconsistency? For if the principle of indiscernibles is to be taken seriously, then there can be *no* other way of telling two monads apart except through their qualities.

Leibniz is clearly in some difficulty here. On the one hand, he does not wish to say that numerical identity reduces to qualitative identity; on the other, he does not wish to abandon the principles of indiscernibles. So in an effort to reconcile these two positions he introduces into his argument yet another metaphysical principle, viz. the 'principle of sufficient reason'. It is not logically impossible, he claims, that there should be different specimens of qualitatively indiscernible monads (even if we ourselves might not be able to discern them). If God had so wished, he most certainly could have created duplicate worlds; it is only that in so doing God would have acted without a *sufficient reason*, and this would be contrary to his nature.[6] In other words, the numerical identity of monads is guaranteed by God's own inherent 'rationality'.

But this explanation, apart from implicitly casting doubts upon the ontological interpretation of the principle of indiscernibles, hardly helps to throw much light on the whole issue. Thus the principle of indiscernibles now seems to reduce to the thesis that if there were duplicate monads and duplicate worlds, *we ourselves*, relying on our own cognitive resources, would not be in a position to distinguish them. This evidently does not apply to God, who is said to be able (although unlikely) to create duplicate worlds. But the point is that we are not told why the distinction between particular and species-identity makes sense at all.

So the problem remains unresolved. Leibniz was quite right, of course, to reject the view that a sufficient criterion of numerical

---

[6] Cf. Letters to Clarke, the 'Fifth Paper', 25: 'When I deny that there are two drops of water perfectly alike, or two other bodies indiscernible from one another, I do not mean that it is absolutely impossible to suppose them, but that it is a thing contrary to Divine wisdom and consequently that it does not exist.'

identity of things can be defined in terms of the conditions under which we distinguish between their respective positions in space, but he himself had no better explanation to offer. All he did was to invoke the dubious metaphysical principle of 'sufficient reason' in order to ensure the existential uniqueness of his monads and secure a basis for a meaningful distinction between numerical and qualitative identity.

(c) Particulars as bundles of qualities

The two theories to be discussed next are of more recent date and, essentially, represent attempts to modify Leibniz's and Kant's theories, respectively, in an effort to salvage what is regarded as the sound core of these theories by stripping them of their philosophically undesirable features. Consider, first, a theory which takes its clue from Leibniz, while at the same time trying to dispense with Leibniz's dubious metaphysics. The main effort in this theory is concentrated on exposing the logical superfluousness of the idea of substance as a 'metaphysical substratum', which still lingers on in – and complicates – Leibniz's conception of the monad. There is no need, it is argued, to postulate any such substrata in order to account for the idea of particular identity. Leibniz, unaccountably, still clung to the traditional idea of substance, notwithstanding his own 'principle of indiscernibles'. Yet, it is claimed, all that he really needed were attributes, or more accurately, *qualities*.

Consequently, in this theory (which was put forward by Bertrand Russell)[7] the place of Leibniz's monads is taken by what are called 'bundles' or 'complexes' of 'compresent qualities'. A bundle of qualities is said to represent a 'complete complex of compresence' if all its qualities are 'compresent' and if nothing external to the bundle is compresent with all the qualities within it. It is this 'completeness' that is said to individuate a particular, although not in any 'absolute' sense. For – it is argued – the assumption that such 'complexes of compresence' are unrepeatable, i.e. do not occur more than once, is an empirical proposition, not an analytic truth. Although this proposition is unlikely ever to be falsified, nevertheless one cannot maintain that it cannot in principle be false.

This leads to some perplexing conclusions. Thus, according to Russell, since the possibility of a recurrence of the same 'complexes of

---

[7] See Bertrand Russell, *Human Knowledge*, London 1961, Pt. IV, Ch. VIII.

compresence' cannot be excluded (there is no equivalent of Leibniz's principle of sufficient reason to ensure their numerical uniqueness) we must accept that propositions about order in time, such as 'If A precedes B, B does not precede A', 'If A is before B and B is before C, then A is before C', etc. are merely *empirical propositions* and not inviolable *a priori* truths. Propositions about order in space too should be interpreted in the same manner. Thus, Russell argues, although it may make good empirical sense to say that a 'complete complex of compresence' (a given 'particular' cannot be 'to the north of itself', 'above itself', etc., these situations cannot be excluded on *a priori* grounds. A reduplication of such complexes while empirically unlikely is not logically impossible.

But all this, to say the least, is highly confusing. For what sense exactly can be attached to a statement that a given particular is 'to the north of itself' or that it 'precedes itself'? If the expressions 'to the north of itself' or 'precedes' are taken in their usual sense, then this is plain nonsense. And if they are not taken in their usual sense, how should they be understood? It is implied that the same particular (the same 'complex of compresence') can be in two different places, or 'recur' at different times. But this abolishes, in effect the distinction between particulars and universals, while leaving us with the problem of explaining just what is meant by 'different' places and 'different' times.

But there are two further objections that might be raised against this theory: one of them concerns compresence, the other completeness. The relation of compresence, we are told, has two aspects: psychological and physical. In physics it means 'overlapping of qualities in space-time'. In a psychological context it means the compresence of simultaneously experienced qualities – visual, acoustic, tactile, etc. – which are part of one momentary experience (referred to by Russell as 'I-now'). Although the relation is the same in both cases, the psychological aspect of compresence has the epistemological priority and it is by considering the 'private compresence' of the parts of one total momentary experience that we must begin in trying to explain the possibility of an objective order in physical space-time.

But the concept of compresence is far from clear. If it implies that no time-lag is detectable between elements of an experienced 'complex', then this is true only in a very limited sense. Take, for example, the perceptual experience that I have while looking at this bunch of carnations arranged in a vase on the table in the middle of the room. I see this 'complex' as one whole. But while I am looking at it my eyes constantly wander from one flower to the next, pausing at some, ignoring others, picking out the details of their shapes and colours. Finally, without taking my eyes off the flowers, I may move the vase closer, or walk around the table and look at the flowers from different angles. The scene will keep constantly changing. As a result, I shall experience a succession of different 'complexes of qualities' but I shall still be looking at the same bunch of flowers. Yet how do we decide in such a case what is compresent with what? Different qualities and complexes of qualities are registered by me in a temporally extended sequence; none the less, they are all part of the wider experience of looking at this same bunch of flowers which I assume to exist 'out there'. Indeed it is hardly possible to speak meaningfully of any qualities as 'compresent' in such cases without positing a re-identifiable 'transcendent' object. But this merely brings back the idea of particulars as distinct from qualities or (mere) configurations of qualities, and we find ourselves up against the very difficulties the theory was trying to eliminate.

Consider now the concept of *completeness*. It is assumed that a given complex of qualities owes its 'individuality' to its completeness. A complete complex, in a psychological context, is said to represent 'one total momentary experience', while in a physical context, it represents a 'space-time point-instant'. But the question is, how do we explain the possibility of change and temporal order from the point of view of such complexes? It is difficult to see, for example, how the relation earlier/later can be made clear sense of without allowing the possibility of developing complexes, i.e. complexes which are not complete, but are rather in the 'process of completion'. But if so, the concept of compresence will have to be revised to accommodate temporal distinctions; briefly, it will have to be interpreted in such a way that it makes sense to speak of qualities occuring in a temporal sequence as part of a particular's 'biography'. However, if this is accepted, then we end up again with the concept of a particular as some kind of a temporally extended 'peg' for qualities – a view which the theory was directed against in the first instance.

(d) A unitary system of re-identifiable particulars

Clearly the above theory does not come anywhere near providing a plausible alternative to Leibniz's model. Its main aim, as we saw, was to obviate the need for substances as distinct from qualities. Accordingly, particulars were interpreted as complexes of qualities and regarded as being essentially of the *same logical type* as single qualities; with the implication that any significant statement about either is necessarily significant, although, it is conceded, 'probably not true',[8] about the other. But this is a confusion. For if such 'complexes' are to play the role of particulars, they cannot be regarded as being logically on a par with single qualities. If they both were of the same logical type, then we could not hope to be able to clarify the distinction between numerical and species identity and the possibility of order in space or time.

But consider now a different theory which takes its clue not from Leibniz but from Kant, while at the same time trying to eliminate the main causes of the difficulties and problems that bedevil Kant's own approach.

This theory – proposed by P.F. Strawson (op. cit.) – rests on the premiss that we possess the idea of a single spatio-temporal system of material things in which every such thing, at any time, is spatially related in various ways to every other similar thing, and that this is in fact the 'conceptual scheme' we use and rely on in making the world intelligible to ourselves. At the same time, it is strenuously denied that the idea of such a unitary spatio-temporal framework in any way necessitates a Kantian distinction between phenomena and noumena. Kant, as we saw, held that the unity of the phenomenal world can be accounted for only if space and time are interpreted as forms of our intuition, not as properties of things in themselves, but that for this very reason we must accept that there is an extra-phenomenal as well as a phenomenal side to reality, with things in themselves being inaccessible to cognition. The theory under discussion rejects this as a 'doctrinal fantasy' of transcendental idealism. If noumenal things did exist, there would be no possibility of defining a 'principle of individuation' for them in any case. As regards the phenomenal world, the meaningfulness of references to identical particulars presupposes the possibility of logically adequate criteria of re-identification, and such criteria, in turn, can operate only within a unitary spatio-temporal system; conversely, the idea of such a unitary system presupposes the possibility of particular-identification. In short, particular-identity,

[8] Cf. op. cit., p. 325.

the logically adequate criteria of re-identification and the idea of a unitary spatio-temporal system, are all regarded as *analytically interlinked* concepts.

This thesis is now used as a basis for an attack on scepticism. A sceptic wishing to challenge our belief in the existence of re-identifiable objective particulars in space and time, it is argued, cannot present his case coherently, for his doubts would amount to a 'rejection of the whole conceptual scheme within which alone such doubts make sense'. For suppose there is no numerical identity except in cases of continuous observation. Then instead of a unitary spatio-temporal system we would have scores of mutually independent systems, each corresponding to a particular stretch of continuous observation. As a result, we would no longer be able to use the concepts of material things in the way we normally use them and the question whether something observed on one occasion is identical with something else observed on a different occasion *would not even arise*. In other words, the sceptic, if he is to make himself understood, cannot avoid relying on the conceptual scheme that he is overtly attacking, and if so, his argument collapses before it can even get off the ground.

It has been objected against this kind of reasoning that it really misses the point the sceptic is trying to make. The sceptic, it is argued, may well concede that the conceptual scheme that we use and rely on makes sense only if we posit the possibility of re-identifiable particulars, while at the same time insisting that no proof can be supplied of their *actual existence*. The fact that our conceptual scheme is inseparable from the idea of such particulars, he might argue, does not testify to their existence *per se*.[9]

I don't think that this objection is fatal to the above theory. If it is accepted that we are in possession of logically adequate criteria of particular-identification, I do not see how one could deny that such criteria are ever fulfilled; for how else would we know that they are indeed adequate? In this respect, the theory seems to me to be perfectly consistent. My own objection is different, and concerns the attempt to make the actual availability of such criteria a condition of meaningfulness of the idea of numerical identity. As I have argued all along, although a consideration of possible criteria is important in

[9] See Barry Stroud, 'Transcendental arguments', in *Journal of Philosophy*, Vol. LXV, No. 9, 1968.

a wider context, the idea of numerical identity cannot be literally 'defined' in terms of the criteria of re-identification of particulars, which means that we shall have to look elsewhere for an answer to our problem.

Can we confine our interest to species-identity only?

To sum up, none of the four theories discussed above seem capable of providing a satisfactory clarification of the conditions of intelligibility of referring to something as numerically the same. Kant tried to link the idea of numerically identical particulars with the idea of one space and one time, both conceived by him as the a priori forms of our intuition. The theory discussed last, in a similar spirit, links the idea of particularity with the idea of a 'unitary spatio-temporal framework'. Both these theories rely on the individuating properties of place, without however offering a satisfactory clarification of the concept of place, or indeed of the *origins* of the idea of numerical identity. Leibniz took a different route and looked for clues to particularity within the monads themselves, but the only 'criterion' he was able to produce was his 'principle of indiscernibles', and eventually he was forced to introduce the additional metaphysical postulate of 'sufficient reason' in order to safeguard the existential uniqueness of his monads. Russell, quite properly, rejected such an artificial device, but was himself unable to offer a more credible solution. He merely maintained that the non-recurrence of the same complexes of qualities was a probability, not a certainty. But since the principle of indiscernibles remained in force in his theory, there was no means of telling two identical complexes apart in any case, and the whole idea of particularity remained as obscure as it had ever been.

Confronted with such a situation, with no sure indication as to how, if at all, a satisfactory clarification of particular identity might be found, we might be tempted to think that the best course to follow is to try and see if we can make do without relying on this awkward and intractable concept. Why, it might be asked, is the concept of particular-identity, as distinct from purely species-identity, at all necessary for a complete description of the world? Might it not be possible to interpret all references to ontological existents along Platonist lines in terms of references to species of one kind or another, and the characteristics of species; thereby providing a proof that the basic ontological existents are, in fact, species, and that the 'problem of individuality', in the final analysis, reduces to the problem of species (or quite generally: qualitative) identity?

In order to see why this assumption is untenable, it is sufficient to consider what is involved in making identifying references to species. In using the phrase 'the same A' in relation to a species I am already implicitly acknowledging the distinction between the species in question and its exemplifying instances. If it is meaningful to say 'the same colour', then it is so only on condition that we can meaningfully speak of different *specimens* of the colour in question, or, at the very least, of different occasions on which this colour is talked about, or referred to as the 'same'. In general, the phrase 'the same A', where A is descriptive of a species F, presupposes the possibility of intelligibly saying 'the same instance of F' and 'a different instance of F'; or 'the same F-specimen' and 'a different F-specimen'.

But quite apart from this, the very concept of an ontological existent, qua 'ontological', is analytically interlinked with the concept of individuality. To posit an object in the modus *per se* is to posit it as something determinate and existentially unique. At the same time, existential uniqueness, as was shown earlier on, cannot be defined in terms of place in an objective space; rather the concept of place in an objective space *presupposes* the idea of existential uniqueness. This was clear to Leibniz but not at all to Kant, although Leibniz, not suprisingly, found it difficult to provide a satisfactory clarification of the conditions of intelligibility of the idea of existential uniqueness, or explain why should there not be duplicate universes, and was finally reduced to appealing to the idea of a rationally acting God.

A structural approach to an analysis of individuality

So the problem before us is this: that whereas the distinction between numerical and qualitative identity is both logically and epistemologically indispensable, this distinction cannot be defined in terms of any set of criteria under which individuals are re-identified and distinguished from species. This, it should be stressed again, does not mean that the question of the criteria of numerical identification is irrelevant to a consideration of the meaning of this distinction. Evidently in positing a given object as an ontological individual I am at the same time committed to accepting that contextually there must be certain criteria whereby such an individual can be meaningfully referred to as numerically the same. Yet the meaning of individuality is not exhausted by any such set of criteria. It is perfectly possible to conceive of different types of ontological individuals, but there is no such 'principle of individuation' as might enable us to pronounce any given type as basic in an absolute sense.

Consequently, rather than allowing ourselves to be drawn into a metaphysical wild-goose chase we should concentrate instead on exploring the structural features of the minimal conceptual apparatus upon which any significant choice of ontological objects must depend. This cannot be accomplished, however, without a thoroughgoing phenomenological analysis of the modes of experiencing that underly meaningful identifying references to such objects. For an object to exist in an ontological sense is to exist in its own right and not merely as an object of thought, but it is not to exist independently of the conditions under which it may be thought of and identifyingly referred to as that particular object and no other. Which means that ontological object-categories have to be analysed in conjunction with certain experiential modalities. It is futile to try to clarify the idea of individuality via a 'universal' principle of individuation of ontological existents. The idea of individuality and the idea of specificity have to be seen in conjunction with such ideas as the idea of possibility and the idea of unity of biographical time, both of which point to certain *experiental modalities*. All these ideas, I shall argue, are structurally interdependent, and their meaning can be fully elucidated only by exploring their structural interconnectedness.

It is towards experiences, then, that we shall have to direct our analytical gaze. However, before embarking upon an analysis of experiences it is necessary to discuss the last of the three 'ontological' categories mentioned earlier, i.e. the category of *plurality*.

4. The Problem of Pluralism

Any identifying reference in respect of any topic presupposes a distinction between numerical and qualitative identity. It also presupposes the possibility of meaningful references to different topics of discourse. For if it is meaningful to say in respect of something 'the same A', it must equally be meaningful to say 'not the same A', 'a different A'. Moreover, if it were not possible to refer to different topics of discourse, there would be no occasion for referring to anything as 'the same'.

But the question is, what is involved in the assumption that there are different *ontological existents* not just different topics of discourse; what conditions must be fulfilled before such an assumption can make clear sense? And furthermore, what is the justification for making it? Why should there be a plurality of ontological existents rather than just one? Can the dispute between ontological monism and ontological pluralism be resolved, and how?

It is not easy to decide how best to tackle these questions, and the difficulties that we came up against in discussing the problem of individuation of particulars partly explain why. The idea of particular-identity, as we saw, cannot be defined in terms of the conditions under which objects are re-identified as numerically the same. In a similar way, the idea of plurality cannot be defined in terms of the conditions under which objects are differentiated from each other. Rather, it seems, any attempt to define the conditions of differentiation already presupposes an understanding of the idea of plurality, and this is where the main problem lies; for what makes such an understanding possible?

There is no question that we normally accept that both 'the same A' and 'a different A' can be significantly used in relation to ontological existents. We accept this even before we are able to formulate any criteria under which things can be correctly described as 'same' or 'different'. But what conditions must be fulfilled for such references to be significant? It is useful, but by no means sufficient to point out that if 'the same A' makes sense, so must 'a different A'. This applies to any topic whatever. What needs to be explained is, what makes a meaningful use of such phrases possible in regard to ontological existents, and such explanation cannot be provided without a detailed analysis of the problem of relations and of the concept of objectivity. However, we shall have to begin, first, by considering certain monistic objections.

The thesis that there is only one substance

Traditionally the notion of ontological independence and self-sufficiency plays a key role in monistic arguments. The basic premiss, usually, is that whatever exists in a fundamental sense does not depend upon anything external to itself for own existence and is in every way self-sufficient, which is regarded as analytically true. A corollary of this, it is claimed, is that there really can be only one fundamental existent, for if there existed more than one, then the individuality of each would, at least in part, depend upon its relations with others, and hence none could strictly be regarded as ontologically independent.

The mode of presentation of this argument often varies, but not very radically. Spinoza, for example, links the idea of independence with another principle – he calls it an 'axiom' – viz. that 'everything that exists exists either in itself or in another'.[1] To exist 'in itself' is to be self-subsistent, non-adjectival, non-parasitic, upon something else; the characteristics that traditionally have been associated with substance. To exist 'in another', on the other hand, is a typical feature of the modes or states of substance. Only that which exists 'in itself', he argues, exists in an ontologically fundamental sense. Expressed differently, if a thing exists genuinely *in se* (i.e. if it is a true substance), then a description of its defining features cannot involve references to anything outside that thing; by the same token, if what purports to be a description of a substance involves references to different substances, then it cannot be regarded as a genuine description of any substance. A substance, in short, is a closed, wholly self-contained and independent system, with all its attributes and modifications being explicable from its own essential nature. It is both 'in itself' and is 'conceived through itself' – i.e. it is that 'the

---

[1] *Omnia quae sunt vel in se vel in alio sunt.* Ethica I, Axiom 1.

conception of which does not need the conception of another thing from which it must be formed'.[2]

Monistic inferences are thus derived from a fusion of the idea of substance with that of independence. Although such inferences are not always logically entirely unimpeachable, given the above premises, the pluralist case becomes difficult to defend and on balance the only reasonable option seems to be Spinoza's own unitarist alternative, viz. that there is only one substance which is in fact identical with the whole of reality, and that the only plurality there is or can be is the plurality of 'attributes and modifications'.

It will be necessary however to consider in more detail certain general logical features of monistic reasoning, and I shall do this in a moment. First, I wish to make a few preliminary critical observations about the formulation of the monist thesis. The immediate difficulty that one encounters is this. If substance is identical with the whole of reality, it is not any discrete thing; but if it is not any discrete thing, it is not clear what sense can possibly be attached to the assertion that there is 'only one' substance. To claim that there is only one substance sounds like an answer to the question 'How many substances are there?' and Spinoza's conception of substance is such that this question *cannot be properly asked.* To ask 'How many substances?' is just as ungrammatical as asking 'How many rednesses?'. Substance, being the whole of reality, cannot be 'counted'. In this respect there is a certain similarity – hinted as, incidentally, by Spinoza himself – between substance and attributes; both substance and its attributes, according to him, are 'infinite' – i.e. they are (unlike discrete things) not limited by anything external that is of the same nature as themselves. It follows that the question 'How many substances?' is strictly meaningless, for given the way 'substance' is defined, it is *logically impossible* that there should be more than one.

Nor is this all. Thus it is an infringement of logical grammar to use phrases such as 'the same substance', for the word 'substance' (in the context of Spinoza's theory) has the status similar to that of a proper name and hence strictly cannot be employed as a general term. To speak of the 'same substance' would be just as ungrammatical as to speak of the 'same Socrates'. More so, in fact. For while 'Socrates' might on occasion be deliberately turned into a general term – as

---

[2] ibid., Def. 3.

happens, for example, in sentences like 'He is another Socrates' – 'substance' cannot be significantly used in such a way at all. Furthermore, it is not possible to talk about the 'type' of thing substance is without actually talking about the substance itself, for substance is by definition one, and any suggestion that there might be different specimens of it is incoherent. But if so, it is not clear how substance can be regarded as an entity at all. It is not a universal, and it is not an ontological individual in any ordinary sense. If it can be significantly talked about, it seems, then it is only as some kind of state, or situation, an ontological 'event' perhaps, certainly not as an entity. The point is that the whole idea of substance as an entity breaks down; which is of course the opposite of what Spinoza originally intended.

The monistic thesis and the doctrine of the internality of relations

But consider now more closely the structure of the monist argument, in particular the monist treatment of relations. The principle of independence in monist reasoning is usually coupled with an attempt to interpret relations as a sub-class of properties and expressive of certain purely internal features of their terms, or what is sometimes referred to as the doctrine of the 'internality of relations'. Although there have been philosophers – Leibniz is an obvious example – who have tried to reconcile this view with the idea of a pluralist ontology, it is clear that if conjoined with the principle of independence the doctrine of the internality of relations provides a powerful support for the monist thesis. In what follows, I shall briefly outline the monist theory of relations. Then I shall examine some criticisms of the monist position from a pluralist point of view, trying at the same time to bring out the presuppositions that underly such criticisms and showing that a clarification of these presuppositions demands a critical exploration of certain new philosophical topics that have not been touched on hitherto.

The problem that we are confronted with here has two aspects, and might be expressed in the form of the following two questions: (a) Is it possible to bridge the difference between relations and properties by treating all relations as 'relational properties'?, and (b) Can 'relational properties' always and unconditionally be regarded as intrinsic to the terms that have them? The doctrine of the internality of relations gives an affirmative answer to both these questions. It is maintained, accordingly, that an ontological existent can be fully described and distinguished from any other similar existent in terms of its properties alone, and that its 'relational' no less than any of its other properties are part of its essential description. Thus the fact, if it is a fact, that the cat is on the mat, in an ontological sense, and contrary to what ordinarily might appear, is just as essential to the identity of the cat as any other of the cat's properties. Without the relational property of being on the mat at a particular time the cat would not be the ontological individual it is. And the same *mutatis mutandis* applies to the mat, insofar as the mat qualifies as a self-subsistent ontological entity. Speaking generally, if an ontological object x stands in a relation R to an ontological object y then it is a necessary, not a contingent fact about x that it is R-related to y; with the converse being true of y in respect of x.

The key assumption here remains, of course, that the identity of an ontological existent, or, more accurately, its ontological individuality, depends upon all of this existent's properties, and hence that if any of them were different from what they happen to be, the existent itself would be different. 'Properties' are meant here to include both relational and non-relational properties. It is a consequence of this view that if two things are related to each other in any way, then neither of them, strictly, can be said to be ontologically independent of the other, for in such a case neither of them can be fully described without presupposing the existence of both. If now 'independence' is regarded as essential to basic existents, it is clear that nothing that depends upon a relation to something external to itself qualifies as a basic existent in the true sense of the word.

It follows that nothing short of the complete reality can be a 'basic existent', for a description of any 'finite' thing inevitably involves references to things external to itself. In other words, the doctrine of the internality of relations together with the thesis of the independence of substance seems logically to lead to the position of ontological monism; conversely, the monist thesis seems necessarily to presuppose the thesis of the internality of relations.

Before commenting, let me now briefly sketch out by way of summary the salient points of the monist argument. The whole argument might be presented as proceeding, essentially, in three main stages.

The first stage involves an attempt to show that relations really are a class of properties, i.e. that relations do not represent a logically independent category of their own. The second is an attempt to demonstrate that relational properties presuppose the existence of non-relational properties of one kind or another, but that the converse is not necessarily true (a possible exception being some reflexive relations). The third and final stage involves the claim that relational properties are merely a special class of qualitative properties of a single substance.

The first stage, it should be noted, does not necessarily rule out the possibility of ontological pluralism, unless it explicitly includes the thesis of independence of substance; it merely involves a rejection of the view that properties and relations are two mutually separate and incommensurable categories, with relations allegedly being purely 'extrinsic' to (and hence making no difference to the essential nature of) their terms. There is clearly no logical inconsistency involved in claiming, on the one hand, that relations must be regarded as a sub-species of properties (in the broad sense of the latter term), and assuming that the world is an agglomerate of many different entities, on the other. Quite the reverse, it is possible expressly to link the concept of 'relational properties' with a (suitably modified) pluralist thesis by arguing, for example, that the possession of a relational property of a certain kind necessarily entails the existence of more than one thing in the world.

But consider now the second stage of the argument. With his opening salvos the anti-pluralist has, if anything, merely forced his opponent to modify his own position somewhat, not to abandon it. But now he goes into an all-out attack, arguing that whereas relational properties presuppose the existence of certain non-relational, or 'qualitative', properties, the latter properties do not necessarily demand the existence of any 'pluralistically committed' relational properties at all. Thus if x is round-shaped, or metal, say, x is not necessarily related to anything outside itself in virtue of being round-shaped or metal. Nor is it necessary to know any of x's relational properties in order to understand what it is for it to be round-shaped or metal. On the other hand, to describe a person as a 'friend', or a 'colleague', or a 'cousin', etc. is implicitly to presuppose the existence of non-relational features of some kind or other, physical and/or non-physical characteristics, actions, attitudes, etc., without which such descriptions would not be applicable, or even make sense.

The central claim in this phase of the argument, then, is that an ostensibly relational statement depends for its meaningfulness and truth upon the meaningfulness and truth of certain 'non-relational' subject/predicate statements, but that the opposite is not necessarily the case. In order that it should be possible to assert correctly 'This tree is taller than that tree' it must be possible to assert correctly 'This is a tree' and 'That is a tree'. But the two latter statements do not presuppose any irreducibly relational facts as a condition of their own truth. Nor does their intelligibility (irrespective of their truth or falsehood) necessarily depend upon the intelligibility of some other statements that might be characterised as 'irreducibly relational' – in the pluralistic sense of 'relational'.

The need to emphasise here the 'pluralistic' sense of 'relational' arises because not everything that is usually classified under the heading of 'relations' involves a pluralist commitment, or allows of pluralist inferences. The relation of identity does not, for example. And the same applies to all relations in which the subject relates himself to himself. Jones loves himself, blames himself, is his own severest critic, is conscious of what he is doing, etc. are all examples of reflexive relations which have no pluralist import. Similarly no pluralist inferences can be drawn from 'mental' relations such as desiring, believing, etc. From the monist point of view, if there can be any 'irreducible relations', they can be found perhaps only among *non-pluralist* relations such as these.

However, it is the third and final stage of the argument that reveals fully its strategic aims. For the idea put forward is not merely that 'pluralistically committed' relational properties are not as basic as qualitative properties, but that all properties and relations can in the end be assimilated to qualitative properties of one sort or another. The world, it is argued, can in principle be described without using any 'pluralistically committed' terms at all. But if this is possible, the conclusion must be that, basically, there can be only one ontological existent, and that all properties are merely qualities – or, using more convenient words, 'states' or 'modifications' – of that one existent. If a given thing x is related to a given thing y, it is argued, this must be seen as having to do with the intrinsic nature of x, and the intrinsic nature of x can, in the final analysis, be fully understood only as a feature of the whole to which it and everything else belongs. There is only one genuine subject – the whole – and the idea of a pluralistically structured world is an ontological misconception.

Properties and predicates

What is wrong with this argument? A typical objection against it might be that it involves an attempt to settle a metaphysical issue without first clarifying the conditions under which such an issue can be meaningfully discussed. Surely, it might be said, we ought to begin by asking questions not about the ontological features of properties but about the logical characteristics of *predicates*. It is improper to ask whether relations can be 'assimilated' to properties or whether all properties might not after all be explicable in terms of 'qualitative properties'. We should ask, rather, what kinds of *predicates* there are and whether it is possible to obliterate such logical differences as do exist between them.

Predicates, however, fall into two main categories: one-place, or monadic, and more-than-one-place, or polyadic, predicates. Someone asks me what cherries look like and I pick one from the basket and say 'This is a cherry'. My sentence consists of a demonstrative pronoun, which acts as an *ersatz* name and fulfils the function of the subject, and a predicative expression. The predicative expression on its own is incomplete; it requires a name, or an *ersatz* name (as in our case), or some kind of designating phrase in order to yield a complete sentence. Only one such object-referring expression is needed to make the sentence complete. There are no other object-referring expressions involved. One object is sufficient for 'cherry' to 'hook on'. Here we have an example of a 'monadic' predicate.[3]

But evidently not all predicates are of this kind. I can say 'This is a cherry' and everyone understands what I mean, but I cannot very well say 'This is an offspring' without committing a grammatical impropriety, except perhaps as a contextually forgivable elipsis when it is already clear whose offspring is being talked about. 'Offspring' demands an answer to 'Whose offspring?'. It is a relation, a polyadic predicate, and requires more than one object to 'hook on' to. Every predicate-term falls into one of these two categories. Which category a given term belongs to, this can be shown by explicating its internal grammar, i.e. by showing how the term in question can be

---

[3] I use the word 'predicate' here in the sense of a term – a general noun, for example – that can be predicated of something, and distinguish 'predicates' qua terms from syntactical 'predicative expressions'. Predicates as *terms* can, of course, be part of grammatical subjects.

appropriately used in a sentential context.

Returning now to monism v. pluralism, the central issue, expressed in terms of predicates, reduces to the question whether we can somehow make do without any polyadic predicates, except perhaps those of the 'reflexive' variety? Why are monadic predicates not sufficient for a complete description of the world?

It might seem that it is sufficient merely to formulate such questions in order to know the answers. For evidently we need both reflexive and non-reflexive polyadic predicates, as well as monadic predicates, if we are to be able to describe at all adequately the world around us. To suppose that all such predicates could be replaced, or reduced, to a single type is plain nonsense.

The alleged irreducibility of spatio-temporal relations

Yet it is not nonsense. There is no question, of course, that we make use of relational or 'polyadic' predicates of the most diverse types, and that we would be hard put to it to express what we wish to express without them. Nevertheless it is by no means certain that the use of such predicates necessarily commits us to an anti-monist stance. The fact that we find the use of such predicates convenient and essential for our purposes does not prove that they are indispensable in an absolute sense: viz. that the world as a matter of logic cannot be completely described without them. Briefly, what needs to be shown if the anti-monist argument is going to work is that it is *in principle* impossible to remove such predicates from the relevant contexts and substitute for them some other predicates without any loss of truth. Or, to put it in another way, it is necessary to demonstrate that at least some non-reflexive relations are *logically* irreducible.

It is sometimes claimed, and more often tacitly assumed, that spatio-temporal relations belong in this category, and that, accordingly, relational expressions such as 'to the left of', 'before', etc. should be treated as logically basic simple symbols. Sometimes, as in Kant's theory, the idea of irreducibility of spatio-temporal relations is defended on general epistemological grounds and is regarded as being inseparably interlinked with the idea of an all-embracing unitary space.[4] But as is already clear from what was

---

[4] Kant's well-known example is the relation of incongruence. The

said in the last chapter, the irreducibility thesis, plausible though it may appear at first sight, remains highly vulnerable to criticism and requires important additional assumptions if it is to be taken at all seriously. More than that: it might even be argued that any attempt to 'prove' the irreducibility of spatio-temporal relations already presupposes, rather than helps to vindicate, the basic principles of a pluralist ontology. Let us now consider this a little more closely.

The irreducibility thesis, in its general outline, might be summed up thus. Empirical statements concerning spatial and/or temporal order – e.g. that x is to the left of y, or above y, or that it precedes y in a time series, etc. – do not involve attribution of certain purely intrinsic properties to x or to y, i.e. properties that might be described as part of their essential description (qua self-subsistent ontological entities). If they did, such statements would be analytic, not empirical. But more important still, in making such statements one is not asserting anything that could conceivably be interpreted in terms of non-relational, or 'qualitative', properties of the objects concerned. And if so, then, given that such statements are sometimes true, it necessarily follows that there is more than one entity in the world.

Yet this does *not* necessarily follow. For even if it is accepted (ignoring, or rejecting, any arguments to the contrary) that spatio-temporal relations are not, or not wholly, explicable in terms of intrinsic and qualitative properties of related things, there still remains the problem of accounting for the *objectivity* of such relations. The point is that a 'pluralistic' inference is based on the assumption that such relations depict an objective order of things 'out there', not merely our own impression of such an order, and this is precisely where the main difficulty lies. To begin with, we have to draw a distinction between spatial and temporal relations within a 'phenomenological' space and time, and spatial and temporal relations within an objective framework. Spatial and temporal relations in a subjective 'phenomenologioal' context, as we saw earlier, can be interpreted in terms of certain internal characteristics

---

left-hand glove does not fit the right hand. My hand and its mirror image, *though equal in all points*, cannot be super-imposed upon each other. This, Kant argues, would be inexplicable if spatial relations were reducible to properties of things in themselves. Two incongruent things are incongruent not qua things in themselves but qua phenomenal objects, sharing the same unitary space which is not a 'property' of any object but a form of our intuition. Cf. *Prolegomena*, Sec. 13.

of the percipient's own experience and are not indicative, or not necessarily, of an external objective order of things. It is quite possible to differentiate between qualitative similarity and numerical difference with regard to items in a phenomenological space; for example, I have no difficulty in distinguishing between two qualitatively similar objects appearing simultaneously in two different regions of my visual field. But this of course provides no proof that there are, or even could be, numerically distinguishable ontological individuals.

But if spatial relations within a phenomenological space can tell us nothing about the numerical diversity of ontological objects, there is even less that can be gleaned in this respect from temporal relations within a phenomenological time. Before and after, within a phenomenological time, separate experiences, not ontological objects, and they do not even separate experiences by number alone. Experiences are part of a biographical time-structure and have different 'positional' values only within that structure. As for the objects posited in individual experiences, they may or may not exist, and they may or may not be ontologically numerically distinct.

So the assumption of an objective order remains crucial to any 'pluralist' argument; but the question is, what makes this assumption intelligible? And furthermore, how do we know that relational statements purporting to depict such an order are in fact sometimes true? If we could say with certainty that they are, then, it seems, we would already know the answer to the problem as to the possibility of a numerical diversity of ontological existents. If, on the other hand, they depict merely a perceptual order within the percipient's own experience, then no argument in favour of ontological pluralism can be based upon them in any case.

Now it might be argued as was done by Kant, for example – that the idea of a non-arbitrary, objective, order is built into the very concept of an external object; that one cannot significantly refer to external objects qua external without acknowledging by implication the existence of such an order; and in a sense this is of course true. In Chapter 2 I argued in a similar vein that the concept of an ontological existent involves the idea of non-arbitrariness, in the sense that by positing something as an ontological existent, i.e. as existing in its own right and not merely as an object of someone's thought, we are by implication positing this something as a potential subject of a non-arbitrary subset of predicates from among an indefinite number of meaningful predicates. Yet none of this is quite sufficient to clarify the concept of an objective order. For what we need is not only the idea of non-arbitrariness but the idea of error and the (logical) possibility of correction of error by third persons. The concept of an objective order demands the possibility of certain criteria of objectivity, such that I might be corrected by others on a given occasion, should I for any reason fall foul of such criteria. The question of criteria of objectivity is a complex one, and it is not easy to decide what criteria are valid in what context.[5] But if it was only I myself and no one else who could decide whether or not an error has been committed in a given instance, then the distinction between 'subjective' and 'objective' order would have no meaning. In other words, in order to make sense of the concept of an objective order we have to postulate the possibility of 'witnesses' other than ourselves.

Reverting now to spatio-temporal relations, the assumption of their irreducibility to monadic predicates is linked with the assumption that they depict an objective order, and if such relations are taken to depict an objective order, then it is clear that we shall have to assume the possibility of a plurality of biographically distinct points of view, occupied by different percipients, before we can make any significant inferences about the ontological distinguishability of their terms. It follows that it is not enough simply to appeal to the 'differentiating power' of spatio-temporal relations within an objective framework. The question that has to be asked first, is: How is such a framework possible? What makes the idea of an objective order intelligible?

Are there any logically irreducible relations?

To put it differently, if spatio-temporal relations are to be appealed to in support of the thesis that there can be numerically, not just qualitatively, distinguishable ontological existents, it is necessary, in the first place, to clarify the conditions under which such relations can be significantly claimed to reflect the structure of an objective world, and in trying to do so we are likely to find that in some form or other we need to assume what such relations are supposed to explain. What is more, this remains the case even if, following Kant, numerically distinguishable external objects – i.e. objects of 'outer sense' – are regarded simply as phenomenal objects or 'appearances',

---

[5] See more about this in Chapter 10.

not as 'things in themselves'.

But consider now some other polyadic predicates which, on the face of it, seem more resistant to a 'reductivist' analysis, and provide what seem to be a more reliable indication of the philosophical untenability of an anti-pluralist stance.

Suppose that x and y are numbers, such that x is greater than y; then it would appear that there is no conceivable way in which such a relation could be reduced to qualitative properties of one kind or another, and re-expressed, accordingly, in a form that does not require the existence of both its terms. Evidently it is no use to describe x as having the property of being greater than y; and, correspondingly, y as having the property of being smaller than x. This is not explaining the relation in terms of something else merely re-stating it. Nor is it much help to say that x comes after y in the number series, for this merely involves replacing one polyadic predicate with another, quite apart from the fact that 'after' does not necessarily mean 'greater' unless serial ordering is associated with a relation of magnitude. Notoriously young children learn very quickly how to recite numbers in the right order without having any clear notion of their 'cardinal' properties, and it is only gradually that they begin to associate their respective positions in the number series with a relation of magnitude. But neither is it any more enlightening to say, for example, that 'x is greater than y' means that if we were to set out to construct x and y by some algorithmic procedure, the construction of x would require a greater number of steps; for the question is, what is meant by 'greater'? In short, any explanation of 'x is greater than y', it seems, still leaves us with a two-term relation, whereas the reductivist, if his argument is going to work, needs a monadic predicate.

What is more, where numbers are concerned, it might be argued, any reductivist argument aimed at undermining the logical independence of relations is doomed from the start. For the properties of numbers are determined exclusively by their relations, not by any 'inherent' qualities. The only 'properties' that numbers can have are 'relational properties', and are moreover such as presuppose a basic parity in logical status as between related terms (which distinguishes them, among others, from the so-called 'mental' relations). In short, if there can be any meaningful talk of 'reduction' here at all, it is perhaps only of a possible reduction of properties to (non-mental and logically independent) relations, not vice versa.

Yet clearly this is true only as long as we leave the judging subject out of the picture. The assumption underlying the above argument is that the system of numbers can be described in certain objective propositions, involving no references – implicit or explicit – to any judging subject, or subjects. It is important to realise that the alleged irreducibility of 'greater than' and other similar relations to 'qualitative' properties turns entirely upon this assumption. The point, is that the existence is presupposed of an objective order that enables us to distinguish meaningfully between 'x is greater than y' and 'A judges (thinks, believes, surmises, etc.) that x is greater than y'. Unless this distinction can be meaningfully drawn, the whole argument directed against the thesis of reducibility of relations falls to the ground.

But this merely confirms yet again that the idea of numerical diversity of ontological existents is inseparable from the idea of an objective order, and consequently that a clarification of the former idea depends upon a clarification of the sources and the conditions of intelligibility of such an order.

The possibility of an objective order

So the end result, as before, is that we have reached the end of a particular analytic path only to be confronted with signposts pointing in a new direction. The aim that we set ourselves was to analyse the idea of a numerical, as distinct from a purely qualitative, diversity of existents; to clarify, that is, what is involved in assuming the possibility of there being a plurality of self-subsistent particulars that are numerically and not just qualitatively distinguishable from each other. The monistic position, as we saw, was that such an idea, if closely examined, does not make clear sense, because there can be no unequivocal criteria of numerical diversity. The pluralist arguments, on the other hand, are designed to show that the possibility of such criteria is ensured by the existence of logically irreducible relations; or by the existence of irreducibly relational, and hence essentially 'pluralistically committed', properties.

Both sides in the dispute see the issue of criteria as being of key importance. But, as already emphasised, the problem of meaning here as elsewhere does not reduce to the problem of criteria. We saw earlier on that the idea of numerical identity cannot be explained in terms of the criteria of re-identification of particulars. Similarly the idea of numerical diversity cannot be explained in terms of the criteria of numerical differentiation of such particulars. The point is that the idea of criteria is itself in need of elucidation, and an attempt to provide such an elucidation presupposes a basic understanding of the concept whose explanation is being sought. In any case, the reasons for regarding the idea of numerical identity and that of numerical diversity as significant are not such as might enable us to decide unequivocally whether something observed on one occasion is numerically the same as something else observed on a different occasion, or how many ontological objects are involved in a given case. The source of meaningfulness of these ideas lies in the logical relationships that bind together a cluster of basic ideas into a coherent pattern. Thus if the idea of numerical diversity presupposes the possibility of irreducible relations, the idea of irreducible relations, in its turn, presupposes the possibility of an objective order, and the idea of an objective order (I shall argue) is unintelligible without the idea of a plurality of points of view occupied by different selves.

One of the more obvious disadvantages of the monist position is that it almost inevitably leads to an obliteration of the distinction between essential and inessential, or accidental ('extrinsic') properties, or features of things. Thus the gist of Spinoza's argument, for example, is that whereas in ordinary circumstances we may indeed find it useful and necessary to distinguish between essential and accidental properties, metaphysically such a distinction cannot be upheld. A substance is necessarily such that all its properties are 'essential' properties, in the sense that they all together define its 'nature', and if any of them were missing or were different from what they happen to be, the substance itself would be different. Metaphysically there are no 'extrinsic' as distinct from 'intrinsic' properties of things. All properties without exception must be classified as 'intrinsic'.

But if this is indeed the case, it becomes difficult to explain how significant individuating references can be made to anything that is subject to change; or indeed to make clear sense of any spatio-temporal order concepts. For it is implied that we cannot meaningfully claim that a given object might be different in certain respects without becoming a different individual. We must accept that for any given F, if x has F, x has it necessarily; i.e. all the properties that x has are its defining properties. But a corollary of this is that it is in principle impossible to describe accurately any x as numerically identical at any given stage of its existence, until, that is, its life-cycle has been completed, for its numerical identity depends upon all its properties. In short, nothing that is in the process of development or change, strictly speaking, can be claimed to be numerically the same as long as this process lasts, for existents are individuated only by their full life-cycles. It follows that we can form no clear notion of spatial or temporal order among existents with uncompleted life-cycles; and this, in reality, means not at all.

None of this is intended to suggest, of course, that in each individual case there are certain essential properties which are sufficient to explain the numerical identity of the particular in question. As I have already made clear before, every such particular has certain 'essential' properties which it cannot shed without ceasing to be what it is; but although its having such properties is necessary to its identity, it is not quite sufficient to explain its existential uniqueness.

Understandably, perhaps, there is a strong temptation to try to avoid these difficulties by taking qualities as basic and confining oneself to the idea of a plurality of qualities, with particulars being interpreted as bundles of qualities. But, as we saw, this will not work; for if we are to be able to make significant identifying references to qualities, we need a distinction between qualities and their existentially unique instances, and this raises the problem of determining the precise ontological status of such instances: i.e. what such instances are, and how they can be identified and distinguished from each other. The difficulty with any kind of platonism that claims the ontological primacy of qualities – or any kind of universals – is that in presenting its case it implicitly relies on certain assumptions about existentially unique particulars, which no sooner are made explicit than the whole platonist case is shown to be built on sand. Identifying references to qualities can be made only via the latter's exemplifying instances and the thesis that what actually exists can be described simply in terms of qualities and relations between qualities, cannot be consistently defended.

The idea of a plurality of ontological particulars, on the other hand, seems to be connected with the idea of irreducible relations, and the idea of irreducible relations, I have argued, raises the problem of objective order. It is this problem that we shall have to investigate in some detail. It will be shown, as was already briefly hinted earlier on, that the concept of objective order is inseparable from the idea of a plurality of witnessing selves – a 'self' to be understood here in the sense of an experienced unity of biographical time, *not* as some kind of substantival entity – and the idea of error; and that the latter ideas in turn can be clarified only through a careful study of the nature of *language*.

B. Modes of Experiencing

5. Experiences as Evidential Events

An analysis of the concept of ontological existent, as we saw, brings certain other categories into focus with which this concept is structurally interlinked and demands that we widen the scope of our investigation. The new array of problems that we are now confronting highlights the complexity of the task in hand, while at the same time exposing the inherent weaknesses and the general philosophical insufficiency of an object-oriented ontological approach to the 'problem of reality', the categorial basis of which has been the subject of the past three chapters.

The initial question concerned ontological existents in the broadest possible sense of this term, and the preliminary aim was simply to establish a minimal basis for a distinction between such – as yet unspecified – items and other potential topics of discourse. After potential topics were tentatively divided into meanings and non-meanings, it soon became clear that meanings could not be included into the range of possible existents. There followed a brief discussion of the problem of reference and the distinction between naming and describing. After which an attempt was made to set out the most elementary logical conditions that must be satisfied before anything can qualify as a potential existent. This, in turn, brought into focus the problem of individuation, and it became evident that the success or failure of any ontological 'principle of individuation' depended upon its ability to provide a satisfactory clarification of the distinction between numerical and species identity. Yet a close analysis of the problems seemed to indicate that there could be no foolproof criteria whereby one might decide with certainty whether anything stays numerically identical from one moment in time to the next. In other words, there was no hope of 'defining' this distinction in terms of the criteria whereby individuals might be distinguished from species. This did not mean that a consideration of criteria of application was altogether irrelevant to the meaning of this distinction. It meant only that no criteria (which are always *contextual*, in any case) were sufficient to clarify its meaning.

But where, then, we may ask, does this distinction have its origins? Or, to phrase the question in a Kantian style, what are the 'conditions of its possibility'? The idea of individuality is inseparable from the assumption of the existence of individuals qua *per se* ontological items. Yet this idea is not explicable in terms of the criteria of individuation of such items. What is it, then, that makes it *intelligible*? An answer to this, I shall argue, so far as an answer is possible at all, can be given only through an analysis of experiences from the point of view of the one who has the experiences; i.e. through a phenomenological analysis of the *modes of experiencing*.

What is significant and highly important is that a demand for such a phenomenological analysis seems to result from the logical pressures built into the very concept of ontological existent. As a result of these pressures we are forced to modify somewhat our style of approach in order to shed light upon certain aspects of our main topic which have remained unexplored hitherto, but this modification of style, as will become clearer in the sequel, does not invalidate our earlier approach, but rather structurally complements it.

Phenomenological epistemology and the philosophy of mind

Ontological existents, I have emphasised, are a sub-class of possible topics of discourse. But topics of discourse are constituted as topics of discourse in certain acts of thought; they are targets of certain thought-experiences and cannot be identified, analysed and discussed except in the context of such experiences. Ontological existents are posited in the modus *per se*, but it is in thought that they are thus posited. Moreover there can be no existents that cannot be objects of thought, although, clearly, not all objects of thought qualify as potential existents.

It follows that in order to clarify the background to meaningful identifying references to ontological existents, it is necessary to investigate the manner and conditions in which such existents are constituted as target-topics in relevant experiences. This is the province of what can be most conveniently described as the 'phenomenological epistemology'.[1] It is an area of special problems which do not lend themselves to being handled easily by familiar logico-linguistic techniques and require a different type of treatment. The point is that we cannot circumnavigate or dispose of these problems by resorting to the familiar logical ploy of treating questions about experiences as if they were simply questions about the logical properties of sentences in which we ordinarily talk about experiences. On the contrary, it is only through a phenomenological clarification of the structure of experiences that the logical properties of such sentences can be made fully transparent. However, such a clarification, as might be expected, is hardly an easy task, and requires on occasion a pictorial and 'non-literal' use of words. For we can hardly use language to throw light upon the basis from which language itself derives its meaning, without having to rely on allusion and metaphor. It is a process analogous in some ways to *story-telling*, where the point is made precisely through a sacrifice of the kind of literalness and explicitness which the logician, by the nature of his training, tends to regard as the ultimate requirement of clarity, and indeed an intrinsic feature of truth.

In a sense, we all understand perfectly well what experiences are; it is when we are challenged to explain this understanding that we are at a loss how to put it into words. To call experiences 'mental states', or 'psychological states', or 'states of consciousness', is to use different generic labels, not to give a 'definition'. The difficulties involved in trying to explicate the concept are so insidious and irksome that, understandably perhaps, one is often tempted to say that they are not crucially important and that the problems that can be profitably discussed in relation to experiences are no different

---

[1] Much of the foundational work in phenomenological epistemology was done by Descartes and Kant, but by far the greatest contribution to it was made by Edmund Husserl. However, I shall not attempt an exegetic analysis of the views of any of these philosophers, each of whom had used the results of their respective phenomenological researches to different ends, developing theories that essentially deviate from the course that I am here pursuing. Furthermore, I shall refrain, whenever possible, from using the terms 'intentional' and 'intentionality', widely popularised by Husserl, because they have been employed by different philosophers (including Husserl himself) in different senses, causing a considerable amount of philosophical confusion; preferring the less controversial and more readily intelligible expressions, like 'intended', 'topic-directional', etc.

from those that arise in connection with any other 'natural phenomena'; and, consequently, that the method of investigation with regard to all phenomena, experiences included, is, or at any rate, ought to be, the same.

But evidently this cannot be true. Experiences are not public objects like trees or pencils or clocks. They are not accessible – not entirely, at any rate – to public inspection. I cannot explain the meaning of 'joy' by pointing to someone with glowing eyes and a smile on his face, and saying 'This is an example of joy', as I might explain the meaning of 'tree' by pointing to a tree and saying 'This is a tree', or 'This is an example of the kind of thing that we call a tree'. What I can say in the former case, at best, is 'This is how people tend to look when they feel joyful' or 'This is the kind of physical expression (or behaviour) that we associate with the joyous state'. But this is hardly likely to be very enlightening to someone who has never had, or is incapable of conceiving the relevant experience.

Evidently, experiences cannot be appropriately or adequately described in terms of the categories that are applicable to public objects or events. It is not merely that they are not just another class of public phenomena; it is through nothing but experiences themselves that such phenomena become objects for us. This photograph on my desk is now an object for me in virtue of my perceiving experience. My registering its presence is part of what might be termed an 'evidential event'. A little later I shall address myself to it in an experience of recollection. Moreover I can address myself retrospectively to the perceptual experience as such as well as to the photograph qua photograph, and the logic of my reports will obviously be very different in the two cases. The photograph might be only a dreamed photograph. On closer inspection – this time basing my judgment upon a different kind of evidential event, viz. an experience of disappointed expectation – I might decide that there is really *nothing there*. But nothing can take away the pleasure that I derived from looking at what I took to be a photograph. The experience itself was real enough, and I can retrospectively describe it and analyse it, irrespective of whether its object was real or fictional. Similarly when I recall an experience of fear, the question of the existence or non-existence of the object of fear need not enter into my consideration, for the experience itself may be my exclusive concern.

But the distinction between experiences and non-experiences is based on a *phenomenological insight*, not on any 'external' criteria. We do not distinguish experiences from non-experiences as we might distinguish oranges from apples, viz. by indicating certain characteristics that might enable anyone, including those who have never tasted either fruit, to tell one from the other. Nor can experiences be interpreted quite simply as a species of natural states or events. Furthermore, it is, I shall argue, no less mistaken to regard experiences, as is sometimes done, as being analogous to 'logical states' of certain sophisticated machines; unless such machines are endowed with so many human characteristics (including the capacity of 'empathetic imagination') that a comparison becomes trivial, and the word 'machine' no longer means what it ordinarily means. The point is that the concept of an experience cannot be fully clarified without an analysis of the actual modes of experiencing from the experiencer's own point of view. And this means that rather than attempting to answer the question 'What are experiences?', in the manner of the conventional 'philosophy of mind', we ought to concentrate our attention on the question 'How do experiences occur?', and analyse them qua types of *evidential events*. Whereas the former leads into a philosophical cul de sac and cannot be given any definitive answer, the latter indicates the kind of approach that promises to be illuminating and fruitful.

The categorial straitjacket of conventional philosophy of mind

Yet in a majority of cases it is precisely the *first* of the two questions that dominates philosophical thinking about experiences. To a large extent this is due to a natural tendency, already mentioned earlier, to simplify the whole issue by treating experiences as logically on a par with other phenomena, and hence as being tractable with the help of basically the same conceptual machinery. Accordingly, the central task presents itself as one of deciding just what kind of thing experiences are. Are they some kind of objects; and if so, of what kind? Or are they properties of certain objects; and if so, what sort of properties, and of what objects? Are they irreducibly mental, or are they, on the contrary, essentially physical. Or are they perhaps a bit of both: a species of 'braided' psycho-physical events with the two components inseparably interlinked with one another? Or are they explicable, perhaps, in terms of certain behavioural-dispositional, or functional, or some similar properties which cannot be strictly categorised either as 'physical' or 'mental', but belong rather in a class of their own?

All these options, it should be noted, remain within the basic framework of the categorial schema of objects and attributes, and this inevitably sets limits to what can be achieved by the respective 'philosophies of mind'. There are, first, two basic rival metaphysical theories, mentalist and materialist, and between them a number of hybrid ontological positions, incorporating in various proportions elements from both these views. Then there are theories which try to avoid any direct metaphysical commitment, but none the less conduct their analysis of experiences in terms of certain characteristics – albeit a special type of characteristics – of physical bodies. None of these 'philosophies of mind', I shall argue, are able to offer a satisfactory clarification of the concept of an experience. Given their basic categorial 'frame of reference', the central issue for most of them becomes one of defining the criteria of significant ascriptions of experiences – which in practice invariably reduces to the problem of defining the general truth-conditions of ascribing experiences to *others*. But the concept of an experience cannot be satisfactorily clarified in this way. In what follows, I propose to examine some of the reasons for this, without going into a detailed exegetical discussion of the theories concerned, my purpose being merely to establish a sufficient platform for a phenomenological analysis, which is to follow.

Two rival metaphysical theories of experiences

Consider, first, what might be called the radically mentalist viewpoint, which is shared by both ontological idealists and ontological dualists. The position of the ontological idealist is that the 'physical world' is merely a modification of non-physical reality, and consequently that, in the strictest sense, there are no non-mental phenomena (although 'mental' has to be taken here in a very broad sense); whereas the classical dualist view is that there are two fundamentally distinct types of phenomena, one physical the other mental, which though irreducibly different are nevertheless ontologically on a par. Both sides are agreed that experiences cannot be explained in terms of physical attributes of physical bodies. They begin with the essentially sound premise that no physical property that one might have is a logically *sufficient* condition of one having a particular experience. But having done so, they go on to argue that experiences, being essentially mental, cannot be properly ascribed to non-mental subjects, and immediately expose themselves to a question about the true identity of their bearers and the criteria under which experiences can be ascribed to them. If, as seems clear, such criteria cannot be defined in terms of any physical properties, how should they be defined? When someone complains that he has a toothache, or attributes a similar condition to another person, what exactly is he saying? This question is particularly embarrassing to the ontological dualist. The ontological idealist, given his general metaphysical premises, can at least argue that what we regard as 'physical bodies' are really no extra-spiritual entities, for all entities are either spiritual or are explicable in terms of attributes of such entities, and although his position gives rise to all kinds of difficulties, he can, on the whole, present his case a good deal more consistently than a dualist can. The dualist (I am here thinking primarily of the Cartesian type of dualism) insists on the ontological separation of physical from non-physical phenomena and is led to postulate a non-physical subject distinct from the body in an effort to explain the meaning of experience ascriptions. But the immediate problem confronting him, of course, is how to explain the assumption that we normally make about the causal link between experiences and bodily states. If my toothache were an event analogous to, but entirely separated from the neuro-physiological process that accompanies it, it would make little sense going to a dentist in search of relief. The dentist cannot see my toothache, only my ailing tooth.

But if the dualist has difficulties explaining ascription of experiences, so does the materialist. The materialist denies the existence of a fundamental ontological bifurcation among phenomena and interprets experiences as a species of neuro-physiological events (or, in a wider sense, as a sub-class of physical-chemical processes). There are no phenomena, no 'occult' mental properties, he argues, that cannot be analysed in a physical causal context. The material causal links may not always be readily perceivable, but they are there all the same. Frequently we tend to be led astray by the fanciful language of introspective psychology. But nothing can alter the fact that all propositions about experiences can in principle be paraphrased into propositions about certain neuro-physiological events – if not without any sacrifice of meaning, then certainly without any loss of *truth*.

The immediate difficulty here, however, is one of explaining just *why* a loss of meaning that seems unavoidable in such paraphrases does not affect the truth-value of the relevant propositions. To put it differently, the problem is how to prove the logical adequacy of the materialist's ascription criteria. What needs to be shown is that the given proposition and its 'neuro-physiological' paraphrase do indeed have the same logical subject and express the same fact. But how can this be shown on independent grounds, i.e. without presupposing the validity of the theory which one wishes to prove? To take the example given earlier, it is necessary to show that the statement about the toothache can indeed be paraphrased into a statement about the corresponding neuro-physiological event (and hence that the occurrence of the latter event is a logically adequate criterion for ascribing the experience in the given instance), and this cannot be done without making use of the premises which such a proof might be expected to underpin.

A re-statement of the materialist theory

However, it is necessary to consider this in a little more detail, for it might be argued that a rather better case could be made out for the materialist theory than the dismissive remarks of the preceding section seem to suggest, provided certain additional facts are taken into consideration. As far as the radically mentalist view is concerned, there is clearly very little that might be said in its favour. If the mentalist position can be coherently presented at all, then, it seems, it is only in the context of an idealist ontology based on the assumption that reality as a whole is non-physical. As part of a dualist doctrine, the mentalist theory merely becomes a source of equivocations and obscurities. For consider again what is being claimed. It is claimed that there exist two radically different species of phenomena, one of which is entirely inaccessible to physical observation. The experiencer, it is argued, has a privileged access to his own mental states, denied to external observers; i.e. he 'knows' them in a sense in which no external observer can ever 'know' them. From this the inference is drawn that what he thus knows cannot be physical states, or explicable in terms of such states, for physical states are necessarily publicly accessible. Mental phenomena are correlated with physical phenomena, but the two species of phenomena are ontologically independent of each other, and there is no direct causal interaction between them. However, the problem is that, if this is true, there is nothing whatever that I, in my capacity as a subject of experiences, can coherently and unequivocally say about myself as a corporeal subject (not even that I do have a body); and hence that, strictly speaking, the theory itself cannot be clearly stated!

A more effective argument, on the other hand, can (or so it seems) be constructed in support of the materialist theory. For example, we might begin by first attacking the mentalist notion of 'privileged access'. The mentalist assumes that mental states are irreducibly mental in virtue of the fact that in all their essential aspects they can be known only by 'introspection'. But surely there are no 'acts of introspection' that could in any intelligible sense be said to be identifiable independently of their objects, analogous to 'acts of extrospection'. To say 'I am in pain' is not to enunciate the knowledge of the *proposition* that I am in pain. It is to transmit a signal that is, in a sense, part of pain behaviour. If someone makes a knowledge claim in respect of a proposition, it is meaningful to enquire about the criteria of such knowledge. But if Jones says 'I am in pain', it is inappropriate to ask 'How does he know he is?' The question of his knowing, or possibly failing to know that he is in the state he says he is in does not arise.

But if so, we are entitled to ask what sense, if any, can be attached to claims to knowledge about one's own 'private' mental states? Surely (so the argument might be continued) the interesting cases of knowledge are those which permit meaningful questions about criteria, and such cases necessarily involve states of affairs that are in some sense publicly accessible.

There is, in addition, one further point that might be made. If there are exclusively private events, in the sense that they are in principle, and not just empirically, inaccessible to more than one observer, it might be argued that such events could not be intelligibly claimed, let alone shown to be, subject to any laws, and this means that no rational explanatory model could be constructed for them. Laws are of the essence public; i.e. they can be intersubjectively monitored. If a law is such that there are no criteria whereby an independent observer might decide whether it is obeyed or deviated from, the law in question cannot be called a 'law' in any intelligible sense.[2] In other words, if we wish to insist on a

---

[2] This argument, essentially, is derived from Wittgenstein's argument against 'private language' which will be discussed later. See Chapter 8.

fundamental ontological bifurcation of phenomena into experiences and non-experiences, with the former allegedly being inaccessibly private and independent of the latter, we have to give up the belief that all phenomena without exception must be capable of a rational explanation. The two positions are not mutually compatible. Briefly, an attack on the mentalist view of experiences might be mounted by linking the idea of publicity of phenomena with the idea of rational explanation, with a view to demonstrating that rationality is incompatible with privacy.

None of this, it should be noted, actualiy *proves* that there can be no exclusively private events. The argument merely highlights the fact that there can be no objective criteria whereby such events might be identified. Nevertheless it is this kind of reasoning that has given powerful impetus to various versions of the 'mind-body identity' theory, including the one sketched out briefly in the preceding section. Let us now look at this version more closely.

It is claimed that reports about experiences are, at root, truth-functionally equivalent to reports about certain neuro-physiological processes. If a person says 'I am in pain', he is not reporting the occurrence of some spectral non-physical event distinct and independent of anything that might be going on inside his brain; or rather he cannot justifiably *claim* to be so doing. For if such a ghostly event does take place *in addition* to the neuro-physiological process of the given sort, there is no way in which such an event could be independently identified. Moreover, since such a ghostly event is by definition inaccessible to external observation, it is *in principle* impossible to provide an independent criterion for its identification. But if so, there is no real justification for supposing that such an event takes place. It is far more reasonable to assume that experiences and neuro-physiological processes are one and the same thing under two different guises; viz. that there is only one basic type of event involved here, not two, and that this type can be subjected to a rigorous scientific investigation.

This assumption, it is emphasised (largely in an effort to meet the kind of objection that was raised earlier on), does not imply that it must be possible for experience-reports to be literally translated into, and replaced by, reports about neuro-physiological processes. The identity thesis merely means that experiences are as a matter of fact neuro-physiological brain processes, not that the terms descriptive of experiences are replaceable by terms descriptive of such processes in all contexts without any loss of meaning. Evidently 'pain' and 'the brain process of type F' have different logical grammar and cannot be used interchangeably, except in a heavily qualified sense. Besides, a person who uses the word 'pain' in reporting his experience of pain may be totally unaware of the existence of brain processes; which means that no paraphrase of his statement in terms of such processes can pretend to reproduce accurately his purported message. Yet none of this undermines the validity of the identity supposition. There was a time when it was not known that lightning was an electric discharge, but this did not make the statement 'Lightning is an electric discharge' any the less true.

But this argument, rather than helping to strenghten the materialist thesis, merely helps to expose its main weakness. For consider what is being claimed. It is claimed that experiences are as a matter of contingent (not logical) fact identical with neuro-physiological brain processes. 'Pain is the brain process of type F' is to be treated analogously to 'scientific identifications' such as 'Lightning is the electric discharge of type F', 'Light is electromagnetic radiation (of such and such a wavelength)', 'Water is a hydrogen hydroxide', 'Heat is molecular motion', etc., all of which are empirical, not necessary, truths. But this, to say the least, is confusing. 'Scientific identifications' are hypotheses that are subject to tests under certain specified conditions, and may be corroborated or discomfirmed by relevant evidence in respect of those conditions. If there is no fundamental difference between such 'identifications' and the materialist identity thesis, this thesis too becomes merely another empirical hypothesis which is open to similar tests and might conceivably be overthrown by adverse evidence; or it might even be shown to be meaningless if our criteria for evaluating evidence should radically change.

The point is that if the identity theorist puts forward his thesis as an 'empirical hypothesis', it is difficult to take his materialism seriously. Empirical hypotheses may conceivably be corroborated to a very high degree, but they remain probability statements, and while they may prove successful in certain contexts, they may not work in others, and however firmly they may be accepted today, they may just as firmly be repudiated tomorrow. If the same applies to the identity thesis, this thesis ceases to be philosophically interesting.

If, on the other hand, the materialist wants his thesis to be taken not simply as a pragmatic rule, whose value is to be judged solely in

terms of practical results – a view that a practising neur-
ophysiologist might take, for example – but as an ontological thesis
about the nature of experiences *per se*, then he would have to say, at
the very least, that being a brain process of a certain sort is a *necessary*
condition of being an experience; that nothing ever can be an
experience unless it is a brain process. Yet how can such a claim be
proved? How can it be shown that there cannot be pains that are not
brain processes? For all we know, there might be. On the face of it, at
least, it does not seem self-contradictory to suppose that there are.

As it happens, even if such a proof were forthcoming, this would
still not be quite sufficient to vindicate the identity thesis. For unless
it can be shown that being a brain process of a given sort is a *sufficient*
as well as a necessary condition of being an experience, there might
be other characteristics that experiences necessarily possess, and
some of those characteristics conceivably might not be physical.

In short, the identity theorist is in some difficulty explaining his
own materialism. If he wishes us to take his materialism seriously,
he has to say that in principle it is impossible that there could be
experiences that are not brain processes. He cannot allow the
possibility, however remote, of his materialism being false tomorrow.
But if so, it is not clear what he means by calling his thesis
'contingently true'. Alternatively he will have to confine himself to
the more modest claim that experiences such as are actually had by a
certain class of individual are identical with brain processes, but not
necessarily or universally so; in which case again he will have to face
the problem of substantiating his claim, as well as having to explain
how can a materialist belief be reconciled with the implication that
there might be experiences that do not allow of such an
interpretation.[3]

---

[3] The view that the materialist identity thesis cannot be coherently
claimed to be true without being claimed to be necessarily true, was
powerfully argued for by S. Kripke (Cf. *Naming and Necessity*, Oxford 1980).
As may be gathered from the above I am broadly in agreement with this
view, though not quite for the same reasons. Kripke's argument is couched
entirely in terms of his doctrine of 'rigid designators' (which was referred to
in Chapter 2), but I think that in this case it is merely a question of whether
or not we should take the materialism of the identity theory seriously. Also I
do not accept Kripke's claim that 'scientific identifications' such as 'Water is
H_2O' (given they are true) represent necessary identities. First of all, such
propositions, however well corroborated, remain empirical hypotheses and
must be treated accordingly. Secondly, even if 'Water is H_2O' is true *tout*

There is, it would seem, only one way in which the materialist might be able to reconcile his general materialist approach with the view that the identity thesis is a contingent proposition, and hence in principle a falsifiable hypothesis, viz. by stipulating in advance that any evidence that might have a bearing on the truth-value of this proposition, whether it be positive or negative, must be publicly accessible. In fact, he will have to take his argument against privacy, outlined at the beginning of this section, a stage further and maintain that the assumption that there are inaccessible private events is not just indemonstrable but incoherent; and consequently that the 'falsifiability' of the thesis that experiences are brain processes can only mean that experiences might be public phenomena of a *different sort*. In other words, whatever experiences might be, they are necessarily public events.

But the difficulty with this line of argument is that it in effect presupposes what the identity theory is ostensibly designed to prove, viz. that there is no basic ontological bifurcation of phenomena into those that are publicly accessible and those that are exclusively private. This general thesis, it needs hardly stressing, is not comparable to empirical hypotheses of science. It cannot be compared with such hypotheses, because it is in principle impossible to define the 'public' criteria whereby the evidence conflicting with this thesis might be identified, and hence the question of its objective empirical falsifiability cannot be significantly raised. It is a *philosophical* thesis, and if it can be validated at all, it can be validated only with philosophical arguments, but apart from the general criticism of privacy referred to earlier (which is not sufficient for his purpose), the materialist has no other arguments to offer.

Logical behaviourist and functionalist approach

But now the following view might conceivably be put forward. The plight of the two theories of experiences discussed so far, it might be said, is due simply to bad metaphysics. Unquestionably both the radically mentalist and the radically materialist theory run into unsurmountable problems, and neither represents a philosophically tenable position, but the reason for this lies in their uncritical

court, or has the probability 1, in respect of all actual water anywhere, it is still possible to conceive of a substance which we would be prepared, with good reason, to call 'water' even if it had a different chemical composition.

metaphysical commitment, not – or not principally – in the way the questions which they are purporting to answer are phrased. For the basic issue still remains the same. we still want to know what kind of things, or properties of things, experiences are. All that is needed are better, more critical and logically altogether less vulnerable, answers.

I do not think that this is true. However, it is necessary to examine this view with some care, for it raises important problems of method. I shall at the same time have an opportunity to expand and clarify some of my earlier brief remarks relating to this topic. The crucial assumption underlying the present view is that the schema of objects and properties of objects, in general, remains an appropriate and adequate framework for analysing experiences. The defects and errors of metaphysical theories, it is assumed, leave the value of the schema as a conceptual tool for an analysis of all phenomena, experiences included, fully intact. It is only a question of using this schema to the best advantage, while at the same time taking the necessary precautions to avoid the pitfalls of idealist and materialist metaphysics.

Let us tentatively accept this, and begin by addressing ourselves first to the question of classification. It seems fairly obvious that experiences must be excluded from the class of objects. Designating expressions purporting to refer to experiences, as a rule, can be paraphrased out of the relevant contexts without any great difficulty and without any damage to truth, even though we often find it convenient to use them. If someone says 'The hunger I felt a moment ago is now gone', he is merely announcing in a dramatic fashion the happy circumstance that he no longer feels hungry. The function of the pseudo-naming phrase 'the hunger I felt a moment ago' in this instance consists mainly in conveying the importance that the utterer of the statement attaches to the fact that he expresses, and this indeed may be intended as an essential part of the message. But this in no way obscures the difference that exists between the logical grammar of such an expression and the logical grammar of, say, 'the man I saw a moment ago', for all their surface similarity.

If, however, experiences cannot be classified as objects, they must be some kind of properties of objects. But what kind of properties, and what kind of objects? How can we answer this question, while at the same time steering clear of any direct metaphysical commitment?

On the face of it at least, this seems hardly possible. Consider the way in which we normally talk about experiences. We attribute experiences to beings which we assume can be intersubjectively identified by their physical characteristics. In fact, we go further than this, by regularly associating experiences with certain physical causes. I now have this sensation of sweet smell which I instantly recognise as a smell of ripe apples. I am moved by the experience to direct my attention to the fruit bowl. I say 'These apples smell nice'. It is quite true that I can be mistaken: this smell may be due to an entirely different cause. What I see as a fruit bowl full of ripe apples may be merely an optical illusion. But I still identify this smell as characteristic of ripe apples. I say to myself, as it were: 'This is what ripe apples smell like. There must be some ripe apples somewhere in the room.' If I fail to find any, I shall conclude that some other thing must have been responsible for my having this sensation and continue my search. My assumption is that there must be a thing or substance of some sort which has the property of giving off this sort of smell and is responsible for causing me to have the experience that I have.

The natural reaction, then, is to look for an explanation by linking experiences with certain physical properties of physical things. Nor, of course, can we afford to act differently. When in pain, we seek help on the assumption that the unpleasant sensation can be removed by a medical intervention directed at a particular part of the body. The doctor asks: '*Where* does it hurt?' Admittedly not all sensations, not even all sensations of pain, are instantly traceable to a specific part of the body. This is even more true of feelings and emotions. In general, the more complex the experience the less clearly localised it tends to be. Yet even in such cases, as shown by numerous idiomatic expressions involving references to 'blood', 'heart', 'gall', etc. the tendency is to look for some thing or substance whose physical characteristics or physical condition at the relevant time might help explain the mental states or attitudes in question.

All this seems to lend support to the materialist view, and is in fact often used in justification of materialist inferences. It does not, of course, actually vindicate the materialist thesis. For all it shows is that, given the way we normally talk about experiences, we accept by implication that there is a close link between mental states and certain physical states, and moreover that the former can be triggered off and influenced by the latter. It does not show that we are committed to accepting the reductivist materialist thesis about the basic identity of physical and mental attributes.

So the question is, what kind of attributes are experiences? One possibility, it seems, of avoiding a materialist, or, for that matter, any crude metaphysical, commitment about the nature of experiences, with all the ensuing perplexities and problems, is to adopt a 'logico-behaviourist' approach and treat statements about experiences as logically equivalent to statements about behaviour, or dispositions to behave, and concentrate accordingly on an analysis of behavioural criteria for application of 'mental concepts'. Thus 'Jones is angry', it might be argued, should be treated neither as descriptive of some occult irreducibly mental occurrence, nor, in a materialist fashion, as essentially reporting a neuro-physiological event, but simply as reporting Jones' angry-like behaviour, or disposition to behave in an angry-like manner.

The immediate attraction of this approach is that while it ostensibly helps to obviate the need for making metaphysical claims of any sort, it nevertheless enables one to continue talking in terms of *observable* properties of *observable* bodies. The materialist makes the absurd attempt to interpret statements about experiences as being truth-functionally equivalent to certain statements about physiology. By contrast, the logico-behaviourist approach merely involves trying to elucidate how mental concepts perform their function in the context of ordinary discourse, where they are as a rule associated with propensities and dispositions to behave in certain ways. It is hoped, at the same time, that in this way it might be possible not only to provide a criterion whereby statements about experiences can be tested for truth – the materialist has this goal too – but that an analysis can be supplied of their meaning as well.

Unfortunately the project does not work. It fails chiefly because of the difficulties involved in deciding just what behavioural criteria are appropriate for what concepts. Such criteria may differ considerably in different 'linguistic communities', and are in any case subject to change. It follows that it is not possible to make any general statements about what constitutes a meaningful or appropriate use of a given 'mental concept'. But even if the behavioural criteria are defined strictly contextually, they may not necessarily provide a reliable instrument for testing the appropriateness or the correctness of application of a mental concept on a particular occasion. The reason for this is that the behaviour or a disposition to behave in a certain way under certain specified conditions is determined to a large extent by the kind of goals and motives that the agent concerned happens to be guided by; which means that the same kind of experience, in different agents, differently motivated, may result in different kinds of behaviour; and, conversely, the same kind of behaviour may for the same reason be associated with very different types of experience.

It is largely the need to cope with this very difficulty that has been instrumental in the development of the so-called 'functionalist' theory of mind, which I shall now discuss briefly. The basic idea put forward is that an analysis of mental states must take into account what is called the 'functional organisation' of the subject of those states. The concept of functional organisation is explained by analogy with certain complex problem-solving machines, in particular those capable of generating and testing theories, including theories about their own structure. What is being offered, in effect, is a machine analogue of the mind, with the mind-endowed organism being compared to a computing mechanism – referred to as the 'probabilistic automaton' – capable of making choices and evaluating the likely consequences of its own actions. The functional organisation of such a 'probabilistic automaton' is specified by its 'machine table', i.e. its basic operative programme, which gives 'transition probabilities' as between one logical state of the machine and the next, and generally governs its reactions relative to 'sensory inputs'. The behaviour of such a machine is thus determined not simply by the kind of input it receives but by certain parameters in its machine table, which in human language correspond to values, assumptions, beliefs, etc. These parameters are an essential ingredient of the 'functional organisation', and may differ from machine to machine. Thus it is quite possible that two similar 'probabilistic automata', if subjected to the kind of sensory input that in either case normally produces a functional state know as 'pain', will behave differently if one of them, say, places a higher value on concealing pain than on revealing it.

It is argued, accordingly, that both the materialist and the logical behaviourist theory are wrong. The materialist theory is wrong because what matters is not the type of material in which a given 'probabilistic automaton' is cast, but the latter functional organisation. It is perfectly possible for two such machines to undergo similar functional states in response to similar inputs (stimuli) even though their chemical and physical composition may be radically different. The logical behaviourist theory is wrong because the criteria of application of mental concepts cannnot be defined simply in terms of behaviour but have to take into account the functional organisation of the subject of mental states if they are to be at all adequate.[4]

Does the functionalist theory succeed where the other two theories fail? The answer to this, it seems to me, must be that it does not. Its main advantage over the other two theories is that it draws attention to an important point which they both tend to overlook but which is clearly relevant to any consideration of the truth-conditions of experience-ascriptions. Thus in order to establish what psychological state a given organism, or 'probabilistic automaton', happens to be in, it is not enough just to observe its behavioural responses to certain types of 'sensory inputs', or to analyse the minutiae of its physiology; what we need to study is the structure of its basic *operational system*. Yet this does not quite solve the problem either. For while the occurrence of a particular functional state (which the familiarity with the operational system enables us to detect and accurately describe) may be a necessary condition of a correct experience-ascription, it is far from being a *sufficient* condition, i.e. it does not, indeed cannot, fully reveal the intrinsic structure of the experience. Let me give an example.

Imagine a highly computerised washing machine whose functional organisation includes the capacity to monitor its own activity and alter or modify its own operations within a given range of available options at any given time during the performance of a particular task. The machine is continuously processing its own 'sensory inputs', and its 'decisions' at any given stage, whether to proceed or not to proceed along a given course, whether to initiate a different work sequence, bypass or omit a particular operation that in the circumstances proved unnecessary, switch itself off, etc. are based on its own estimates in the light of the available data of the likely consequences of such actions, and are in conformity with the general master plan enshrined in its 'machine table'. Then, if the functionalist model of mind is correct, there is no logical reason why such a washing machine should not qualify as a sentient being, and hence as a valid candidate for experience-ascription. To take a fairly

---

[4] Cf. H. Putnam, *Mind, Language and Reality, Philosophical Papers*, Vol. 2, Cambridge 1979, Chs. 18-21.

commonplace case, if the machine detects the presence of a foreign body within its works, say a piece of loose metal tumbling around together with the washing and pounding the sides of its drum, but calculates that the possible damage that might result from it is not likely to exceed certain pre-set limits of tolerance and decides to complete the operation, then it behaves no differently from a person who, having considered the options available to him, decides to complete his walk despite the discomfort caused by the stone in his shoe; and the fact that we use the word 'discomfort' in the latter case but not the former becomes merely an indication of a linguistic prejudice that has its roots in the way our civilisation has developed and our present society works.

But this cannot be true. Our reluctance to apply a mental concept to the washing machine is based on the assumption that the machine *does not have* the experience that the silently suffering walker has, even though they might be 'functionally isomorphic' in some ways. Our discrimination against the washing machine as a possible candidate for experience ascription is not so much a 'sociological' – although, of course, it is that too – as an 'epistemological' discrimination. It rests on the supposition that whereas the subject of mental states 'knows' his own experiences in the sense that no external observer can know them, the machine qua machine can hold no secrets for anyone. It is conceivable, of course, that in a given case such a discrimination might prove unfounded. But if it does, it is because the machine in question is more like ourselves than a simple inspection of its functional organisation is ever capable of revealing, and hence, in a sense, it is not a machine at all.

Experiences as evidential events

Both the logical behaviourist and the functionalist approach are avowedly anti-metaphysical. They are both inspired by the desire to circumvent the barren metaphysical dispute between mentalism and materialism about the 'true nature' of experiences. Yet what they in the end provide, in effect, are merely two different version of what might be described as 'materialism without tears'. While rejecting any crude reductivist metaphysical claims, they nevertheless couch their respective anlyses entirely in terms of publicly identifiable properties of publicly identifiable objects (identifiable, that is, on the basis of certain public, intersubjectively operable, criteria).

Essentially their's is a 'third person's view' of experiences, focusing as it does on the 'external' rather than 'internal' aspects of mental states. Yet if an analysis of experiences is to produce philosophically interesting results, it has to begin not with an analysis of a third person's accounts but with an analysis of *one's own* modes of experiencing. This is not to say, it needs hardly stressing, that that third person's accounts are uninteresting or unimportant. If no third person's accounts were possible or intelligible, we could not successfully transmit, paraphrase and exchange reports about experiences in the manner we do. Nevertheless the crucial point remains that our ability to understand a third person's accounts of experiences, in the final analysis, depends upon our ability to have, or to conceive the possibility of having, the relevant experience, or experiences, ourselves.[5]

It follows that it is a mistake to begin by asking, what kind of things, or properties of things, experiences are? It is precisely because it begins with this kind of question that the philosophy of mind, as conventionally pursued, tends to generate more puzzles than it solves, and proves incapable of providing a secure theoretical foundation for practical psychology. In the end, the psychologist is left very much to his own devices; relying, as he in the normal course

---

[5] The point is delightfully illustrated by a story from *Grimm's Fairy Tales* (translated into English, not very adroitly, as *Shiver and Shake*; its original title is *Märchen von einem, der auszog das Fürchten zu lernen*). The story is about a somewhat dim-witted young lad who had never in his life experienced any fear and was unable to understand what people meant when they talked about 'being frightened'. This troubled him a lot. His elder and much cleverer brother, who was his father's favourite, kept saying that he was terrified to go near a churchyard at night, and during long winter evenings, when scary yarns were being spun around the fire, people would say 'It makes my flesh creep!' But he would merely sit in his corner puzzling over what they meant. As it turned out, his handicap proved quite an advantage, for it enabled him to break the spell of an enchanted castle and claim the hand of the King's daughter in marriage as a reward. But the grasp of fear continued to elude him, until eventually his princess, aided by her resourceful chambermaid, managed to surprise him. While he lay asleep in his bed, they fetched a bucketful of ice-cold water from the stream that ran through the Palace garden and put into the bucket as many gudgeons as they could catch. Then they tore off his bedclothes and emptied the bucket, fish and all, all over him. He jumped in fright, shivering; then suddenly he realised what had happened, and was overcome with happiness and gratitude. *Ja*, he announced, *nun weiss ich was gruseln ist*. Now I know what horror is. The story does not say whether they lived happily ever after.

of events invariably does, on his own hunches and common sense insights, and constructing working models for specific sets of circumstances, without concerning himself too much with wider theoretical issues.

By contrast the approach that I am here advocating is 'epistemologically' oriented (in the broad sense of 'epistemological'). It involves treating experiences as modes of experiencing from the experiencer's own point of view; as events, that is, through which certain things become evidentially present to us in a particular manner. It involves acknowledging the special status of experiences vis-à-vis other phenomena: viz. the fact that they are not just another type of natural event but the very medium through which witness is borne to such events, and hence through which the world becomes an 'epistemological event' for us.

In short, any attempt to settle the dispute between the 'mentalist' and the 'materialist' interpretation of experiences, philosophically speaking, is pretty much a pointless exercise. Neither interpretation works. 'Experience' does not denote a class of objects or naturalistically conceived events. Nor is 'experience' comparable to adjectival general terms like 'round' or 'blue-eyed', or to abstract general terms of adjectival or, for that matter, verbal provenance. This is not to deny that we do ascribe experiences to certain entities, and moreover that we ascribe to these same entities physical properties as well. But logically ascriptions of experiences are not analogous to ascriptions of physical properties. Indeed experiences cannot, without important qualifications, be categorised as 'properties of things' at all. The metaphysical misconceptions discussed earlier on demonstrate the dangers involved in an uncritical acceptance of such categorisations. It is sometimes argued that the appropriate way to use experience words is in adverbial positions where they modify certain behavioural verbs. Thus to ascribe an experience to Jones is to say something about the way Jones behaves or does things. It is to say that he smokes nervously, pronounces words carefully, or sings joyously; with the emphasis on 'nervously', 'carefully' and 'joyously'. This approach has a lot to commend it, provided of course we bear in mind that the adverbs concerned are indicative of certain states which are not in all their aspects accessible to external inspection, and hence cannot be entirely unequivocally identified on the basis of external (behavioural) criteria. This does not alter the fact that we do rely on external criteria in ascribing experiences to third persons, and moreover that such criteria are quite indispensable. Yet the meaning of experience ascriptions cannot be defined in terms of such criteria *alone*. The point is that the intelligibility of ascription of experiences to third persons – unlike the intelligibility of ascribing physical properties to them – presupposes the ability to exercise *empathetic imagination*. Without empathetic imagination no experience ascriptions make clear sense and the 'external' criteria are of little use. In a sense, it is solely in virtue of their capacity to exercise empathetic imagination that men are distinguished from machines.

6. Experiential Modalities and the Structure of Reference

It is now necessary to consider in some detail the structural features of certain elementary types of 'evidential events', i.e. the structural features of certain basic experiential modalities. In my analysis I shall avoid making any ontological pronouncements about subjects of experiences. In particular, I shall refrain, as far as I can, from making any references to other persons' experiences. Also I shall postpone discussion of the differences between ascribing ownership of experiences to oneself and to others. What needs to be clarified first are the minimal conditions of intelligibility of experience-ascriptions to anyone at all. Accordingly, the emphasis in my discussion throughout will continue to be on the question 'What is phenomenologically involved in an experience occurring?' rather than on the logical implications of saying that one has an experience. (The latter topic will be dealt with in Section C: *Objective Order*.) The logical implications of ascriptions of experiences to oneself and to others cannot be made fully transparent without a phenomenological elucidation of the modes of experiencing that make such ascriptions intelligible in the first instance.

Now it might be objected that this represents a rather narrow view of experiences. The factors that determine the actual content of an experience, it might be argued, are not always and necessarily wholly internal. Consider, for example, what might be termed 'cognitive experiences', such as perceiving, remembering, recognising, something. etc. We cannot, in any accepted sense, be said to be perceiving x unless x actually exists. If a person claims to 'see' a fictional object, his experience strictly is not that of seeing. We cannot claim to 'remember' an event that never took place. Nor is it possible to 'recognise' a thing that is not there. But if so, then the person concerned in such cases cannot be the sole arbiter as to what kind of experience he is in fact having. His own phenomenological resources, so to speak, are not sufficient to enable him accurately to identify it. To put it differently, truth or falsehood of an experience report, in so far as the latter incorporates a truth claim, depends upon external circumstances as well as on the phenomenological features of the experience, and the person making such a report may be unaware of, or might misjudge, the relevant facts. What is more (so it might further be argued) two contents that are phenomenological-ly completely alike may have different truth conditions. Suppose a patient says to his doctor 'It hurts here'. Then it is not inconceivable that, when he makes a similar statement on a subsequent occasion, its semantic properties will be very different even though *phenomenologically* the situation may be exactly analogous; for 'here' might turn out to refer to a different part of the body (or in the case of pains that are sometimes 'felt' in amputated limbs, to no part of the body at all). There is certainly no purely phenomenological criterion that would enable the patient to say with certainty 'It hurts here *again*'.

What reply can be given to this? First, it must be conceded that in considering the truth-value aspect of the content (as expressed in a proposition) in such and similar cases certain assumptions have to be made that go beyond the internal phenomenological structure of the experience. Nevertheless this does not diminish the importance of a phenomenological analysis. Thus it is the phenomenological features of the content that provide a clue to the actual behaviour of the subject of the experience. It is because 'It hurts here again' that the patient is looking for, or expects to be given, the same kind of medicine as on a previous similar occasion, even though it may turn out that what he now needs to relieve his pain is something entirely different. In addition, we have to bear in mind that although the patient himself may misreport his own experience, those on whose advice he relies – his doctor, say – in turn base their judgement on their own evidential experience, i.e. on the manner in which the reference of 'here', as this word is spoken by the patient, is evidentially present to *them*. But most important of all from an epistemological point of view is that the phenomenological structure of the content helps to throw light upon certain basic ideas that are implicit in any classification of objects of knowledge, viz. the ideas of individuality, specificity, possibility, etc. It is therefore the *how* of experiencing that we have to scrutinise first. Rather than confining our interest exclusively to the semantic properties of the bits of language in which experiences are reported or talked about, we must begin by focusing attention on the internal features of experiences themselves, i.e. on the manner of their phenomenological occurrence.

Methodological solipsism and realist commitment

The approach I am advocating here should not be confused with what is sometimes referred to as 'methodological solipsism'. As I have already indicated, I do not think that the contents of mental states can in all cases be characterised independently of any relation that such contents might have with the 'external' world. Nor am I suggesting that for the purposes of psychological explanation all (literally all) that is needed is to work out a detailed phenomenological taxonomy of such contents. (Notice, incidentally, that on a phenomenological taxonomy 'It hurts here', as spoken in two different contexts, can carry a type-identical content irrespective of how different the referents of 'here' may turn out to be in the actual world. On the other hand, the contents of 'It hurts here' and 'It hurts in my tummy' can never be phenomenologically type-identical even though they may express the same fact.) My aim here is not to inquire into the theoretical foundations of psychology, but simply to give a phenomenological description of certain basic modes of referring, with a view to clarifying the key ideas that enter into the very concept of an object.

Methodological solipsism goes back to Descartes and his experiments with doubt. Descartes pointed out that since phenomenologically there is no means of unequivocally distinguishing between the state of wakefulness and dreaming, it is conceivable that our experiences might remain as they are even if no external world existed at all. In the *Meditations*, he writes: 'At the present moment … I look upon this paper with eyes wide awake; the head which I now move is not asleep; I extend this hand consciously and with express purpose, and perceive it; the occurrences in sleep are not so distinct as all this. Yet I cannot forget that, at other times, I have been deceived in sleep by similar illusions; and, attentively considering those cases, I perceive so clearly that there exist no certain marks by which the state of waking can ever be distinguished from sleep, that I feel greatly astonished; and in amazement I almost persuade myself that I am now dreaming.'[1]

The idea, briefly, is that the common sense realist assumption is vulnerable to sceptical arguments if only because, phenomenologically, it cannot be shown to make any difference. It was this Cartesian type of reasoning that provided the main inspiration for the so-called 'method of bracketing', which is central to Husserl's Phenomenology, even though Husserl's aims were somewhat different from those of Descartes. Descartes was using his method of doubt in an effort to beat the sceptic at his own game. His method of doubt was designed to establish an area of certainty within the mind itself. An attempt at a universal doubt leaves the doubter with the residual certainty of his own existence qua thinking being. Husserl's own method of 'bracketing' (which comes under the larger heading of what he called the 'phenomenological reduction'), on the other hand, does not involve an attempt at overthrowing the common sense realist thesis, merely rendering it inoperative – placing it 'within brackets' – with the aim of bringing the 'noematic content' of experiences into sharper relief. It is not, Husserl claims, an attempt at 'universal denial', like the Cartesian doubt, merely an act of suspension of all considerations relating to the actual existence or physical nature of the objects 'out there', as a preliminary to an uncluttered description of the intrinsic features of what is 'phenomenologically given'.[2]

Nevertheless, although Husserl insists that his method does not involve a rejection of the 'thesis of the natural standpoint' (as he called it), merely its phenomenological 'disconnection', the underlying assumption is that this thesis need not feature in essential descriptions of experiences at all, and I don't think that this is a feasible proposition in the long run. A wholesale application of the method of 'bracketing' can only lead, as it did, incidentally, in Husserl's own case, to grave idealist distortions. The realist thesis cannot be kept forever imprisoned within 'brackets', and has to come

---

[1] *Meditation I.* There have been attempts to reconcile the position of methodological solipsism with the demands of a naturalist psychology via a 'computational theory of mind' (See J.A. Fodor, *Methodological solipsism Considered as a Research Strategy in Cognitive Psychology*, in *Mind Design*, edited by John Haugeland, 1981), but such projects fall outside the scope of my present topic.

[2] Cf. E. Husserl, *Ideas – General Introduction to Pure Phenomenology*, tr. W.R. Boyce Gibson, London 1958, Section 31.

out of confinement at some stage. Rather than trying to keep it out of circulation at all cost, we should confront it and try to elucidate its underlying *rationale*, and this, in turn, as I shall argue later on, will have to involve the assumption of other selves.

However, having said this, I hasten to add that there is a limited role for 'bracketing' as a temporary expedient, and in the present chapter I shall make use of it for the specific purpose of highlighting certain referential modalities before probing into their existential roots. I begin, first, with a general phenomenological analysis of experiences.

Non-reflective forms of experiencing

In a broad sense, any form of awareness qualifies as an experience, although the word 'experience' is most naturally associated with what might be described as a focal event within a certain *area* of awareness – an area of awareness consisting of whatever happens to be perceptually registered simultaneously with, but not as centrally, or as clearly, as a given event. (The distinction between focal experiences and areas of awareness, as will be seen later on, is essential to an understanding of the flow and interconnectedness of experiences in the context of biographical time.)

Experiences involve a greater or lesser intensity of awareness; they are registered with a greater or lesser degree of clearness, with a greater or lesser amount of detail; but unless they are registered in some form there can strictly be no experiences. The concept of experience is inseparable from the concept of memory. Nothing can qualify as an experience unless it can in principle be recollected as part of a biographical time structure. But if nothing whatever is registered, there is nothing to recollect, and hence no experience to talk about.

Nevertheless, it has often been argued that 'registered' does not necessarily mean *consciously* registered. While it is trivially true, it is said, that nothing can be recollected in memory that had not been previously registered in some way or other, it does not necessarily follow that only consciously registered events can leave memory traces. A great many things happen to us at any given time, but only a very tiny fraction of this ever becomes part of our conscious experience. Yet the amount of what is actually stored in memory often exceeds the amount of what is consciously registered. And if so, there is no reason why we should not be able to speak of 'subconscious', or even 'non-conscious', as well as 'conscious' experiences. After all, associative memory chains can be built on the basis of conditioned reflexes, often via subliminal stimuli, and hence without involving consciousness, let alone self-consciousness.

To this one further objection might be added. In our own time it has become a universally accepted practice to apply the concept of memory to electronically operated systems for storing and retrieving information, even though the concept of consciousness within such systems has no discernible meaning. Some of these systems are characterised by a very high degree of complexity and sophistication and, once set in motion, are capable of functioning as entirely self-contained operational units. The registered data are stored on a selective basis and recalled when needed by a complex self-triggering mechanism. As a result, such systems, as well as absorbing all the relevant information, are capable of responding appropriately to external circumstances within the general scope of their programme. But there is nothing in all this that could with any degree of clearness or justification be called a 'conscious experience'.

These objections are misplaced, first, because the concept of memory makes clear sense only against the background of *our own experience of time*. This fact cannot be sufficiently stressed. Without the lived experience of the passage of time the concept of memory ceases to mean what it normally means and reduces to an atemporal order concept. To speak of acts of memory from the point of view of an electronic mechanism, i.e. disregarding the significance that its operations may have within a human context, is just about as appropriate as to speak of a tree 'remembering' to grow fresh leaves each spring or to say of nitrogen that it 'remembers' to react with hydrogen under certain conditions, producing ammonia.

Secondly, the above objections are misplaced because they are based on the assumption that experiences, if they are anything at all, must be explicable entirely in terms of properties of physical things, and I have argued that such an approach tends to lead into a metaphysical cul de sac, by encouraging a reductivist analysis of experiences, rather than helping to clarify the real issues. The real meaning of ascription of experiences to certain public, or publicly identifiable, entities has yet to be explained, and in order to do this it is necessary first to consider experiences qua experienced modalities of awareness.

If we adopt this approach, however, it is clear that we must reject the terms 'non-conscious', or 'sub-conscious', experience as strictly inappropriate. Every experience qua lived experience is self-monitoring to a certain degree, although the extent and intensity of self-monitoring activity may be strictly limited. At this instant I am sipping coffee from a cup that was placed before me only a few minutes ago. I feel fatigued. My attention is not focused on anything in particular. As my eyes wander aimlessly around the room I feel with every sip that I take the strong tang of black unsweetened coffee in my mouth coupled with a sensation of pleasant warmth, but I do not reflect on any of these. I do not say to myself 'This is a cup and I now drink coffee from this cup and I now have the characteristic taste of black unsweetened coffee in my mouth' – although, if asked, I could easily describe the experience. And, of course, I can remember it.

Moreover I can remember an experience even if I am not quite sure how to describe it. Thus I can recognise an experience as being similar to another, earlier experience without necessarily being able to put a name to it. I am certain that this pleasant smell now reaching my nostrils is the same kind of smell that I felt on a previous occasion, although I cannot quite identify it. This smell is familiar to me, just as countless other experiences are familiar to me. I recognise them as being similar to the experiences I had in the past, even before I begin to describe them. Sometimes I say to myself 'I felt like this before' or 'I have seen something like this before', and sometimes this is all I do, or can say. Occasionally the experience is entirely new and unfamiliar and is difficult to describe in any case. But it is not necessary that it should be clearly described at the time, or even described at all, in order that it might be remembered, or that a similar experience might be recognised on a subsequent occasion.

There is, then, it seems, a primitive form of awareness, in which certain things, activities, mental states, etc. that happen to stand out in a given situation are registered in a non-reflective way, i.e. without an act of conscious targeting at any object qua object. As I take a sip from the cup I instantly recognise the taste and continue drinking, without reflecting on my action. It is possible that I do not know the name of the drink, or can no longer remember it, but none of this is likely to spoil my enjoyment. When I came into the room a little earlier on I made straight for my desk and sat on the chair, without pausing to reflect on what I was doing with each step I took.

I had a feeling of familiarity with my environment. The chair was a chair and the desk was a desk. I had seen them both before. There was no need for me to say 'This is a chair' and 'That is a desk'. I implicitly 'knew' what they were and behaved accordingly.

But the absence of any conscious directedness to objects can also be a feature of what is normally regarded as intellectual activity. Imagine a reader immersed in an absorbing book, oblivious of the world around him. At times he may be vaguely aware of a slight feeling of discomfort which comes from sitting too long in one position. He may even, at the periphery of his consciousness, be registering the murmur of a subdued conversation going on near-by, the muffled noise of a door being pushed open and swinging back and forth on its hinges. But he is registering these noises without clearly identifying them. His attention is focused upon the unfolding story in the book. He reads rapidly but with comprehension. In all this, he is not conscious of directing himself upon any object. Nor does his understanding of what he reads *necessarily* depend upon his addressing himself to something in an objectifying experience. Suppose he came across the following bit of writing: 'All was quiet. It was gradually getting dark ...' He might stop for a moment and picture in his imagination a quiet landscape with hills fading into the dusk. But he can understand the atmosphere that this short description seeks to convey even without such images. It is not essential that he should always direct himself explicitly to certain objects in order to be able to grasp the sense of what he is reading.

Or think, for example, of a pianist playing a piece of music with consummate skill and utmost concentration. He is producing a stream of sounds and is himself, as it were, riding with the stream. He is fully conscious of his own activity, but is he relating himself to any object? His awareness of what he is doing does not imply an explicit topic-directedness. He does not reflect (or not necessarily) on the score, or on his own performance. The awareness that he has is of a non-reflective kind.

The monitoring activity and topic-directedness

It is clear that there are different degrees of being 'conscious of something', and that at the lower end of the scale, at any rate, being 'conscious of something' does not mean consciously directing oneself upon an object. Nor does it involve the consciousness of a self as the subject of the experience. Rather it is as if certain things and events are being registered in an unmediated *per se* modus, revealing themselves just as they are, in their pure 'uninterpreted' form.

Yet we ought to be careful how we talk about such experiences if we wish to avoid creating a serious philosophical confusion. Sometimes an exaggerated philosophical importance is being attached to such experiences. It is maintained that they are *existentially fundamental*, that they form the ground layer of all mental acts, and that they should be the primary topic of a philosophical analysis. A philosophical elucidation of these experiences, it is claimed, will take us beyond the subject/object dualism into the sphere of pure 'existential' facts; it will show that the subject/object distinction is not at all a primary distinction, but an epistemological construction which tends to obscure what in the *ontological* order comes first.

But, of course, in order to be able to describe these experiences, i.e. to able to say what *kind* of experiences they are, it is necessary that one should be able to address oneself to them – as we ourselves have just done – in *objectifying reflection*. They have to be recalled – or perhaps the right word is 'reconstructed' in one's memory. To the extent to which they are 'states of consciousness' they cannot be meaningfully said to exist except as potential topics of reflective attention within a biographical time series. An experience, I have argued earlier, must be capable of being remembered. We cannot very well say of someone 'He is frightened, but is in principle incapable of remembering the experience' without in effect confusing a state of consciousness for a piece of mindless behaviour.

Subject to these qualifications we may divide experiences tentatively into two main classes: those which are topic-directed and those which are not (or at any rate not explicitly) topic-directed. The targets of topic-directed experiences may be non-experiences or they may be other experiences. Thus in acts of perception we can address ourselves to non-experiences such as chairs and tables, while in acts of memory, for example, we can address ourselves 'objectifyingly' to past experiences, and in acts of imagination to types of possible experiences. And, of course, we can and frequently do address ourselves in monitoring reflection to current experiences, focusing our attention on selected sections of the total field of awareness at any given time. We shall see, however, that the manner of targeting at experiences has its own peculiar features which profoundly distinguish it from the manner of targeting at non-experiences.

Topic-directedness as an experiential modality

Consider, first, topic-directedness as an experiential modality in a very general way. Topics of topic-directed experiences are constituted as potential targets of different temporally separated experiences. I am now focusing my attention on this ruler on my desk and in so doing I am positing something that transcends my current experience of perceiving it; something that can (possibly) be perceived again, described in different ways, remembered, etc. – in short, something to which I can address myself in different experiences at different times. As a matter of fact, I shall, in a moment or two, use this very same ruler to draw a line on the sheet of white paper before me. And I might even use it to scratch my forehead while pondering over a problem, or try to bend it to test its elasticity, or simply to listen to the sounds it makes as it jerks back to its original position. Or suppose I merely think of a certain object, or try to picture it in my imagination. Again the distinction will have to be made between the experience and the object (the 'topic') of the experience. If I can address myself to an object once, I can, in principle, address myself to the same object a second time, but I cannot re-live (literally) the same experience. It should be noted that the distinction between an experience and its object is independent of the considerations of the actual existence of the object concerned. It is not necessary that the object aimed at in a given experience should exist in the actual world before this distinction can be meaningfully drawn. The assumption that we can address ourselves to the same object in different experiences – for example, in different acts of memory – is a constitutive part of *any* act of object-positing.

The usual objection to this, as we saw earlier, is that only in the case of actually existent objects it is in principle possible to define certain *criteria of identification*, and that if talking of identity of objects makes any sense, it does so only in the light of such criteria. The answer to this is simply that we cannot even begin to talk about such criteria unless it is assumed that we can address ourselves to the same object (qua topic) in different experiences, for we could not say what the criteria are for. Nor, without this assumption, could the question regarding the actual existence of objects be coherently raised, for there would be nothing whose existence could be meaningfully asserted or denied.

Topics, then, are constituted qua topics within certain experiences as potential targets of different, temporally separated experiences. This is the first and the most general observation that can be made about topic-directed experiences.[3] But not all topic-directed experiences aim at their topics in the same way; nor, of course, does the topic-directedness as such ensure the ontological existence of the topics aimed at.

Aiming in an individuating fashion

It should be made quite clear at the outset that the purpose of the present analysis is solely to identify the characteristic features of certain basic types of topic-directional modalities, not to investigate the conditions of re-identification of topics aimed at. As an illustration of one such basic modality, consider some examples of experiences ostensibly targeted at individuals.

My attention now is focused firmly upon the object in front of me. In my perceptual experience this object is singled out and separated from its background. I gesture towards it, and say 'I want that chair'. I am addressing myself to this one object and no other, this unique specimen in front of me. My topic is not, or not primarily, 'something that φ-ies', but 'this φ-ing x'. I am aiming at it in an individuating fashion, before making my existential assumptions about it explicit, and before making any attempt to puzzle out the criteria for its identification.

Now 'this φ-ing x', of course, may turn out not to be φ-ing at all. It may turn out to be a table, or something quite different. Moreover it is possitle that there is nothing there. If I discovered that there was no chair, I would have to say 'What I wanted was what I *thought* was a chair'. In other words, the object of my desire was not what I took it to be at the time. Yet this is a retrospective judgment which conceivably may itself be incorrect. The point is that phenomenologically my desire at the time was targeted in an

---

[3] I am using here the term 'topic-directed' in preference to 'intentional', because, as I explained earlier, 'intentional' and 'intentionality' have been used in different contexts and have acquired different shades of meaning in different theories. The concept of topic-directedness, on the other hand, is unequivocal and seems perfectly adequate for the job.

individuating fashion. Most important of all, it is only through such and similar experiences that the individuality of the chair, if indeed one happens to be there, becomes graspable at all.

But the object of my individuating experience need not be a physical thing qua physical thing, an object, say, that I happen to need and wish to use for a certain purpose, or simply want to move out of the way. Suppose I am merely looking at a particularly striking photograph of a chair, or a painting of a chair. In each case I have in front of me a physical particular, but my primary interest is not necessarily in anything physical. It is possible, of course, that the photograph, or the painting, shows a really existing chair and in certain circumstances I might wish to specially emphasise this fact. Thus I might point to a photograph of a fine Chippendale mahogany chair and say 'This is the most valuable piece of furniture that I possess'. On the other hand, I might look at the same photograph merely as a chair-photograph. My interest, that is, might be confined exclusively to the chair qua shown in the photograph. Suppose that I am looking at it in the context of a photography exhibition. The target of my objectifying interest in such a case is not any material thing. I am not addressing myself to any physical chair, not even to the particular photographic print before me. There may be any number of duplicate prints, but the object of my interest remains the same, whichever of them I look at, and it is this object, this 'ideal individual', that is the subject of my aesthetic judgment.

The same applies to paintings, although here the almost unsurmountable difficulties involved in any attempt to produce an exact replica give a special value to the original. Nevertheless there are very good photographic reproductions and we have no difficulty in accepting that in looking at a reproduction of a given original we are looking at the same (*numerically* the same) work of art. The value of the original derives from its being existentially linked with its creator; it has nothing to do with its artistic value. When I look at an original – say van Gogh's well-known painting 'Gauguin's chair' – from an aesthetic point of view, I am not addressing myself to the circumstances in which this painting came into being, or to Gauguin's chair, or to the physical properties of the painted image on the canvas, but to the represented 'ideal' individual and the significance that this individual has in the context of human aesthetic experience.

None of this, of course, can obscure the fact that such ideal individuals are accessible only via physical particulars; that the two are closely interlinked. Nevertheless, they involve two different modes of looking at individual objects, two different experiential modalities, and it would be a mistake to suppose that statements expressive of one of these modes can be explained in terms of – or 'reduced to' – statements expressive of the other mode. It is frequently argued, and more often implied, that only physical particulars are really basic and that all references to individuals, in the final analysis, are explicable in terms of references to physical particulars. But there is no way in which such an assumption could be vindicated from the point of view of experiences. It is important that this be clearly emphasised. Any argument in support of this assumption would have to be based on a metaphysical premiss that essentially incorporates the conclusion which the argument seeks to establish, and hence it would be of little use.

Quite a different problem, however, is the problem of whether and in what conditions an object aimed at in an individuating experience can be said to exist in its own right: viz. whether and in what conditions it exists *per se* in the way in which it appears (or is posited) in a given experience. To illustrate some of the difficulties involved here, let us consider a series of still pictures projected onto a screen in rapid succession, e.g. a film shown in a cinema. We see certain figures moving about on the screen; we do not see single frames. We address ourselves in individuating experiences to these figures, but the figures, looked at from a different point of view, are merely sets of discrete pictures on a film track. In other words, what is posited as numerically identical from one point of view may not be numerically identical from a different point of view; similarly what is seen as numerically distinct on a given occasion may, in different circumstances, appear as numerically one and the same thing. This raises the question, how do we decide which criteria are appropriate and valid in what circumstances, and, in general, how do we explain the distinction between what is objectively the case in a given situation and what merely seems to be the case. These problems require that we widen the basis of our analysis still further and explore the conditions of objectivity (see Chapters 8-10).

But consider now a different example. Suppose the target of my objectifying interest is not a physical chair or a chair-painting (qua aesthetic object) but my own chair percept, viz. the phenomenological content of my own perceiving experience. I might say, for example, 'The chair image that I now have is much more vivid than any other than I can remember'. The item aimed at in such an instance is not any 'external' object but is an integral part of the experience concerned, and the manner of targeting, accordingly, is 'biographical'. In other words, the item in question is posited as existentially unique in virtue of its belonging to a biographical time-structure. (I shall return to the topic of biographical time in the next chapter.)

Aiming at species

So far I have discussed certain very elementary experiences aiming, or purporting to aim, at individuals. But consider now the type of experiences whose 'topics' are not individuals but universals exemplified by individuals, i.e. experiences directed at *species* or *kinds*. I can address myself to this chair in front of me as an individual (e.g. 'I want this chair'), but I can also address myself to it as an example illustrating a species of objects that I want to distinguish from another species, say that of stools (e.g. 'This is not the kind of thing that we call "stools"') If this chair happened to be displayed in a shop-window, I would normally be expected to see it as the sort of thing available in the shop. But the point is that I can distinguish between an object and its kind even if the object in question be the only specimen available; it is not at all necessary that there should be more than one specimen of a certain kind for us to be able to make the distinction between an individual and its underlying type.

Moreover, it seems, it is possible to direct oneself to a species or kind without necessarily directing oneself to any of its examples. Thus if someone says 'Trout is my favourite fish' he is not necessarily expressing a liking for any particular fish of that kind. Still less is he declaring his partiality to all trouts – although, admittedly, he cannot consistently insist that he likes trout and at the same time refuse to taste any trout whatever. There is, however, no logical inconsistency between his liking trout and his rejecting all trouts that is offered on a particular occasion: his reason may be simply that they do not taste as a trout *should* taste.

Nor is it necessary, it seems, that there should actually exist specimens of a given species, before the species in question, whatever it might be, can qualify as an object of thought. After all new machines, new products, begin their life as blueprints on the designer's desk. The designer is desiging a new type of product, not any particular specimen that may roll off the production line. He is addressing himself to the species as such.

Nevertheless, although the mode of species-directedness quite clearly differs from the mode of individual-directedness, it does not follow that these two modes are entirely independent of each other. On the contrary, they are structurally interlinked. Thus the designer gains a greater clarity about his own idea for a new product only by refining and improving his own *drawings*, and it might be argued, not entirely without good reason, that not until after a prototype or a working model has been actually built can an entirely adequate idea be gained of the relevant species.

Aiming at collectives and groups

It is necessary to stress again that the aim of the present analysis is not to try to decide what kind of objects, in an ontological order, come first, but merely to describe certain experiential modalities; in particular, certain basic modes of *topic-directedness*. The value of such analysis is that it enables us to shed some light on the various subtle differences in meaning which become obscured, or are deliberately swept aside in reductivist paraphrases of statements expressive of such modalities.

Consider now the mode of aiming at collectives and groups. We are confronted here with what appears to be a radically different situation to the one we encountered in earlier cases. Suppose a customer in a shop on being offered a number of different shirts to choose from says simply 'I want all of them. The lot.' He is not addressing himself to an individual shirt; nor is he addressing himself to each shirt individually. Nor is he 'aiming' at the species 'shirt on the counter' qua species. The target of his objectifying interest – and hence his topic – are the members of this species collectively, in the plural. This is what he means by 'the lot'.

In fact, when we use the word 'all' we frequently think 'the lot'; in other words, 'all the (those) ...which ...'. But the reductivist logicians regard this use of 'all' as inconvenient and misleading. 'All' in the sense of 'the lot' is 'existentially committed', in that it implies that the species in question has members; but, it is emphasised, the species conceivably might be empty, in which case there is nothing to be referred to; or the species might have one member only, in which case again the use of 'all' in the sense of 'the lot', implying the existence of a 'collective' of objects, is inappropriate.

It is suggested, accordingly, that in order to avoid these difficulties all-statements should be paraphrased in such a way that they no longer carry an 'existential commitment', viz. by translating such statements into conditional statements with variables. Thus to assert, for example, that all trouts spawn in fresh water – it is argued – is really no more than to assert that for any *x*, if *x* is a trout, *x* spawns in fresh water. And if so, it follows that in saying something about all members of a species we are not 'addressing' ourselves to any object or group of objects but merely stating a condition which an object must satisfy if it is to belong to that species.

The advantage of this interpretation, as already made clear, is that it can cope with cases when species in question happen to have no members, since the suggested paraphrase by means of a conditional does not make any existential assumptions. However, it would be useless to pretend that *all* all-statements can be successfully dealt with in this manner. It is of course true that in a given case we may find that no collective actually exists, i.e. that the species in question has no members; or that it has one member only. But none of this makes the idea of a collective dispensable. It only means that we have to distinguish between the idea of a class and the idea of a collective. Whereas there can be 'empty classes', there can be no 'empty collectives'.

The idea of a collective, unlike the idea of a class, is structurally linked with the idea of a *whole*. All-statements referring to collectives presuppose the possibility of treating those collectives as structurally distinguishable wholes as well as collections of parts. It is here that the connection between the idea of collectives and the idea of individuality becomes apparent, for collectives qua wholes are merely complex individuals. Thus, for example, I can say various things about 'all the trees in the wood', 'all the pictures in the exhibition', 'all the books in the library', etc., but not unless I can refer to the wood, the exhibition, the library, as distinct, and distinguishable, units. This does not of course eliminate the difference between statements about 'all the members' of such a unit and statements about such units qua wholes. The mode of topic-directedness, and with it the meaning of my statements, changes radically as I switch my interest from the collective qua collection, to the collective qua whole, and vice versa. For example, when visiting an exhibition of paintings I might first look at the exhibition from the point of view of its presentation and then consider the paintings in the light of the fact that they are all watercolours or that they are all painted by the same man. I first look at the exhibits merely as parts of the same visual display and I can express various views about the display *qua* display. But then my approach changes and the thought of the pictures being watercolours or being painted by the same painter becomes the central unifying factor in my evaluation. I am now no longer addressing myself to the display as such, but to the pictures in the display, looking at them as a collection of objects sharing a particular attribute.

It is quite clear that what I shall have to say in each of the two cases will be not just materially but logically different, and there can be no question of bringing the two types of statements under the same logical denominator. A statement about a whole as a whole is not reducible to a statement about 'all the parts' of this whole, nor is a statement of the latter kind explicable in terms of a statement of the former kind. At the same time, it is evident that the intelligibility of statements of one kind depends upon the intelligibility of statements of *either* kind.

This needs to be clearly stressed. When stating something about 'all the constituents' of a given collective I am at the same time presupposing the possibility of intelligibly referring to this collective as a whole (a complex individual), and conversely any statment about such a whole presupposes the possibility of making significant all-statements about its constituent parts. These two kinds of statement, though logically very different, are nevertheless structurally interdependent. Furthermore, it is important to emphasise that statements involving references to 'all the constituents' of certain wholes, unlike other all-statements are 'existentially committed' and require a different treatment. (Some implications of this are discussed in Chapter 13.)

The indeterminate mode of aiming and the idea of possible objects

Finally, it is necessary to say a few words about experiences directed at objects in an indeterminate sort of way – not aiming, that is, at any specific individual, or any species qua species, or any collective for that matter, but vaguely at any object of a certain kind. When I point to a chair and say 'I want this chair' I am addressing myself in an individuating experience to a specific chair; but when I say merely

'I want a chair' I am not addressing myself to any particular chair – I just want something that satisfies the conditions of being a chair: any chair, no matter which. The mode of topic-directedness in this case is deliberately vague and imprecise.[4] Because of the inherent indeterminacy of their aiming, experiences of this kind – unlike the experiences discussed in the preceding sections – cannot form a basis for significant identificatory references to objects. Thus if I say simply 'I want a chair' I cannot say after a while 'I still want the same chair', since no specific object was aimed at by me in the first instance.

All I can say is 'I still want the same kind of thing'; but in saying this I am merely giving expression to my continuing desire to have an object of the same species. My topic is not a concrete individual existent, nor is it the species qua species, but quite literally 'an object, no matter which, that satisfies the given description'; if F be the species, then my topic is 'a possible specimen of F'.

In other words, if I am addressing myself to objects at all in such cases, I do so only under the aspect of *possibility*. I am on the look out for possible exemplifying instances of F, and of course it may be that there are no such instances. Conceivably there might not be any chairs at all. But unless the idea of 'possible specimens' made sense, I could not intelligibly claim, in a given case, that none existed.

Furthermore, the idea of 'possible specimens' is involved in the very distinction between individuals and species. For suppose there is a chair in front of me, and I say merely 'I want something like this'. Although I am looking at an individual object, I am looking at it merely as an exemplifying instance of a species which I assume can be instantiated by other specimens as well. My 'topic', in fact, is these other possible specimens. I want 'something like this', another object of the same kind. What is more, the idea of 'something like this' is an essential underlying ingredient of any act whereby I differentiate a given individual from its species.

The idea of *possible* objects, *possible* worlds, etc. plays a vital role in

---

[4] Language here can be an uncertain guide. Linguistically the presence of an indefinite article in front of the relevant noun usually indicates the indeterminateness of reference, but not always. From the point of view of experiences there is a vast difference between 'I see a chair' and 'I want a chair', even though grammatically they seem perfectly alike. If I see a chair, I see a particular chair, but if I merely want a chair, it is possible that any chair will do.

philosophical arguments, but its true significance can be made plain only by first exploring the idea of possibility as an *experiental modality*, and this means pursuing the kind of analysis that has been briefly outlined above. What is for us here of particular interest and importance is the close structural links that such an analysis helps to reveal between the idea of possibility involved in the indeterminate modes of topic-directedness and the ideas of individuality and specificity; in addition, of course, to providing us with useful clues for a clarification of the meaning of fiction.

Experiential modalities and their underlying ideas

In conclusion, our discussion of experiential modalities may be summed up as follows. First, all experiences are self-monitoring to a degree, but not all experiences are explicitly topic-directed. There is a distinction to be drawn between the non-reflective and the reflective modes of experiencing. Our ability to understand the *per se* modus of existence, in a sense, depends upon our ability to understand this distinction. Yet this distinction is itself an act of reflection. Experiences occurring in a non-reflective mode have to be reconstructed in acts of memory. The point to bear in mind is that the non-reflective mode of experiencing is retrospectively projected qua non-reflective in a *reflective* consciousness.

Secondly, topic-directedness involves a degree of conceptualisation usually associated with the use of language. The activity of reflection is a form of conceptual activity whose outward manifestation is a linguistic exercise of concepts. Nevertheless, it would be a mistake to go a step further and argue, as some have done, that conceptual thinking is literally identical with a use of language; for if this were so, we could no longer attach any clear meaning to the distinction between human language and animal language, or generally between concept-exercising and non-concept-exercising languages. I shall have to say more about this in a later chapter.

Thirdly, topic-directedness does not necessarily involve directing oneself to any specific ontological individual. In certain cases, as we saw, things are aimed at in an indeterminate sort of way. Yet the common feature of all such experiences is that they are directed at something that essentially transcends the confines of any single experience of aiming. When I say 'I want a chair' I am not addressing myself to any particular chair. It is just possible that there are no chairs anywhere. But none of this alters the fact that I want something, an object of a certain sort, that transcends any particular experience of wanting; something that is capable of being wanted on different occasion, rejected, etc. In short, something that can be a self-same object-topic of different experiences at different times.

It is important to note moreover that the mode of topic-directedness cannot always be identified by simply inspecting the syntax of the statements concerned. Sometimes we aim at specific individuals, and sometimes we do not aim at any specific individual, but this is not always clear from what we say on a particular occasion. Consider the following example. Suppose someone says 'The Minister for the Environment is a member of the Cabinet'. It is not immediately evident from the statement whether he is expressing a belief *de re* or a belief *de dicto*. If his intention is to make a statement about a particular person whom he knows from personal acquaintance, or knows about, or at least assumes exists and could be clearly identified in some way, then he is expressing (or purports to be expressing) a belief *de re*. But this may not be his meaning. The object of his belief may be simply the *proposition* that the Minister for the Environment is a member of the Cabinet, irrespective of whether the post is actually filled at the time, or by whom. In such a case his belief is *de dicto*; in other words, he is not addressing himself to any specific individual at all.

The value of this distinction is that it helps to draw attention to the difficulties involved in approaching an analysis of topic-directedness from a purely 'syntactical'point of view, instead of looking at it from the standpoint of the modes of experiencing. As the example given above shows, it is not possible adequately to analyse the topic, and hence the meaning of what is said on a particular occasion, in complete isolation from the speaker's own intentions and beliefs.[5]

Fourthly, and finally, our discussion seemed to indicate the existence of certain structural links between the ideas of *individuality, specificity, unity* and *possibility*, involved in the types of topic-directional

---

[5] That the distinction between *de re* and *de dicto* beliefs implicitly exposes the inadequacy of an exclusively 'syntactical' approach is, interestingly enough, completely overlooked by some philosophers who otherwise make much of this distinction in their criticism of the phenomenological conception of intentionality. See, for example, J. Hintikka, 'The intentions of intentionality', in *Essays on Explanation and Understanding*, edited by Manninen and Tuomela, 1976.

modalities with which we have been concerned. While the differences between these modalities remain both considerable and extremely important, there seem to exist certain relations of logical dependence between their underlying *ideas*. However, this immediately presents us with a fresh problem. For if these ideas are interlinked, the inevitable question is, what makes these links possible? What are the conditions of *intelligibility* of such links?

An answer to this, as I shall try to show in the following chapter, can be found only through an analysis of experiences in a *biographical context*. In other words, in order to gain a clearer insight into what lies behind the different directional modalities it is necessary to explore the manner in which experiences occur and link up with each other as events in biographical chains. It is experiences themselves in their 'natural habitat' that must now be our topic, and as is already clear from our analysis so far there are considerable difficulties awaiting us on the road ahead, for experiences qua topics of topic-directional modalities cannot be treated on a par with non-experiences. In addressing ourselves to experiences qua evidential events we are addressing ourselves to certain modifications of lived time. Experiences are biographical in the sense in which non-experiences are not, and indeed cannot be. The chair I am addressing myself to in my perceptual experience is not, nor is posited by me as part of my biography, but the experience of perceiving a chair cannot be coherently thought of except as part of a biographical time-structure. It is here that we shall have to look for clues in trying to answer the above questions.

7. Unity of Biographical Time

The mode in which experiences present themselves to us phenomenologically as topics, as has been pointed out, is biographical. They are recollected, reflected upon, analysed, as events in a biographical series. They represent modifications of biographical time.

All understanding of time begins with experienced time, and experienced time involves a differentiation and an implicit awareness of the mutual interconnectedness of past, present and future in a biographical series. The phenomenological distinction between these three temporal modes thus goes together, and is indeed inseparable from, an experience of the *unity* of time as biographical time.[1]

My argument in what follows will be that any references to ontological existents qua identical topics of topic-directed experiences presuppose this unity of biographical time. Conversely, it is only through positing certain object-topics (things, events, or whatever) as identical reference points of its 'acts' that this unity maintains itself in existence as a unity. Ontological targets, in short, are essential to its own survival. Useful hints about this can be found in Kant, although, as I shall explain later, there are basic differences between what I here call 'the unity of biographical time' and Kant s own concept of the 'trancendental unity of apperception'.

A further aim of my analysis will be to expose the links between the unity of biographical time as an experiential unity, and the idea of private ownership of experiences. Finally, an elucidation of the

---

[1] After I had completed the first draft of the present chapter I re-read, after many years, Husserl's *Phenomenology of Internal Time-Consciousness*, hoping for some new insights, and, to my disappointment, found the book singularly unhelpful. Although Husserl devotes a lot of space to minute descriptions of the various aspects of temporal flux, his analysis is diffuse, bitty, and on the whole unenlightening. My own analysis in what follows forms an integral part of the structuralist argument that I am presenting in this book, and follows a different route.

phenomenological structure of this unity will, it is hoped, help to throw more light on the experiential basis of intelligibility of the idea of individuality and the idea of specificity, while at the same time helping to clarify the position of the self as a lived unity of experience relative to 'mere objects'.

The unity of biographical time, it should to be stressed again, is an experiential modality. It is not itself an ontological existent; it merely modifies one. It is not any kind of metaphysical ego-substance. Nor should it be confused with the psycho-physical ego-subject, although the word 'I' which such a subject uses to refer to himself, in part at least, serves to indicate just this unity (qua experiential 'modality'). In fact, it is precisely this part of the connotation of 'I' that resists analysis and largely accounts for the loss of meaning involved in paraphrases of the statements in the first person singular.

Although my primary interest here is not in the word 'I' but in the unity of biographical time, it may nevertheless be helpful, for the reasons just stated, to take a brief look at some uses of this word in ordinary language and the difficulties to which they give rise. This will at once enable me to throw the 'modal' aspects of my analysis into clearer relief.

First person singular

In what follows, I shall be concerned with the word 'I' exclusively in the context of an I-utterance. The function of 'I' in direct speech is to refer to its utterer on each occasion of its utterance; which means that the designatum of 'I', and with it the meaning of a particular I-utterance, will depend upon who is doing the uttering. Notoriously this poses problems for the logical grammarian. Thus 'I' – and along with it all other indexical expressions whose meaning is affected by the circumstances of their use, such as 'now', 'this', 'you', 'here', 'there', 'yesterday', etc. – do not seem to fit in with the customary division of logical terms into proper names, or 'object-words', and concepts (if, that is, concepts are interpreted 'predicatively', in the Fregean sense). Grammatically 'I' is classified as a pronoun, but the implied suggestion that its role is merely to serve as a stand-in for a noun is misleading. One needs only to think of the form of words used occasionally in personal statements intended for official purposes: 'I, the so-and-so, etc.', where the personal pronoun fulfills a function that is readily distinguishable from that of the proper name or the noun phrase by which it is followed. 'I' clearly is not simply a name surrogate. Rather, as we have just seen, it helps to establish a reference of a name, although a name, once introduced, unlike 'I', does not change its designatum with its user. Nor can 'I' be classified as a general term in any ordinary sense of the word, for one cannot point at someone and say 'This is an I' But neither can 'I' be quite compared to syncategorematic expressions like 'equals', 'and', 'but', etc. which receive what meaning they have only in combination with other words within the sentential contexts of which they form a part, and signify nothing on their own. Such expressions are characterised by the kind of intrinsic fragmentariness that does not attach to 'I'. Thus, unlike 'I', they cannot be given in answer to a question, except perhaps to refer to themselves qua symbols. That 'I', by contrast, is possessed of a certain logical completeness, makes it similar to a name, although this does not obliterate the profound differences that divide it from names in other respects.

The point is not only that 'I' designates exclusively its utterer but that it does so in a way which makes it impossible for the utterer to replace it with the name by which he is commonly known, without altering the meaning of what he says. If Jones, in answer to a question, says 'I am called Jones', he is providing an information about himself which may or may not be true, but if he should say instead 'Jones is called Jones' he might provoke an amused chuckle, or worse. Nor of course is it possible to avoid all equivocation and safeguard oneself from trouble by replacing 'I' with 'this person now' or 'the person who is now speaking'. 'The person who is now speaking is called Jones' can be taken to refer to a third party, whereas 'I am called Jones' cannot (unless it is used as part of a quotation). Nor can one be certain to have injected a sufficient dose of precision into the paraphrase by adding 'the person who is now speaking *to you*', for it is not uncommon to be addressed by several people at once.

None of this, needless to say, detracts from the fact that in communicative interchange we often paraphrase other people's statements into a third-person mode, without thereby distorting the substance of the messages conveyed. If Jones should say to me 'I am called Jones', I do not falsify his statement if I say to a third party 'He (or 'This man') is called Jones'. If the question should arise as to who was meant by 'he' or 'This man' I might add 'the person standing next to me, or use some similar descriptive phrase. Clearly if intersubjective communication is to be possible at all, it must in principle be possible for such paraphrases to report the same facts. Admittedly there might be disagreements about the criteria of identification. What is more (as was shown earlier), no such criteria are entirely foolproof. Nevertheless, provided the context is not too complex, an agreement as to who or what is being referred to on a particular occasion usually presents no problems. Thus, in normal circumstances, 'the person standing next to me' is perfectly adequate to identify Jones. Nor indeed will Jones himself hesitate to accept this as an accurate reference to himself. As a rule, he will quite willingly accept a large number of other 'third-person descriptions' of himself as well. Indeed he *must* do so if he wishes to communicate. At the same time, it is clear that statements in the first person singular cannot always be paraphrased in a third-person mode, with their meaning or truth-value remaining intact. In particular, *Jones himself* cannot abandon the first-person idiom and talk about himself in a third-person mode without creating a confusion.

In short, the meaning, and possibly the truth-value, of paraphrases of first-person statements will depend upon who is doing the paraphrasing. The reason for this is clear. Whoever speaks in the first person does not refer to himself as he might refer to an object. He is not simply transmitting a neutral piece of information about himself; he is performing an act of reporting. And while it is true that in an intersubjective context what he says can be translated into an impersonal third-person mode, his performative act cannot be so translated, and to the extent to which such an act enters into the meaning of what he says, something inevitably will be forfeited in the translation.

First-person reports thus point back to the conditions of their utterance. Not all such reports, of course, literally contain the word 'I'. The more inflected a language, the less often the word 'I' is used. However, the logical structure of such reports remains unaffected by this, for the one who makes such a report is by implication broadcasting his own authorship of it. He is reporting something in a biographical manner. When he says 'I' he is making this explicit; and although others can say 'Jones' or 'that man over there', when he himself says 'I', he is not using 'I' as he might use an ordinary name or 'object-word' but is giving expression to a mode of experiencing without which no act of naming would make any clear sense at all.

Experiences and the structure of time

Let us now return to experiences and try to analyse the manner of their occurrence in a biographical context.

Certain things are happening now, at this moment in time. I am writing this sentence now. I have this sensation of sweet smell now. I hear music from the room next door now. Also I remember listening to a record of similar music some time in the past. I further remember that at that time too I was writing something – a letter to a friend to which I have not received a reply. At the same time, I hear someone climbing up the steps and while continuing to write these lines, wait for him to reach the door.

This is a complex situation in which several events seem temporally to overlap; yet my 'mode of directedness' alternates respectively from present to past, from past to present, from present to future. I am experiencing these events as a temporally extended complex of several interlocking strands which are retrospectively recognised as part of the same 'situation'. As to what counts as part of the same situation, this will depend on what the focal event, or events, are on a given oocasion, or on what the main topic of my interest happens to be at the time. There is no restriction of principle on the number of elements that a situation may contain.

But let us concentrate for the time being merely on the 'mode of directedness'. In the above example, my attention oscillates between something that is happening now and something that occurred in the past. I hear this music now. I am addressing myself to this event in the modus present. A moment ago the sensation of sweet smell occupied my main attention. The sensation is still there, but is not, at the moment, my focal preoccupation. I am listening to a stream of sounds forming themselves into a recognisable musical phrase. The phrase develops into a many-layered theme. All the while I am instinctively looking ahead of the stream of sounds, anticipating the future course of music, filling out the gaps, trying to pick out the characteristic sound patterns. This activity is interspersed with intervals of reflective attention directed at the ongoing experience itself. Thus I am conscious of this experience as the dominant feature of my current situation, surrounded along the periphery with a penumbra of other less important concerns. I identify this experience as 'listening to music'. If what I heard was merely an irritating cacophony of sounds, I would have characterised the experience as 'listening to noise'. An act of reflective attention whereby I register an experience as happening in the modus present necessarily involves an act of 'characterisation'. This characterisation, to begin with, may be of a very general sort. Thus I might describe the sensation that I am having merely as 'pleasant' or 'not pleasant'. Sometimes I am unable to say more. Sometime I am not sufficiently interested to find out. But usually the characterisation is more specific than this, and the information we are able to give about the relevant experience correspondingly more exhaustive. Often we address ourselves in several successive acts of characterisation to the same current experience. Thus I may, to begin with characterise my current experience simply as a pleasurable acoustic sensation, and then proceed to identify this pleasurable sensation as listening to a piece of organ music, and then identify it as an experience of listening to the *Toccata in D minor* by Bach.

Such characterisations, of course, are not always correct. I may be wrong in supposing that the music that I am now hearing is organ music, and I may be wrong about the *Toccata*. If I want to be cautious as well as precise, I shall have to phrase my experience-reports in terms of belief. I shall have to say 'I believe that I am now hearing organ music, and ...' However, this may not always be necessary. Thus the situation changes if I am merely interested in whether the experience concerned is pleasurable or not pleasurable. In such a case the only mistakes that can occur, it seems, are those arising from the wrong use of words. If the acoustic sensation that I am now having gives me pleasure, it would be an odd thing to say 'I believe that I find the acoustic sensation that I am now having pleasurable'. I might say, at best, 'I believe that the correct word to describe the experience that I am now having is 'pleasurable' '. But this implies that a certain 'prelinguistic' identification had already taken place. (I shall revert to the question of corrigibility of experience-reports in the next chapter.)

I am registering this acoustic sensation in the modus present. But my attention is never static; it moves backwards and forwards, following the sensation as a moving target, reconstructing various segments of its trajectory and anticipating its future path. The sensation, although registered in the modus present, is nevertheless temporally structured. As I listen, the acoustic scenery is continuously changing, with new sounds flowing into my attention, lingering on for a while, and then sliding into the half-shade of the immediate past and finally disappearing to make room for new arrivals. The experiential present is a continuing bridging process between past and future. I am looking ahead as well as behind me, expecting certain things to happen, and, of course, sometimes I am mistaken; the musical composition might not be the one I thought it was; the anticipated harmonies might never materialise; the whole experience might take an unexpected new turning, or be suddenly brought to a halt by some outside interference. Virtually anything might happen – except the world as a whole disappearing into nothingness (which, I shall argue, is a logical, not just an empirical, impossibility). Obviously the range of possibilities in any situation is vast, although the range of actual anticipations is contextually limited by such factors as past experience, theoretical assumptions, personal desires and inclinations, etc. Nevertheless it is when the expected does not happen that reality presents itself as a problem, and there is no doubt that it is precisely the sense of disappointed expectation that provides the experiential basis of intelligibility of the idea of *fiction*.

The experience I am currently undergoing is structured segment of my biographical time, with acts of recollection and acts of anticipation extending backwards and forwards the temporal lines issuing from the experiential present. Just now I remember that I heard a similar piece of music before. I remember the circumstances in which I heard it, and also that the listening to it had a very similar effect upon me then as it does now. This change in reflective attention from present to past brings a new element into the situation. In addressing myself to an experience as a 'past experience' I am addressing myself to someone's past; in this case *my own past*. I am thinking of this experience as an integral part of my own biography. That I can be wrong in assuming that I had a particular experience in the past is of course quite obvious, but in the present context immaterial. What matters is that I do as a matter of fact direct myself to certain experiences in the past modus, and that this inevitably involves positing such experiences as part of a biographical time-structure; i.e. that I cannot refer to an experience as a 'past experience' without at the same time referring to it, in effect, as part of *someone's past*.

Moreover, without the possibility of recollecting past experiences there would be no occasion for referring to any experiences as 'present'. In the example just given the contrast between what is happening now and what happened in the past is dramatically highlighted by the switch in the mode of directedness. It is important to note that the possibility of such a switch in the mode of directedness (from present to past and from past to present) is presupposed by any act in which I ascribe certain experiences to myself.

Is an atemporal view of experience possible?

There might, however, still be one or two lingering doubts about the kind of approach that I have outlined above. Why, it might be asked, is it absolutely essential to link an analysis of experiences with an analysis of experienced time? Why do we need to concern ourselves with experienced time at all? Consider again the example of an electronic machine: a computer, say, capable of recording and giving precise account of all its operations. The monitoring device within the computer incorporates a clock mechanism, which is synchronised with our own clocks and calendars, so that by asking the computer appropriate questions we can find out exactly what it was doing at any given time. The memory circuit operates something like this. After receiving the appropriate signal (the question) the computer performs a number of operations, scanning and rejecting a wide variety of stored data, until it finally comes up with the information asked for. Its 'reply' involves tracing the link between the relevant incident in its history – a particular operation – and the corresponding operation in the monitoring device. An 'act of recollection' in such a case, then, reduces to a process whereby a one-to-one correspondence is established between certain members of two different series: one series involving the 'basic' computer operations, the other a clock-and-calender mechanism.

What is more, it is not necessary that there should actually exist a causal link between these two series of events. It is quite conceivable that the two series might run along strictly parallel lines without there being any direct connection between them at all. In any case, it is possible to describe the computer's keeping record and 'recollecting' its own operations entirely in terms of serial order concepts; using terms such as 'before', 'after', etc. merely as markers indicating the numerical positions of individual members in the corresponding series relative to each other, not to suggest a 'flow' of time. The operations of the computer, in other words, including the operation of 'recollection', can be described in an entirely atemporal way; dispensing with tensed verbs in favour of the 'tenseless present'. And if such a 'tenseless' description can be given of a computer monitoring and 'recollecting' its own operations, why should not the same kind of description be possible in regard to experiences?

The answer to this is that this might indeed be possible if experiences could be treated strictly on a par with other phenomena. But if it is accepted that experience represent 'evidential events' (and hence 'modes of consciousness'), then an analysis of experiences cannot be separated from an analysis of experienced time. This is not to say that in 'timing' experiences we do not need to rely on contextual correspondences and serial order. In the example given above the monitored operations are 'timed' in relation to certain events that take place in the clock-and-calendar mechanism with which they are contextually linked. In a similar way, experiences can be 'timed', or 'temporally located', via certain external events with which they are contextually connected. But what is at issue is not the method of timing but the *understanding* of time. We address ourselves to certain experiences as present experiences, to certain others as past experiences, and yet others as possible future experiences. The distinction between past, present and future, however, cannot be defined in terms of any contextual correspondences between events. Indeed it cannot, in the strict sense, be 'defined' at all, only phenomenologically elucidated. It is intelligible only from *one's own experience of time*.

Unity of biographical time

The problem confronting us, briefly, is this. If we approach experiences as just another class of natural events for which a principle of ordering needs to be defined, then inevitably we must look to certain contextual correspondences, using either causal relations as our guide, or rely perhaps on such things as spatial proximity, structural links, etc. But the important thing to remember is that in defining order with the help of such correspondences we are not defining time. On the contrary, it is the experienced time that represents the necessary precondition of an understanding of the temporal aspects of any order so defined.

Experiences, as was pointed out earlier, are focal events within certain situations which contain a penumbra of concomitantly registered, or half-registered things, features, events. In a relatively simple experience, e.g. a short-lived but intensely felt sensation, the penumbra of awareness may not extend very far beyond the experience itself. With more complex experiences, the surrounding penumbra is usually larger. In addition, the whole pattern of awareness often changes, with the focal event subdividing into a number of smaller events and the attention oscillating between them and pursuing them with uneven intensity during the course of the experience.

Depending upon the intensity of concentration, the context in which a given experience is embedded can vary in its breadth and complexity. When attention slackens, the nature of the context changes. The context may now include many things which were previously excluded by the selective power of attention. Often the structure of the context may change considerably during the life-time of a single experience. Moreover, in certain cases it is essential that changes in the 'contextual penumbra' should occur if duration is to be part of the experience. Thus if my attention is attracted, say, by an evenly pitched continuous sound, it is only as a result of the various contextual changes accompanying the experience that I am able to retain the awareness of this experience occupying a specific stretch of my biographical time.

But suppose now that this evenly pitched continuous sound begins to modulate, is joined by other sounds at various intervals, and that together they begin to form themselves into what I recognise as a musical phrase from a familiar musical composition. The 'topic' of my experience now changes. The experience becomes more complex; and whereas earlier it was the fluctuations of attention and the changes in the context that accounted for the duration being part of the experience, now the dominant event itself seems to have a temporal structure on account of its very complexity. Having heard the composition in question before, I am able to report my present experience as 'listening to the *Toccata in D minor*'. There are other things going on around me, but it is this music that now claims my main attention. All the while I am looking ahead of the stream of sounds, as well as remembering what had just gone by, connecting and reconnecting in my mind the various parts of the unfolding musical whole. The characteristic opening phrase of the *Toccata*, alone, is sufficient to excite a keen awareness of a temporal structure. I expect this phrase to be repeated in a slightly modified form, and then repeated again lower down the scale. I am *waiting* for this to happen. Of course, I may not be familiar with the piece. In such a case my expectations will be far less precise. But if I do have expectations as to the future course of the experience, this is only because I apperceive what I hear as a developing theme or a whole (an event) in the process of completion.

There are two things that have to be distinguished here: (a) the posited musical event, and (b) the experience of listening. The musical event is posited by me as an objectively identifiable event set in an 'objective' time; although of course, it may turn out to be merely a figment of my own imagination. The experience itself, on the other hand, remains a constituent part of my own lived time, irrespective of whether the event actually takes place. Now what needs to be emphasised in this connection is this: that the manner in which the external event is posited is conditioned by, and makes sense only in conjunction with, the manner in which the relevant experience occurs within the context of the lived biographical time; and conversely, the manner in which the relevant experience occurs within the biographical time can be clearly apperceived only in contradistinction to the externally posited event.

Consider this more closely. The posited event (which may be only a series of modulated sounds coming from a recording machine), although posited as temporally structured, is not conceived as an integral part of any biographical chain. Like spatial objects, it is posited as 'external', and hence in principle equally accessible to – and identifiable by – any number of independent observers. Such an event, usually, is part of a larger pattern, but it is not logically necessary that it should be connected with any other event or series of events. On the other hand, it must be possible, at least in principle, to describe any such event in its entirety. Which means that there can be no infinitely lasting external individual events, although there can be infinitely repeatable event-types.

By contrast, experiences are part of open-ended biographical series, which could in principle be *indefinitely extended*. (Death as an end of lived biographical time is an empirical fact, not a necessary one.) The lived biographical time is as open-ended as a series of real numbers is open-ended, and it can as little be treated as an ontological object or event existing in the modus *per se*. Its unity comes from its temporal sense. It is a unity based not on any limits, but rather on the capacity to think *beyond* limits, and continue doing so.

At the same time, it is clear that the idea of an open-ended series, such as that of biographical time, makes sense only by contrast to the idea of external, objectively describable, temporally bounded events. The two ideas are in fact structurally interlinked, in the sense that the intelligibility of either depends on the intelligibility of both.

Unity of biographical time and unity of consciousness

It is now necessary to compare what I have here called the 'unity of biographical time' with the epistemological concept of *the unity of consciousness*, which especially in its transcendental versions sharply deviates from the notion with which I am here concerned. The best way to make this clear is to consider Kant's epistemological approach.

The guiding idea underlying Kant's approach is that of an order-generating activity of a cognitive agency. It is through a cognitive subject bringing the manifold of intuitions (Kant also speaks of 'representations')[2] under certain concepts that order emerges out of chaos. However, since the objectivity and necessity of such an order, according to Kant, cannot be accounted for in terms of what is actually accomplished, or may be accomplished, by any single empirical subject, there is a need for a universal transcendental model – the 'transcendental subject' – which reigns over the whole field of possible experience. As will become apparent presently, I reject this idea as misleading, not least because it encourages the misconceived notion of concepts as being spontaneously created and imposed upon the world by an 'order-loving' mind rather than being of the world, anchored deeply in its structure.

Let us begin with Kant's analysis of consciousness. 'It must be possible' – Kant argues – 'for the "I think" to accompany all my representations; for otherwise something would be represented in me which could not be thought at all, and that is equivalent to saying that the representation would be impossible, or at least would be nothing to me.'[3] 'I think' must be interpreted here as meaning 'the reflective consciousness of myself having a given experience'. But if

---

[2] Kant uses two terms: *Anschauung* and *Vorstellung*, which are usually translated as 'intuition' and 'representation', respectively, although perhaps they could often be more naturally rendered as 'perception' and 'idea'.

[3] *Critique of Pure Reason*, B 131 f.

so, the above premiss seems to reduce to the analytic proposition that I cannot meaningfully describe any representation as 'mine' unless I can think of it as 'mine', which is true enough but hardly helpful. However, Kant gives this proposition a special transcendental twist. Briefly, he thinks that he can show three things: (a) that a 'self-ascription' of representations presupposes the possibility of uniting different representations in one consciousness; (b) that only through uniting different representations in one consciousness the idea is generated of an identical self-consciousness as a principle underlying all activity of synthesis; (c) that the unity of consciousness (which manifests itself through the activity of synthesis) is a universal and necessary condition of all knowledge of objects.

It is the *last* of these propositions that reveals Kant's main intention. What he wants to do is to demonstrate the existence of an analytical link between the unity of consciousness and knowledge of objects. Knowledge of objects, he argues, presupposes the possibility of unifying different representations in one consciousness. This unification, however, has to follow certain rules. Knowledge cannot result from a haphazard combination of representations, but depends rather upon certain objective rules of synthesis which are valid for everyone. It follows that, at least as far as knowledge of objects is concerned, what actually occurs in a single consciousness is of interest only to the extent to which it accords with what must happen in *any* consciousness that has, or can rightfully claim to have, such knowledge. Kant, accordingly, draws a distinction between a 'subjective' (or 'accidental', 'contingent') and an 'objective' (or 'necessary') unity of consciousness. It is the latter that he honours with the august title 'the transcendental unity of apperception'. The word 'apperception', it should be noted, here stands for the consciousness of an identical self in the synthesis of the manifold; which is why Kant also uses the term the 'transcendental unity of *self-consciousness*'. In short, he tries to combine the idea of objectivity with that of the unity of consciousness, and what emerges is an abstract transcendental counterpart of the empirical subject of knowledge.

But all this surely is unnecessary. Such a 'unity of consciousness' as does, or can, exist, it might be argued, is always and inescapably an experienced unity, and it is just this experienced unity – or what has been referred to as the unity of experienced biographical time –

that underlies all experience of objects. All that we are really committed to accepting is this: that references to identical objects (or events) presuppose a unity of biographical time, and that such a unity, in turn, depends upon the possibility of positing identical objects, viz. that the idea of identical objects qua topics of topic-directed experiences and the idea of a unity of consciousness qua unity of biographical time are structurally interlinked; that neither of them is possible, or intelligible, without the other. There is no need, in addition, to postulate a transcendental super-subject to account for the necessity and universal validity of such structural links.

Kant's preoccupation with the problem of objectivity

Kant's arguments, however, are ingenious and highly complex, and we must subject them to a closer analysis in order to show just why they won't work.

Knowledge of objects, Kant emphasises, is inseparable from the idea of a non-arbitrary, objective order. In making a knowledge claim in relation to an object we are by implication accepting certain constraints, certain rules upon which an identification of that object necessarily depends. Or, as Kant himself puts it '...our thought of the relation of all knowledge to its object carries with it an element of necessity; the object is viewed as that which prevents our modes of knowledge from being haphazard or arbitrary, and which determines them *a priori* in some definite fashion. For in so far as they are to relate to an object, they must necessarily agree with one another, that is, must possess that unity which constitutes the concept of an object'[4]

The concept of an object thus goes hand in hand with the idea of an objective order, and to the extent to which our knowledge-claims purport to reflect such an order they inevitably aspire to objective validity. It should be pointed out at once that to Kant 'objective validity' means the same as 'necessary universal validity'; they are, he says, *Wechselbegriffe*, so that if a judgment is objectively valid, it is necessarily universally valid, and vice versa.[5]

This view of objectivity has a direct and vital bearing on his

[4] ibid., A 104 f.
[5] Cf. Prolegomena, §19.

conception of the transcendental unity of apperception. I shall now try to explain this by synoptically reconstructing the salient points in his reasoning.

His starting premiss, as we saw, is that knowledge of objects involves bringing the manifold of intuitions/representations under certain concepts. Concepts, essentially, are rules for ordering, synthesizing and identifying certain manifolds. They are cognitive tools whereby the understanding organises the manifold of sense into an objective experience.

His next step is to ask, how is use of concepts possible? What are the conditions that make an employment of rules qua rules possible? A rule is such that it can – in principle, at least – be repeatedly used, or else it is not a rule. In order that I may justifiably claim to 'know' how to make a cake, I must be able to understand the procedure involved in making it as an in principle repeatable recipe. Similarly, knowledge of objects presupposes the possibility, in principle, of making a repeated use of the same rules, the same concepts. Concepts are repeatable recipes for unifying and reproducing certain manifolds. But the idea of such repeatable conceptual recipes is unintelligible without the idea of unity and identity of consciousness. (Kant, incidentally, makes no clear distinction between the unity and identity of consciousness.)

This completes the second stage of his argument. But it is evident that this still falls far short of providing a justification for introducing the idea of a 'pure' or 'transcendental' subject (or 'pure Ego'). Admittedly, there can be no intelligible idea of 'repeatable' rules and no meaningful references to reidentifiable objects without a unity of consciousness. But this surely applies to any topic whatever, and the only unity of consciousness required is that of an empirical subject.

It is at this point that Kant appeals to the idea of *objectivity*. The final stage of his argument is an attempt to show that the concept of objective order necessitates certain universally valid concepts and principles and that the very idea of such universally valid concepts and principles presupposes a *transcendental* unity of consciousness as a condition of their possibility.

But the difficulty is that it just is not clear what such a transcendental unity of consciousness might involve over and above the assumption of the universal validity and interconnectedness of such concepts and principles. Kant was, in effect, justifying each of these two things in terms of the other, and his argument throughout remained essentially circular. In trying to clarify the transcendental conditions of the employment of concepts as instruments of organisation and objective order Kant looked to the 'transcendental unity of apperception' for a clue, but he could make sense of the 'transcendental unity of apperception', it seems, only by appealing to the necessity and universal validity of certain concepts and the *a priori* laws associated with them.

Transcendental apperception as an abstract model of a cognitive subject

His argument thus fails to achieve its purpose. He began by pointing out that experience of objects presupposed the possibility of the empirical manifold being unifiable in a single consciousness. The idea of an object, he argued, was inseparable from the idea of a numerically identical self-conscious subject of experience. As it happens, I myself act as such a subject when I ascribe the various experiences that I have to myself. However (he argued) this was just a contingent empirical fact, which could be fully understood only in the light of a transcendental model of a cognitive subject. It was here that the oddity of his reasoning became apparent. For while basing his analysis, in effect, on certain experienced situations, he couched his argument throughout in terms of formal transcendental conditions. As a result, everything, in a sense, was turned upside down. The experienced unity of consciousness was seen as something that had to be made intelligible with the help of the idea of a 'necessary' unity of consciousness. The notion of an empirical subject was seen as being in need of an elucidation from the standpoint of the 'transcendental subject'. The empirical self-ascription of experiences became merely an imperfect illustration of the claim that the universal transcendental subject lays on the whole domain of possible experience. My own acts of positing external objects became fully intelligible only in the context of the relationship between the transcendental subject and the transcendental object, or the 'object in general', etc.

In short, his argument amounted to an attempt to show that certain historical, empirical states of affairs can be made sense of only on the basis of his own abstract transcendental model. But by employing his own method of questioning, it is of course possible to turn the sharp edge of his argument against his own position by simply asking: What makes such a transcendental model itself *intelligible?* What makes its employment *possible?* No sooner are these questions asked than it becomes evident that we have to retrace our steps, and revert to where the whole inquiry originated in the first place, i.e. the 'empirical' self-consciousness.

The point is that Kant's transcendental model is itself in urgent need of elucidation. The transcendental unity of apperception, or the transcendental unity of self-consciousness, is presented as the 'transcendental subject of knowledge'. But, as we saw, this transcendental subject is just nothing without the apparatus of certain concepts and principles which, according to Kant, define the area of what can be known. These concepts and principles are said to be 'necessary and universally valid'; indeed they must be so, if the notion of a transcendental unity of consciousness, and, along with it, the idea of a necessary unity of experience, are to make much sense. But this only means that we are faced with the task of showing that, as a matter of fact, *there are* such concepts and principles.

So the whole model remains problematic. If there is no possibility of demonstrating the necessity and universal validity of any categorial schema of knowledge, there is no way of justifying the assumption, or indeed making clear sense of the idea, of a transcendental subject of knowledge; in other words, nothing much has been achieved.

Private ownership of experiences

The central point of difference between the approach that I have been advocating and Kant's approach might be summed up by saying that whereas Kant thinks of the concepts in terms of which the phenomenal world can be made intelligible as instruments of the cognitive mind and of the unity of explanation as an expression of the unity of the cognitive mind, I regard such concepts as expressive of the world's own modes of being, and look for a unity in the structural interdependence between such modes.

However, I must return to the concept of the experienced biographical time. This concept unfolds basically into the following three propositions. (a) If E is an experience, E is part of a biography; (b) different experiences can belong to the same biography; (c) a biography is a one-directional process in time. A consequence of (c) is that every experience occurs only once.

That experiences (qua evidential events) occur biographically accounts for the exclusively 'private ownership' of experiences and distinguishes experiences from public objects (as existents *per se*). We can, of course, and do, make objectifying references to our own and other people's experiences, reflect upon them, analyse them, discuss them. Moreover we are able to analyse to some extent, as well as report about, our own experiences while they are actually happening. Provided I am articulate enough, I can give a running commentary on my own mental states and attitudes and describe them in minutest detail, possibly just as vividly and as accurately as any 'external' object. But none of this diminishes the difference in ontological status between experiences and intersubjectively accessible public items. My experiences are slices of my own lived time and are, in this sense, inalienably mine as no 'external' object can be. I cannot coherently assume that experiences that I have might exist *independently* of my owning them. Experiences belong exclusively to whoever happens to have them; but the same is not true of objects, including my own body. It is conceivable that the same body can successively serve as a vehicle of different selves, although no two selves can occupy the same body simultaneously (they might conceivably occupy simultaneously different parts of the same body, but not the same body in its entirety).

The particularity of the self

The biographical occurrence of experiences thus holds a key to the idea of individuality. Experiences qua modifications of biographical time are existentially unique events in unique biographical chains. Moreover the unity of such a biographical chain is itself, first and foremost, an experienced unity, and the uniqueness of such a chain is an experienced uniqueness. Without this experienced unity and experienced uniqueness the idea of individuality of ontological existents – their numerical identity – would make no clear sense. In other words, an act whereby I posit an individual existent as an identical subject of a non-arbitrary set of predicates must be seen in conjunction with the manner in which experiences occur within a biographical context. The posited ontological individual, in a sense, represents an externalised form of the unity of experienced time. At the same time, it is only through such acts of 'externalisation' that this unity constitutes itself as a 'self'. It asserts its particularity and maintains itself in existence by projecting itself into a public place via its own 'body'. Thus I am making an individuality assumption in relation to my own body; meaning in particular that its position can be determined in relation to other bodies in terms of certain spatial coordinates. But it is only in conjunction with certain modalities of experienced biographical time that such spatial determinations begin to make sense. On their own, they mean nothing at all.

Consider this in connection with what was said earlier about the use of the word 'I'. 'I' names the speaker in the context of an I-utterance. Nevertheless naming does not necessarily mean individuating; one can name a species without thereby individuating any of its specimens. Nor of course is naming the same as describing, even though, as we saw earlier on, names are frequently initially chosen for their descriptive content, and moreover a name cannot name any individual that cannot also be descriptively referred to. When the biblical God says 'I am that I am' he reveals nothing about himself. What he says, in effect, is 'I am I', and of course everything is exactly what it is, and not another thing. If 'I' particularises anything in such an instance, it does so only in the context of an experienced unity of biographical time. Descartes's *cogito* is in this respect considerably more informative than the statement of the biblical God, even though Descartes having specified the *ego* as the thing which thinks goes on to draw the wrong conclusion that its entire essence consists in thinking.

All this underlines the complexity of the concept of individuality. The concept of individuality, I argued earlier on, cannot be explained in terms of any criteria of individuation. This does not mean that we can entirely dispense with such criteria. In fact, as a little reflection will show, no individuality assumptions can be coherently made in respect of anything, without at the same time accepting that some contextual criteria can in principle be defined. If an individual can be not only named, but descriptively referred to, it must also be possible to define criteria whereby the individual concerned might be contextually identified. The point is simply that the problem of individuality does not *reduce* to the problem of criteria; that an attempt to formulate a criterion of individuation, on the contrary, presupposes a degree of intelligibility of the idea that is being defined.

But an understanding of the idea of *specificity* too is grounded in the structure of the experienced biographical time. The experienced biographical time, as has been shown, is essentially open towards future; while there is always the possibility of its being abruptly ended, there is also the possibility (however unlikely) of its being indefinitely extended in one of an unlimited number of possible directions. And it is precisely because of this essential openness of the lived time that we are able to select an experience, or a series of experiences, and consider them as examples of the kind of experiences that might occur again, i.e. as specimens illustrating certain species of possible biographical events.

C. Objective Order

8. The Concept of Objective Order and the Publicity of Language

The topic to which we must address ourselves next is that of objective order. The discussion of the principle of individuation in Chapter 3, as we saw, raised certain fundamental problems which made it necessary to cast our nets wider and explore the basic modes of experiencing. Similarly the issues highlighted in the course of our discussion of ontological pluralism demand that we broaden the basis of our inquiry further still and scrutinise the conditions of meaningfulness of the idea of an objective order. All these issues are variously interconnected; they intersect and intertwine with each other, revealing a closely knit pattern of certain fundamental categories and ideas.

The thesis that was discussed in the chapter on pluralism (Chapter 4), it will be recalled, was this: that there exist irreducible non-reflexive relations, and moreover that the very existence of such relations is sufficient to account for the possibility of a plurality of ontological objects. It was shown that this thesis presupposed the possibility of an objective order – a vital condition without which no such relation can be meaningfully described as 'irreducible'. So the problem presented itself of clarifying the conditions that make the assumption of an objective order significant; and, as will soon become apparent, in order to provide such a clarification a different kind of pluralist hypothesis in turn becomes necessary.

We all accept as a matter of course that there is a significant distinction to be drawn between 'This is how things seem to me' and 'This is how things are' types of claim, even if disagreeing with reasons that may be given in justification of such claims in any given instance. Yet what is it exactly that makes this distinction meaningful? What makes it necessary? Clearly it will not do to say simply that this distinction makes sense because there are things external to experiences, and that the manner in which I perceive such things on a given occasion may not correspond with how things actually are 'out there'. This assumption is itself in need of elucidation. Perhaps it is itself an expression of how things 'seem to me'. What, if anything, does confer objectivity upon the 'realist thesis'? In the last chapter, I argued that the unity of biographical time 'knows' itself as a unity by positing certain external object-topics as identical reference points of its own 'acts'. But how can we be certain that such 'external' object-topics are not merely clever projections of a monadic self? Might not their 'externality' be merely a mock externality?

The problem with which we are here confronted, in short, is one of explaining why the world cannot be described exclusively in terms of how things appear to me; or, to put it more dramatically, why the world is not, and cannot be, identical with *my own biography*. What is needed, in other words, is a proof of the possibility of different selves.

Is the subjective/objective distinction universally applicable?

Consider, first, certain cases that seem to cast doubt on the universal applicability of the distinction between 'This is how things seem to me' and 'This is how things are'. If it is assumed that, at any given time, things, in principle, could be different from what they appear to me, then, it might be argued, this surely must be false.

If, for example, I feel tired, or elated, or depressed, this is what my mental state is and a distinction between how I *feel* and how I *seem* to feel, clearly, cannot be significantly drawn here. It would be an odd thing for me to say 'It seems to me that I feel tired, but I could be wrong'; as I might say, for example, 'I believe that my feeling tired is due to breathing in too much carbon monoxide, but I could be wrong'. It is quite possible that there is no trace of carbon monoxide in the air, but if it 'seems' to me that I feel tired, then I feel tired; I *cannot* not be tired.

Similarly – to take another example – it is possible that the book I intend to consult in a moment or two in connection with what I am now writing is not in the bookcase, as I believe it is. But although I can be wrong about the book, I cannot be wrong about my *belief* about the book. I cannot, that is, consistently assume that I might be. I can say 'I believe that the book is in the bookcase, but it might not be there', but *not* 'I believe that the book is in the bookcase but it is possible that this is not what I believe'.

In such cases, then, there seems to be no call for a distinction between 'This is how things seem to me' and 'This is how things are'; and if, as we have assumed, the range of significance of the concept of objective order coincides with the range of significance of this distinction, clearly we shall have to concede that a meaningful application of this concept is subject to certain important restrictions.

The problem, briefly, is this: that the distinction in question presupposes the possibility of things being different from what they appear to me, and hence my asserting something false, i e. the possibility of my being in error. But *prima facie* this seems to depend on the kind of statement I make. If I merely report how things strike me personally at the time of reporting, the question of my experience being possibly different from what I take it to be does not seem to arise. I may be wrong about my *past* experiences, of course. Thus it may well be that the feeling of fatigue that I think I experienced yesterday never really happened. But while it is quite possible that in referring to my yesterday's fatigue I may be talking about something fictional, there is nothing fictional about my currently *thinking* that I had the experience. Or, to take the other example given above, it is possible that I am wrong in assuming that a while ago I thought that the book was in the bookcase, but I cannot consistently believe that my present belief about my past experience might not be what I think it is.

Experience reports are subject to verbal tests

What reply might be given to all this? The first objection that comes to mind is that the above argument fails to take into account the corrigibility of *linguistic reports* about experiences. What is being asserted, it might be said, is something trivial and not very helpful, viz. that if I believe *x*, I cannot at the same time *not* believe *x*. What should have been considered however, are verbal *reports* of belief and *reports* of experiences. While it is quite true that we cannot speak meaningfully about the 'corrigibility of experiences', we have every right to regard experience reports as corrigible. Reports of experiences may be 'personal', but they cannot be 'private', in the sense in which experiences are 'private'. The privacy of experiences consists in their belonging exclusively to whoever happens to have them. But there is nothing 'private' about experience reports; on the contrary, such reports are made with the expressed intention of bringing certain experiences to *public notice*.

Admittedly, the 'publicity' of such reports does not necessarily mean that there is always a clearly defined procedure by which such reports can be independently verified. Sometimes an attempt at verification may involve observations extending over a long period without necessarily producing any conclusive proof of the veracity of such reports. However, there is, it seems, at least one test that can be immediately applied, and this test is the verbal test.

Dictionaries and other similar linguistic works of reference are designed to serve this very purpose. If a dispute should arise over the meaning of a given word,the quickest way to settle the matter is to consult a reputable work of reference. Dictionary definitions record the currently accepted standard forms of linguistic usage. Sometimes the work of compiling dictionaries is entrusted to special institutions which are expected not just to provide a record of the currently prevalent linguistic practice but to lay down explicit rules where the common usage is equivocal or contradictory or where no rules exist; and the works of reference produced by such institutions tend to acquire, or are expressly given, the status of official guide-books in linguistic matters. The point relevant to our discussion is that the existence of such works of reference makes it possible to carry out checks to see whether the words used in experience reports have been used appropriately. If someone complains of suffering from depression and on being asked to state more fully the nature of his complaint proceeds to describe it as a discomfort caused by ill-fitting spectacles, clearly we have every right to question the accuracy of his report.

Of course, verbal tests too may cause problems. Often simple dictionary tests are not sufficient and must be supplemented by other, more complex verbal tests before a clear decision can be arrived at in a given case. Sometimes the same word carries two, or more meanings. Furthermore, words notoriously tend to acquire different shades of meaning in different contexts and this makes the process of checking that much more difficult. There are innumerable shades of meaning that are not, and cannot be, listed in any dictionary. In addition, it is possible to alter the customary meanings of words altogether, as is done, for example, in coded messages. If we are going to use dictionaries, we must know which dictionaries to use.

Nevertheless, it might be argued that these are merely practical problems that have to be tackled as and when they arise. What is important is that so long as there exist certain rules, whatever such rules might be, independent tests can be carried out with a view to determining whether these rules are observed; in other words, no individual user of language can be the sole arbiter of the correctness of what he is saying.

The impossibility of a 'private language'

It is essentially this kind of reasoning that lies behind the well-known argument against the idea of a 'private language'. The argument is due to Wittgenstein, and it may be briefly stated as follows.

Language is analogous to a game played in accordance with certain rules. These rules lay down the standards for the appropriate use of linguistic symbols and linguistic mistakes are judged in the light of such standards. We are free, in principle, to modify the existing rules or introduce entirely new rules into the game, but some rules there must be if there is to be a meaningful distinction between correct and incorrect use. No rules, however, are such that they can be intelligible to one person only. A language as a rule-governed game must be teachable to others. Moreover the very idea of a 'private' rule – 'private' in the sense that no one except myself could ever (logically ever) decide whether it is obeyed or not – is incoherent. In order to be able to understand what 'obeying a rule' means we must be able to understand the distinction between obeying a rule and being under the impression of obeying a rule, and this distinction cannot be drawn from a purely 'private' standpoint. For ' ...to think one is obeying a rule is not to obey a rule. Hence it is not possible to obey a rule "privately"; otherwise thinking one was obeying a rule would be the same as obeying it.'[1] But if it is not possible to obey rules 'privately', there can be no 'private language'.

It follows that I cannot use language without being implicitly committed to accepting the possibility that I might use it inappropriately on a given occasion and that I could be corrected by

---

[1] L. Wittgenstein: *Philosophical Investigations*, Sec. 202.

others. All statements that I make are without exception subject to independent verbal checks. They are by their very nature 'corrigible'. The argument, in short, links the publicity of language with its *corrigibility*.

Corrigibility of linguistic reports and beliefs

Before commenting on this argument, it is necessary to clear up certain ambiguities surrounding the concept of corrigibility. Consider again one of our earlier examples. When a person says 'I feel tired', it is of course possible that he is misreporting his experience simply because he is not sufficiently familiar with the English word 'tired'. But suppose he says instead 'I believe that "tired" is the correct description of how I feel at the moment'. The situation is now different, for he is merely reporting his *belief* about the word 'tired' and what he says may be a true statement of his belief, even though the belief itself may be false.

It is important to draw a clear distinction between these two cases. In one case, it is the appropriateness of the word used that is at issue; in the other, we are judging the accuracy of the expressed belief about the word in question. Of course, it is possible that the speaker's own belief-statement is linguistically inaccurate and, as a result, misreports his own belief. But the point is that a distinction has to be made between verifying the accuracy of his report and evaluating the accuracy of his stated belief.

Consider now the other example that was given earlier. I believe that the book I am anxious to consult is in the bookcase. In saying this I am expressing a belief which may turn out to be false. But suppose I say merely: 'I believe that by saying "I believe that the book I am anxious to consult is in the bookcase" I am accurately expressing my current belief about the book in question'. The latter statement is a statement of belief about a statement of belief. Here too the statement as it stands may be accurate, although the stated belief may be false.

It is necessary, then, to distinguish between the accuracy of *belief-statements* and the correctness of stated *beliefs*. The tendency frequently is to confuse these two things. Yet, as we shall see later, it is essential to keep them separate if absurdities are to be avoided. All linguistic reports, including belief-statements, are 'corrigible': viz. they may be accurate, but need not be. But the same cannot by any means be said of all *beliefs*.

Publicity, corrigibility and generality of language

Let us now return to the argument against 'private language'. This argument involves an attempt to show that the publicity of language – i.e. its accessibility to different users, and hence its intelligibility at different points of view – flows from its corrigibility. Language involves rules, and the concept of rule involves a distinction between adhering to, or 'obeying' a rule and deviating from it. However, I myself cannot be the sole judge of whether a rule is obeyed or infringed. If I were, there could be no meaningful distinction between what seems to me to be right and what is right, and hence no intelligible concept of 'right'.

The argument, in other words, relies on the intelligibility of the subjective/objective distinction in trying to establish the public accessibility of language, i.e. its shareability by 'different selves'. The idea of a private (logically, not merely 'empirically' private) language is untenable because it is incompatible with the distinction between how things seem to me and how things are.

In what follows, I propose to turn the argument around, and try to clarify the subjective/objective distinction through an analysis of the publicity of language. In order to understand the possibility of an objective order we need to assume the possibility of different selves, and here the publicity of language might provide us with a clue.

The immediate consequence of this reversal of route is to bring the aspect of generality of language into focus. Before a language can be publicly accessible, it must possess a degree of generality. Before others can correct my mistakes they must understand what I am saying; above all, they must understand the rules, and the 'public accessibility' of rules is inseparable from their *generality*.

Generality of language and the plurality of selves

Indeed it might seem at first sight the 'publicity' of language flows entirely from its 'generality', and consequently that in trying to explain the idea of a plurality of selves it is only the aspect of generality that needs to be taken into account. After all, we use language to transmit and exchange messages with other language users, assuming as a matter of course that what we say can be understood at points of view different from our own before we even consider the possibility of error. Irrespective of the kind of statement we make (the distinction between 'This is how things appear to me' and 'This is how things are' type of claim is irrelevant here) we are implicitly commiting ourselves to accepting the possibility of there being other selves – other subjects of experiences – capable of understanding what is being said, despite being 'biographically distinct' from ourselves. This commitment seems to be imposed upon us by the very *generality* of language.

But if this is the case, then surely there is a relatively comfortable logical short cut to pluralism, making it unnecessary to appeal to the 'irreducibility' of certain relations; in fact, we could, it seem, altogether reject the idea of such relations without abandoning the 'pluralist thesis'. Nor do we need to assume the plurality of anything other than *selves*!

As an attempt to vindicate pluralism without relying on 'irreducibly external' relations this argument would certainly have appealed to Leibniz. Indeed it seems to me that if his idea of mutually independent 'windowless' monads can be defended at all plausibly, than it has to be along these lines. I shall therefore, call the argument *Leibnizian*. It is in my view an important as well an attractive argument, and it deserves to be analysed in more detail in order to show just how far it will stretch and why, in the end, it must fail.

Human and non-human languages

Let us begin by first considering language as a public system of information, taken in the widest possible sense. In the argument against private language, to which we referred earlier, the publicity of language was linked with the concept of rule and the concept of error. But, surely, it might be said, if 'language' is used in the broad sense in which it is very frequently used, i.e. as descriptive of a wide class of both human and non-human systems of information, it is clear that the concepts of rule and infringement of rule do not necessarily feature in every such system.

Every system is built up of certain regularities, and where there are regularities it is conceivable that irregularities might occur also. If linguistic symbols are subject to certain rules, it is always possible that such rules might be infringed. It is necessary however to distinguish between the possibility of a rule being infringed – or error 'committed' – within a given system and the availability of the concept of infringement of rule *within that system.*

Imagine a series of computers capable of gathering, processing and exchanging information among themselves – a system that might, for example, be used in weather forecasting. The chain of computers works as a fully independent system, providing at regular intervals what to us are probability inferences about future weather conditions. What we must ask ourselves now, is this: What does linguistic 'error' mean within such a system? Suppose all computers are working perfectly and no 'rules' are ever broken or deviated from. Are we to say that because of this the computer language of such a system cannot be called a language in any real sense? Why should every system of information necessarily embody the concept of error?

However suppose that malfunctioning does occur from time to time, an altogether more likely proposition. Suppose moreover that the system itself is equipped to deal with such an eventuality, provided that the malfunctioning is on a relatively minor scale and does not disrupt the basic operations on which the survival of the system depends. The computers are programmed in such a way that when a fault occurs, threatening the stability of the system, a special mechanism is put into operation which eliminates the fault and restores the *status quo ante,* or something very near it. Can such computers be said to have the concept of linguistic error?

The answer, clearly, must depend on whether such a system of computers can be regarded as a teleological, rather than a merely causal, system. Within a causal system (qua causal system) there is little room for the concept of rule or infringement of rule. In an animal organism there is a constant flow of information between the receptor cells in its sense organs and the central nervous system, but although the process of coding and decoding of messages follows a regular pattern, the *concept* of a pattern is not itself part of the system. Admittedly this may not be the most ideal illustration of a language system. Yet surely the point that this example helps to bring home remains valid none the less. The flow of information from one point to another while presupposing the existence of certain regularities does not depend on the availability of the concept of a rule. Many animal species, especially the so-called 'social insects' operate highly intricate systems of mutual communication, but we could hardly assume that these systems of communication incorporate the concept of rule and the concept of infringement or deviation from rule.

The point – as we shall see more fully later[2] – is that the concept of rule and the concept of infringement or deviation from rule are linked with the concept of purpose and depend on the availability of the latter concept. But quite clearly this concept is not available in all systems of information. The bee is said to be capable of indicating with great precision where nectar can be found by performing a dance on the honeycomb. Its dance is a very complex social signal which has all the characteristics of a language symbol. But it would mean stretching the imagination a little too far to describe the bee's behaviour as a *purposive action*.

Animal communication follows certain established patterns, just as human communication does, and such patterns can be deviated from by individual members of the species. After all, an animal does not inherit all his communicative skills and it has to acquire many of them, sometimes laboriously, by an extended process of trial and error in the context of group life. A large part of the process of learning inevitably consists in learning how to avoid error. But we must be careful not to confuse what we ourselves from our own point of view see as an error in an animal's behaviour and what error represents in the context of the animal's own life. In a well-known experiment pigeons are taught to recognise words by being rewarded with food pellets each time they peck at the right word from a number of different words displayed before them in succession. From the experimenter's point of view, the pigeon makes a 'mistake' each time it pecks at a word other than the one which releases pellets. But the pigeon does not have the concept of a mistake; it simply goes on pecking randomly at different words until a repeatedly successful outcome in a given case helps to create a sufficiently strong conditioned reflex, so that his pecking becomes correspondingly more discriminating. Every successful effort on its part reinforces the reflex, while a repeated failure weakens it. But the pigeon knows nothing about 'missed opportunities' and the possibility of having acted differently; of rules and the possibility of rules being violated, or ignored, or misunderstood.

A system of information, then, does not necessarily incorporate the concept of rule and the concept of infringement or deviation from rule. Even the highly complex systems which incorporate

---

[2] See next chapter.

sophisticated self-rectifying mechanisms, as we saw, cannot be unequivocally said to include these concepts. Nevertheless they all depend upon certain regularities and repetitions. In short, such stability as they have depends upon the same kind of signals producing the same kind of effects.

'Rules' in such systems reduce to 'regularities' and the concept of error has no real application. In a causal context an 'error' merely exemplifies a 'regularity' (a 'law') of a different sort. What is more, it is clear that every system of information if looked at 'externally' – merely, that is, as a system of stimuli and behavioural responses of a certain type – is open to a causal interpretation in which the concept of error need not feature at all. It is only in conjunction with concepts such as intention, goal, motive, etc. that error enters the scene.

The counterpart of these regularities in the human system of information are the rules that govern the use of linguistic symbols and ensure the 'stability' of the system. Error here has a special status. Whereas an 'irregularity' in a causal context merely points to a different kind of regularity, what counts as an error in the human context cannot be treated simply as an example of a different kind of rule.

Generality and possible experiences

Let us now proceed with our discussion of the view that a pluralist thesis is implicit in the idea of generality of language. The generality of language, as we saw, consists in the fact that language symbols can be used in the same sense at different times and points of view. However, if we are to prove that this does indeed entail the possibility of a plurality of selves, we must prove that no single self can occupy all the points of view that are available, or possible, at any given time.

In what follows, I shall try to construct such a proof. Moreover I shall try to avoid relying on the assumption that there are things other than experiences – physical objects, for example. I shall confine myself exclusively to the aspect of generality and try to establish whether the possibility of a plurality of selves, occupying different points of view, can be derived from the idea of generality alone without presupposing the 'realist thesis'. If a language is 'realistically committed' in the sense of containing words descriptive of things other than experiences, there seems to be no problem; for even if it is assumed that there is only one such thing, this still commits us to accepting that there can be points of view that we ourselves shall never occupy. When I point at this object in front of me and say 'this table', I am addressing myself to something that is by definition simultaneously accessible to different observers at different points of view, as opposed for example, to my saying something about my feeling of anxiety or my fatigue. In other words, I accept implicitly that it is meaningful to speak of points of view which are co-existent with, but different from, any one that I myself might occupy at any given time.

But the question is, why should a language necessarily contain references to external, publicly accessible, things in order to be *shareable?* 'This anxiety' unlike 'this table' does not refer to any 'externally accessible' particular, but it is none the less intersubjectively intelligible. Why does the 'publicity' of a language have to depend upon the availability in that language of words descriptive of things other than experiences?

Consider, for example, general terms, in particular those descriptive of feelings or emotions, such as 'anxiety', 'depression', 'excitement', 'pleasure', etc. (I am here deliberately selecting words that are not habitually associated with any particular part of the body, but express a general state of mind.) Evidently it must be possible for such terms, if they are to count as part of language, to be used and understood at an unlimited number of different points of view, including those that we ourselves shall never occupy. Consider the word 'anxiety'. This word is not a name of any individual experience or group of experiences; rather it describes a *type* of experience that we may but need not have. It applies to any experience of anxiety whatever, and I cannot coherently claim both that I have understood its meaning and that the experience, or experiences, of anxiety that I myself have had in the past or am likely to have in the future are the only possible experiences of this kind, i.e. that an experience of anxiety could not possibly occur without my having it. On the contrary, I must be prepared to concede the possibility of an experience of anxiety occurring at the time when I do not in fact have it.

Clearly the meaning of a general term cannot be explained in terms of what actually happens in my own biography, and 'anxiety' is here no exception. But is this sufficient to undermine the solipsistic stance? Perhaps all that is needed is to take into consideration what might happen in my own biography – without assuming any experiences that are not, in principle at least, attributable to myself. Surely, it might be said, the generality of a general term such as 'anxiety' is perfectly adequately explained by saying that this term applies to any experience of anxiety that I myself *might conceivably* have. There is no need to postulate the possibility of experiences attributable to other 'selves'.

This is not quite true, however. The central problem here is one of making clear just what it means to say that possible experiences are all 'attributable' to a single self. If a self's identity is determined by what actually happens in its biography, to claim that there can be only such experiences as are attributable to myself is to obscure the very notion of 'possible experience'. For in such a case only the experiences that actually occur within my own biography qualify as possible experiences (there being no other biographies). If *e* is an experience, either I have had it in the past, or am having it, or will have it in the future. But this only shows that 'possible' in this context loses its real meaning. It comes to mean what will happen rather than what might, or could, happen. Which means that on this view we cannot properly speak of 'possible experiences' at all. If all experiences are mine, there can be no meaningful distinction between possible experiences, on the one hand, and those which I am having or will have, on the other.

In short, if all experiences are mine, if no experience can occur without being part of my biography, then (on the assumption that I cannot change my experiences without changing my identity) I cannot speak of there being experiences which I could but will in fact never have. An experience that is not part of my own biography is not 'possible'. If I have an experience, I have it necessarily. Moreover, the only possible order of experiences is the one in which experiences do actually occur, for any different arrangement would mean a different 'biography' and there are no different biographies.

The idea of possible experiences and the possibility of different biographies

Let me now restate the whole argument in a more rigorous form.

If there can be no experiences other than my own, i.e. except those that are actualised in my own biography, then, given that my biography defines my identity, there can be no coherent idea of an experience that I might but will never have. For let *e* be such an experience. Then if *e* can be actualised, it can be actualised only in my own biography. But *e* is never actualised in my own biography; moreover *e* literally cannot be actualised in my own biography, for my own biography by definition consists only of those experiences that I have actually had, or will have, and if it were different from what it is, I would not be the individual that I am. It follows that *e* cannot be actualised at all. But a possibility that cannot be actualised is not a genuine possibility. Hence *e* does not qualify as a possible experience.

It follows *per contra* that if I wish to be able to talk coherently of possible experiences which I myself will never have, I must postulate the possibility of biographies *different from my own* of which such experiences conceivably might form a part. In short, the idea of 'possible experiences', if it is to make sense, requires the possibility of different and mutually independent biographies; and hence of different experiencers occupying different points of view. If *e* is possible, then it is only as *someone else's* experience, not mine.

It is this argument that I said earlier might be used in defence of the kind of monadological pluralism that Leibniz was propounding.

The generality of language and the pluralist thesis

The inevitable question is, is this argument valid? There is one immediate objection that might be raised against it, and it is this. The defended thesis was that if it makes sense to describe *e* as possible, then it is only on condition that *e* can occur in some biography other than my own. But suppose that *e* never occurs in *any* biography. Then surely *e* cannot be coherently described as 'possible' at all, for the underlying assumption is that no self can have a different biography from the one that it actually has. And if so, the distinction between actual and possible in relation to experiences ceases to have any real meaning, and the entire argument becomes a pointless exercise in any case.

However, this objection misses the mark, for what is demanded is not that all possible experiences be actualised somewhere, only that they should in principle be actualisable in different biographies. In other words, it is not claimed that there must as a matter of fact be different biographies, only that different biographies (different from my own) must be possible. The key thesis was that I cannot coherently assume both that *e* is never part of my own biography, and is nevertheless possible *within it*.

In short, it does not follow from the above argument that an experience must actually occur somewhere if we wish to speak of it coherently as 'possible', only that it must be possible for it to occur as part of a biography other than my own. The argument merely seeks to establish a connection between the idea of possible experiences and the possibility of different biographies.

Nevertheless the argument does not work, and it is not difficult to see why. Its main assumption, as we saw, is that any modification of my own biography, however slight, would necessarily entail a change of my identity, i.e. that my identity, ontologically speaking, is indistinguishable from my biography. This assumption is of crucial importance, for if it is in principle possible for me to have experiences different from the ones that I actually have *without* necessarily becoming 'someone else', then clearly I do not need to postulate the possibility of different 'selves' in order to make sense of the concept of possible experience.

Translated into the traditional language of attributes, the gist of the argument might be expressed thus. I am individuated by the attributes I have. If any of my attributes were different, I would not be the individual that I am. Nevertheless I can very well conceive of the possibility of other attributes – some similar, some not similar, to my own – occurring as part of alternative biographies; moreover I cannot avoid postulating the possibility of such attributes. (This follows from the consideration of the generality of language.) But if so, there is no difficulty in explaining the possibility of ontologically different selves.

But the point of course is that it has to be shown first that none of my experiences (or any 'attributes' for that matter) could be different from what they are without my literally becoming a different self. This is certainly contrary to what is normally believed to be true. It also seems to conflict with the conception of the self as being essentially 'open' towards the future. In the preceding chapter I discussed the self in terms of the unity of biographical time. The lived biographical time, I argued, is an essentially open-ended series whose unity derives from its 'temporal sense'. It is an essentially uncompleted series of biographical events which can as little exist *per se* as the series of real numbers can, and must be clearly distinguished from 'ontological objects'. But if the self is to be understood as an essentially open-ended series, a series which is permanently in the process of construction and cannot be 'completed' without in effect ceasing to be what it is – a series, in short, whose future course cannot in principle be fully 'mapped out' in advance – then on what grounds can we claim that every single experience that happens to occur in the history of a given self occurs in it *necessarily* and is vital to that self's identity, i.e. that no self is capable of having experiences different from those that it actually has without ceasing to be the same self?

In fact, the difficulties confronting the above argument go deeper still; for even if it were possible to show that all the experiences that I have are necessary to my identity, this would still not be quite sufficient to vindicate the inference from the generality of language to the possibility of a plurality of selves. What the argument proves, in effect, is merely that there can be biographies different from my own, not that such biographies are biographies of *logically independent* selves. For it may be that no self can exist except as and when posited *by me*. The ability to conceive of possible experiences that I myself will never have, and hence of different biographies, though essential, clearly is not sufficient. It is necessary, in addition, to assume that on any given occasion I could in principle be mistaken in what I claim or suppose about the biography of another self. In short, the idea of logically independent selves is inseparable from the idea of error, and it is this idea and its implications that we shall now have to examine in some detail.

9. Objective Order and Error

The concept of error is inseparable from the idea of an 'external' world of public objects. It is also inseparable from the idea of other selves, existing independently of myself. For to understand what 'error' means is to understand that we can be in error on a given occasion even though we do not believe that we are, and by implication that we can in principle be corrected by others. It is to accept the possibility of certain criteria for identifying and rectifying error, and such criteria, as we shall see, can be defined only with reference to a social context.

Generally speaking, error can be committed in two ways: (a) by entertaining an incorrect belief, and (b) by infringing a given rule, law or standard of consistency, either inadvertently and accidentally or as a result of incorrect belief. Thus it is an error to believe that Mount Everest is in Australia, or that Caesar drowned in the Rubicon, or that there are five prime numbers between one and ten. But error can also be committed by unintentionally mispronouncing or misapplying a word, absentmindedly stepping on someone else's toes, or driving at fifty miles an hour in a built-up area while believing that one is driving within the permitted speed limit. In these and similar cases certain rules are being broken, but not deliberately. If such rules are broken deliberately, then 'error' becomes variously a deceit, a joke, an act or mockery, an insult. As everyone knows, it is not always easy to determine whether an error is a genuine error or something different.

Imagine now a world in which no error is ever committed. It is conceivable, however unlikely, that a world might exist whose inhabitants are convinced that they never make any mistakes and that moreover they happen to be right. They never entertain any incorrect beliefs, nor do they make mistakes due to accidental distractions, oversights, slips of the tongue and such like. Intersubjective transmission of information presents no problems. There is never any cause to question the accuracy of any factual statements, and hence no reason for distinguishing between what merely seems to someone to be the case and what is actually the case. Such disagreements as do arise have nothing to do with facts, but are due entirely to other causes, such as the desire for domination, different views on good and evil, political preferences, etc.

The question that now presents itself is this: if there is nothing logically amiss with such an idea, if such a world is indeed logically possible, what gives us the certainty that our own world is not, and *cannot* be, such a world? There is no doubt that we do have the concept of error. But perhaps this concept is simply a convenient invention on our part; perhaps we use 'error' merely as a handy label for things of which we happen to disapprove. Perhaps we use it merely in order to conceal, or confer a certain respectability to what happens to be, our subjective bias? What makes it certain, if anything, that errors – genuine errors – are not just 'possible' but that they actually occur?

Proof of the reality of error

Strangely enough, it seems that the right to be certain about the existence of error flows from the very belief that we are sometimes mistaken. Most of us are ready to admit that occasionally we hold mistaken beliefs. Now suppose I make a statement to this effect. Suppose I say: 'I believe that sometimes I make mistakes.' Is it possible that I might be mistaken? Suppose I am. Then it follows that my belief is a correct belief, i.e. that as a matter of fact I do sometimes make mistakes. In other words, if my belief is incorrect, it is correct. The assumption that I am mistaken generates a contradiction. Hence my belief is *necessarily* a correct belief: viz. I cannot be wrong in thinking that I am occasionally wrong.[1]

---

[1] This should not be confused with the so-called 'paradox of the preface', which is another interesting corrolary of one's belief in one's own fallibility (and there are yet others, no doubt). The 'paradox of the preface' essentially reduces to this: on the face of it, an author who believes that what he has written in his book is correct but in the light of past experience none the less anticipates the possibility of having made some as yet undetected errors, and in the preface to his work makes a statement to this effect, accepting full responsibility for such errors, acts in a perfectly rational fashion. Yet clearly he cannot consistently believe *both* that his work contains undetected errors and that what he has written is true. So we are confronted with the paradox

Notice that what is here being talked about is the *belief* expressed in my statement, not the statement itself. The statement is true if it reports accurately the relevant belief, false if it does not. What interests us at the present moment, however, are not the conditions of truth of belief-statements but the question of correctness of the beliefs expressed in them.

The conclusion that my belief that I sometimes make mistakes is necessarily a correct belief is, to say the least, highly surprising. We normally assume that beliefs are not self-verifying. We would certainly not expect the belief that we are occasionally wrong to be *its own proof.* Yet this is precisely what the above analysis of my statement seems to show to be the case. I do indeed sometimes make mistakes. Sometimes, but not always. For suppose that I say 'I believe that I am always mistaken'. This may indeed be a true report of my belief, but, as can be easily seen, the belief expressed in it cannot possibly be correct. For if it is a correct belief, it is not true that I am always mistaken. Hence it is necessarily an incorrect belief. Hence I am sometimes right; for example, in believing that I do occasionally entertain false beliefs.

It follows that at least in one instance what appears to me to be the case is actually the case, because it is believed by me to be the case. There are, of course, a great many propositions which I happen to believe to be true and which moreover are necessarily true (all logical truths, for example); but they are not necessarily true in virtue of my own or anyone else's belief. But the above proof seems to show that in some cases at least a proposition can acquire the status of a necessary truth simply by being believed.[2]

---

that one can, apparently, rationally hold contradictory beliefs. (See D.C. Makinson, *The Paradox of the Preface*, in *Analysis*, Vol. 25, No. 6, 1965.) However, in my own proof above, I am not concerned with the possibility of entertaining contradictory beliefs, but with with the *reality* of error.

[2] I might mention in passing an interesting generalisation suggested by the above proof. Let φ be an operator on propositions, such that if p is a proposition, then φp too is a proposition. (In our example above, p represents 'I sometimes make mistakes' and φp 'I believe that sometimes I make mistakes'.) Let us now begin with the following general assumption, viz. 'There is a p, such that φp but p is not true'. Let us call this proposition M. Now clearly there will be many propositions that satisfy the stated condition, but certain propositions, in particular M itself, cannot (logically cannot) satisfy such a condition *irrespective of what φ might be*. This fascinating result can be proved formally, as follows:

The concept of error and the reality of error

The reality of error has thus been derived from a person's belief in his own fallibility. Now unquestionably each one of us finds in our own experience plenty of evidence to encourage such a belief. Just now I need a new sheet of typing paper and look in the box expecting to find some, but there is none there. This morning I was hoping that the clouds would disperse and that there would be a fine day, but the sun never showed up. When a little while ago I wished to turn on the light in the room, I accidentally reached for the wrong switch. The most immediate subjective evidence of error is the disappointed expectation.[3] It is conceivable, of course, however unlikely, that my expectations are never disappointed. I might never commit any errors. But if I should as much as believe that I am sometimes mistaken, then I am indeed sometimes mistaken. Moreover it is logically impossible for me both to believe that I am sometimes mistaken and not to be occasionally wrong.

Similarly it is not inconceivable that all the beliefs that I happen to entertain might be incorrect beliefs. Yet, as we saw, I cannot consistently believe that they are. This is one belief that cannot be incorrect. Although I may be wrong on every single occasion, I am contradicting myself if I believe that I am; in other words, to believe that one is *always* mistaken is to make it logically impossible for oneself to be always wrong.

But the important thing, surely, it might be said, is that we can be in error without believing that we are. The reality of error does not depend upon people actually believing that they are occasionally

------

First, the definitions:

$m(p) =$ def. $\varphi(p)$ & $\sim p$		D 1
$M =$ def. $(Ep)m(p)$		D 2

The theorem to be proved:

$\sim m(M)$; i.e. M does not have the property m.

Suppose to the contrary that $m(M)$; then, it follows:

(i)	$\varphi(M)$ & $\sim M$	by D 1;
(ii)	$\varphi(M)$ & $\sim (Ep)\, m(p)$	by D 2;
(iii)	$\varphi(M)$ & $(p) \sim m(p)$	from (ii);
(iv)	$\varphi(M)$ & $\sim m(M)$	as a particular instance;
(vi)	$\sim m(M)$ Q.E.D.	from (iv).

[3] Disappointed expectation, as was pointed out earlier, provides at the same time the experiential basis for an understanding of the meaning of 'fiction'.

mistaken. The belief that mistakes do as a matter of fact occur may be important, but why should it be necessary? Would I be any less fallible for not entertaining such a belief? If the above proof were all that we could go on, we could no longer claim that errors occur regardless of what anyone thinks, only that they do, provided someone believes so, and this surely cannot be true.

In reply, it is, I think, important to stress the following. First, while there is no doubt that I can be mistaken on a given occasion without believing that I am, it is nevertheless necessary that I should possess the concept of error if an attribution of error to myself by others is to make clear sense. In other words, it is essential that I should at least be able to grasp the possibility of an error occurring. The reality of error thus presupposes the availability of the concept of error. If there was no concept of error, then to all intents and purposes *there would be no error*. This, of course, does not preclude my believing, if I should happen to entertain such a belief, that as a matter of fact I am never mistaken. It is conceivable, however unlikely it may be, that I may be right, although I cannot know for certain that I am.

The second point that must be made concerns the question of criteria. The concept of error is inseparable from the idea of criteria for identifying error, and the idea of such criteria is strictly incompatible with a solipsistic stance. Errors, as we saw, go hand in hand with purposes, and in accepting (as we must) the possibility of certain public criteria of error we are at the same time implicitly accepting the possibility of certain public criteria for verifying purposes. But this, in turn, makes it necessary to assume the possibility of other purpose-conscious selves. What is more, if such criteria are not just possible but actually available, there must be other selves. I shall return to this presently.

Objectivity of logical tests

Let us now look at the above proof from the point of view of its 'objectivity' The conclusion that my belief that I sometimes make mistakes is an 'incorrigible' belief, i.e. that what seems to me to be the case in this particular instance is necessarily the case, was derived from certain considerations of logical incompatibility. My believing that I make mistakes was shown to be logically irreconcilable with my not making them. The certainty of the conclusion rested on the result of a logical test. But why, it may be asked, should a logical test be a sufficient criterion of correctness of any such belief? What confers objective validity upon such a test?

It will suffice for our present purposes to answer this in terms of the minimal conditions of objectivity. If the objectivity claim in respect of a logical test is to make sense, it must be possible, at the very least, for such a test to be performed with the same result at an indefinite number of points of view different from my own. Briefly, to reject the possibility of our being mistaken in our belief that we are sometimes mistaken as logically incoherent, is implicitly to assume that this can be found to be logically incoherent by other epistemic subjects as well as myself.

This assumption is crucial. It may be objected that this is itself a belief that conceivably could be wrong. But this objection is self-defeating. For if the relevant test cannot in principle be performed with the same result at points of view other than my own, then no intelligible sense could be attached to saying that my belief that p – in the above example, my belief that sometimes I make mistakes – coincides with p's being the case, as distinct from p's merely *seeming to me* to be the case.

The point is that in arguing for the reality of error from my belief that I am sometimes mistaken I am not arguing simply 'on my own behalf', or merely expressing a subjective opinion about the matter. I am not saying 'I believe that my belief is a correct belief' but 'My belief is correct'. I am making an objectivity claim on behalf of my proof, and in doing so I am at the same time acknowledging by implication that the proof is open to independent external checks. I am in effect offering it for intersubjective inspection.

For the sake of comparison, consider Kant's view again. Kant, as we saw, treated 'objective validity' as indistiguishable from 'necessary universal validity'; so that, from his standpoint, to say that the above proof is objectively valid is the same as saying that it is necessarily universally valid. But this, to say the least, is misleading. If my analysis is correct, the meaning of 'objective validity' cannot be clarified satisfactorily without a reference to other epistemic subjects, who occupy points of view different from my own. Thus it is not enough to say, with Kant, that the above proof and its corrolaries are 'necessarily universally valid'; unless, that is, it is clearly understood that the proof is valid at points of view which I myself will never occupy. What we must assume, in short, is the possibility of there actually being other epistemic subjects who are capable of reconstructing the proof and coming to the same conclusion as ourselves. What is more, it is necessary to assume the possibility of these other subjects (other 'purpose-conscious' selves) correcting our own mistakes. None of this, however, features in Kant's own analysis of objectivity.

Briefly, the point that I am here trying to make as against Kant is this: that if objective validity is equated with 'necessary universal validity', as he suggests, all that can be said about the above proof is that any rational being, if there are such beings, ought to accept the proof as valid; that no one can reject the proof and claim to have done so on *rational grounds*; whereas the view that I am putting forward is that objective validity demands that it actually must be possible that there should be different epistemic subjects who are capable of reconstructing the proof from their respective points of view and coming to the same conclusion as ourselves about the correctness of the relevant belief. Whereas the concept of necessary universal validity seems neutral with regard to the possibility of a plurality of epistemic subjects, the concept of objective validity is *incomprehensible without such a possibility.*

None of this means, of course, that my belief that sometimes I make mistakes is true simply because other epistemic subjects can reconstruct the relevant proof and come to the same conclusion as myself. What it means is merely that unless it is possible for other subjects of experiences to reconstruct the appropriate proof, it cannot be significantly claimed that what I believe is a necessary truth. In other words, my belief cannot necessarily be true without this possibility, but it does not follow from this that it is necessarily true *in virtue* of such a possibility.

A note on necessary and contingent truth

At this point, I might interject a brief note about the distinction between necessary and contingent truth, in anticipation of the more detailed discussion of the topic of truth later on. What has been said in the preceding paragraph may help to cast some light on the presuppositions underlying this distinction. All truth claims without exception (as will be shown more fully later on)[4] necessarily involve objectivity claims, but not all truth claims presuppose equal

[4] See Chapters 10 and 14.

accessibility to evidence that might verify such claims. If, for example, it is claimed that a given proposition is necessarily true, the assumption inevitably is that the access to evidence must be guaranteed to other epistemic subjects as well as to ourselves, irrespective of place or time. This 'must' is a logical must. I cannot coherently claim that what I believe (viz. that sometimes I make mistakes) is necessarily true without at the same time claiming by implication that this proposition is such that it can be seen to be true by others as well as by myself without any restrictions as to time or place. But the same does not apply to contingent propositions; and, among these, least of all to first-person experience reports. That I now have pain in my left shoulder, though true, cannot be as evident to other subjects of experiences as it can be evident to myself. True though it may be, this proposition is not necessarily true, and moreover it is impossible for it to be necessarily true, if only because its verifying evidence cannot be entirely and unequivocally intersubjectively accessible. Nevertheless such propositions too incorporate objectivity claims, and to the extent to which they incorporate such claims they can be paraphrased at points of view other than my own and subjected to various semantic and formal logical tests.

In accepting that such tests can be performed at points of view other than those that I myself occupy at any given time, I am at the same time accepting that I am not the only one who can check their accuracy, and hence that I can in principle be corrected by others if what I say happens to contravene certain logical standards. I am implicitly acknowledging that there exists an objective possibility of my being in error, even if disagreeing with any corrections that may be made on a particular occasion.

It should be emphasised that what is here being talked about is the corrigibility of the language in which beliefs are expressed or talked about, not, or not primarily, or chiefly, the corrigibility of beliefs. Language, unlike belief, is universally corrigible. Whatever I may say on a given occasion is subject to correction, irrespective of what I myself happen to believe. However – and this, as is clear from our analysis so far, is a point of some considerable importance – I cannot, in the strict sense, be meaningfully said to be in error if I am in principle incapable of grasping that an error has occurred.

The concept of error thus provides a link between the idea of objective order and other selves. At the same time, it helps to highlight the analytical interdependence between these two ideas and the thesis that there exist certain public objects 'out there' external to experiences (or what I have, for the sake of convenience, called the 'realist thesis'; not to be confused, incidentally, with 'radical' or 'metaphysical' realism, which will be criticised later: see Chapter 13.) Let me now comment briefly on these analytical connections.

It is often argued, in an attempt to demonstrate the untenability of a Cartesian 'autarchic' view of mind, that a commmitment to the existence of an 'external' world is built into the very language in which mental states are reported or talked about. It is a fallacy, it is claimed, to think that what goes on inside our heads necessarily determines 'what we mean and what our words refer to'; and hence that linguistic meaning is explicable simply as a 'mode of intending'. The truth is that semantic properties of thought depend just as much upon external circumstances. For example, the experience that I report by saying 'I feel sleepy now' and another similar experience that I had yesterday may be phenomenologically completely indistinguishable; moreover the words I use may be exactly the same on both occasions; yet 'now' spoken now refers to a different time, and the content of what I say will accordingly be different, although I may be completely unaware of it myself.

But, of course, the tacit assumption underlying such an argument is that the reference of 'now' can be identified independently of the phenomenological context of the relevant experience, viz. by looking at clocks and calenders; and since this already involves a 'realist' commitment, the argument essentially presupposes what it tries to establish. In short, the existence of certain external items which are supposed to be instrumental in determining, or co-determining, the objective content of thought. Now while I do not wish to suggest that circularity can be altogether avoided in philosophical arguments, I certainly do not think that such circularity need be unilluminating or vicious. My own proposal, therefore, was that we begin with the experience of our own fallibility. The subjective experience of error provides the most immediate phenomenological reason for drawing a distinction between subjective and objective order, and for assuming the existence of an 'external' world of public objects. At the same time, it is clear that the latter assumption becomes credible only in conjunction with the assumption of the possibility of other witnesses, other selves. For if I am the only possible witness, everything might be an invention, and the concept of error itself ceases to be clearly intelligible. The subjective evidence of error thus provides us with an insight into certain basic conceptual relationships which transcend the limits of purely subjective belief.

Error and objective order

It is precisely this transcendence of the horizon of subjective belief that represents the most dramatic feature of the above proof. The concept of error, once grasped through the experience that we have of our own fallibility, acquires, as it were, a logical life of its own. If I believe that I am sometimes mistaken, then I am indeed sometimes mistaken; and hence subjective and objective order do not, and cannot, always coincide. What is more, although the proof was couched in first-person singular terms, the intention, obviously, was to demonstrate a general proposition, viz. for any *x*, if *x* believes that *x* sometimes makes mistakes, then *x* is sometimes mistaken. Not just myself, but anyone who holds a similar belief, necessarily holds a correct belief.

In short, the proof was conceived (and executed) as a genuine proof. What I said was not simply 'It is evident to me that when I believe that I am sometimes mistaken I cannot possibly be wrong', but rather 'My belief is *necessarily* a correct belief'. Nevertheless the 'objectivity' of the latter claim depends upon this claim being confirmable at points of view that are not part of my own bigraphy. It is important to emphasise that whoever advances the above proof implicitly presupposes the possibility of such a confirmability.

Another point that needs to be stressed concerns the corrigibility of what is said on a particular occasion. Here our earlier distinction between beliefs and statements of belief becomes relevant. Whereas in certain cases it may make good sense to speak of 'incorrigible beliefs', there can be no incorrigible *statements of belief*. My belief that I am sometimes mistaken, if my proof is correct, is an 'incorrigible' belief. But there is always the possibility, however remote, that I have misreported my belief, or that I have made a mistake in my proof. Although I cannot coherently assume that I could always be mistaken, I might very well be mistaken on a particular occasion. What is more, I cannot at any time be one hundred per cent certain that in expressing my beliefs I have not committed an error of any sort. Certainly I cannot pretend to be the only judge as to whether or not an error has taken place.

Thus the general conclusion is that the concept of error is inseparable from the idea of intersubjectively operable criteria of error. The possibility of an objective, as distinct from a merely subjective, order, demands the possibility of other witnesses, other selves. Moreover, in the final analysis, it is only through appealing to independent witnesses that verifying evidence can be supplied to show that an error has in fact occured in a given instance.

Errors and purposes

In fact, I wish to go beyond this and argue that the actual availability of the criteria of error, so far as such criteria are available, implies the *existence*, not just the possibility, of other selves. However, before saying more about this, it is necessary to dwell a little longer on the link between errors and purposes.

A decision as to whether in given circumstances an action (for the sake of convenience I am here using the term 'action' in a sufficiently wide sense to include any linguistic utterances that a person might make on a particular occasion as well as other forms of goal-directed behaviour) does or does not constitute an 'error' will have to depend upon the consideration of the following factors: (a) its declared, or implied, purpose; (b) its appropriateness to its declared, or implied, purpose; and (c) its consistency with the framework of purposes and rules that represent the context within which the action in question takes place. An action, or part of one, may be judged an 'error' because it is unsuited, or conflicts with, its declared or implied purpose, and hence is incapable of achieving it, or is incapable of achieving it adequately or satisfactorily; or because it clashes with some other contextually accepted purposes or rules.

Errors in such cases, as was stressed earlier, need not necessarily result from incorrect beliefs. Suppose a pianist strikes a wrong note while playing a piece of music which he has played faultlessly many times before. He knows the score well and there is no question of his holding an 'incorrect belief' about the misplayed note. His mistake may have been due simply to a momentary lapse of concentration, a sudden pain in his hand, or some other distraction. Or, suppose that while writing these lines I accidentally make a spelling mistake. I know perfectly well how the word in question is spelt, and on re-reading what I have written I can easily make the necessary correction. The mistake in such a case is not due to any incorrect belief on my part as to the correct spelling of the word; for if it were, I would not see the spelling error as an error. Similarly the pianist (assuming he knows his score) can easily identify his own mistake while listening to a recording of his own performance. In fact, it is quite possible that he was fully aware of what happened the moment the mistake occurred. He knew what he *ought* to have played, but for some unknown reason had failed to do so.

There are two points that need to be borne in mind here. First, the pianists's intention was to play a musical composition. He was performing a goal-directed conscious action, not striking notes on the piano key-board at random simply to pass the time. If there was no intention on his part to reproduce a piece of music, or if, say, he was acting under a hypnotic influence, then, given his audience knew of it, his action would have been judged differently. His discordant note was seen as a straighforward error in the light of his indicated intention to reproduce accurately whatever he happened to be playing at the time.

However, often opinions are bound to differ as to the 'true' meaning of an action within the particular social context within which it takes place, and this brings us to our second point. The pianist's intention may have been merely to make a joke, and his attitude, consequently, will be that there was no error. His audience, however, may take a different view. If, say, he was giving a music recital in a concert hall, an error presented as a deliberate joke would most likely be treated as an attempt to cover up for ineptitude and would cause offence and meet with loud noises of disapproval, while within a comedy show the same event would most likely be greeted with gales of grateful laughter. Evidently it will depend a good deal on the circumstances and the kind of rapport that the pianist has struck with his audience whether a note wrongly played will be regarded as an error or simply as a deliberate impish diversion. Similarly a word wrongly spelt which in a serious context appears as an unfortunate mistake will be seen in a different light if it occurs in a piece of writing intended to amuse the reader with orthographic distortions, although the error may well have been unintended in both cases.

Objective criteria and the existence of other selves

We are thus led back to the problem of criteria. While the subjective experience of one's own fallibility, as I have tried to show, gives one a first insight into the distinction between a subjective and an objective order, the full grasp of this distinction involves a recognition of the possibility of our being in error even if we do not believe that we are. The concept of error is inseparable from the idea of objective criteria of error. The assumption that it is in principle impossible for anyone but myself to decide whether an error has occurred on a given occasion is incoherent.

What is more, error may, but need not, arise from incorrect belief. We might make a mistake simply in formulating our beliefs. Or we might profess to hold certain beliefs which are really incoherent and cannot be regarded as genuine beliefs at all. Suppose someone says 'I believe that I am not I', or 'I believe that I do not believe anything'. It is most likely that his statements would be treated as feeble jokes rather than as a serious expression of belief. As they stand – provided the individual words mean what they normally mean – they do not carry any coherent message, and if it should happen that someone makes such a statement with a serious intention, the appropriate reaction would be to say to him not that his belief is 'incorrect', but that he has not succeeded in expressing one. If we wish to interpret his mistake in terms of incorrect belief, the most that we can say is that his *implied* belief that he has expressed a coherent belief is a mistaken belief.

All this, of course, presupposes the possibility of certain public criteria. The concept of error is unintelligible without the idea of such criteria, and the idea of such criteria, in turn, is unintelligible without the possibility of independent tests, and hence without the possibility of other selves, and also things that are not selves.

Possibility does not imply actuality, of course. I am not suggesting here that the idea of public criteria alone is sufficient to prove the existence of other selves. What I am suggesting is that the *actual availability* of such criteria is incomprehensible without the existence of other selves. The existence of such criteria presupposes the existence of a social context. An 'objective' criterion is a typically social construct and presupposes a degree of intersubjective understanding and cooperation.

As an example, consider the question of consistency in the use of language. Suppose someone introduces a new word into the conversation. On being asked to explain it, he gives a verbal account of its meaning. A little later he uses the same word in a different context and what to his hearer appears to be a different connotation. A dispute ensues. The hearer wishes the definition of the word repeated. If this is done to his satisfaction, he may point out that the meaning originally given to the word is not compatible with the use that this word is being put to in a new context. Disagreements may now extend to other words. Sometimes such disagreements can be settled quickly by consulting a dictionary, or some other public work of reference. But language changes, of course. New words have to be added to the dictionary, old words have to be redefined, changes have to be made in orthography and grammar. Furthermore, as we saw earlier on, there is always a shaded area along the periphery of established usage where no clear rules exist. If the dispute strays into this area, the disputants cannot appeal to any neutral arbitrator, any standard work of reference, and must settle their differences among themselves as best they can. However, their exchanges will lead them nowhere if they fail to observe one basic rule: the rule of consistency of use within the ongoing discourse. For if the speaker who introduced the new word kept altering its meaning each time he made use of it, or if he kept changing the syntax of his sentences just as he pleased, introducing new ad hoc rules as the occasion arose, and failing to observe them next time he spoke, his language would cease to function as an instrument of communication; indeed it would no longer qualify as a language at all.

Naturally this does not mean that the linguistic rules, once laid down, should be adhered to always; it only means that a certain consistency should be preserved within the given context of communication. Certain ground rules, at least, must not be violated. Very well, we might say, but how does one decide whether such ground rules are in fact adhered to or infringed in a given case? The answer to this is that there must already exist certain criteria for identifying infringements of consistency, and that such criteria necessarily presuppose a degree of intersubjective consensus. It is not simply that they cannot be such as to be operable by the speaker alone. This condition must be satisfied in any case. If the speaker alone was capable of deciding when a rule is adhered to or deviated from, then, as Wittgenstein correctly observed, there would be no clear concept of a rule. What I wish to maintain here is not only that the access to criteria for verifying error must in principle be open to others as well as myself, but that a criterion cannot truly qualify as objective *unless and until it is shared*.

A search for objectivity thus inevitably involves looking for intersubjective confirmation. This search is conducted within a context within which a measure of intersubjective consensus *already exists*. The extent of this consensus inevitably fluctuates all the time. New problems bring new conflicts and disagreements, and this often means disagreements about methods and criteria. But the point is that no criterion can meaningfully function as a criterion outside the framework of an intersubjective consensus, however tenuous such a consensus might be. To return to our example, without a social framework of comminication the question of consistency, or lack of consistency, would not even arise. In other words, it is not sufficient to say that a meaningful disagreement between the communicating partners presupposes a certain consistency in the use of language. It is necessary to clarify the concept of consistency, and in particular the conditions that make it possible to claim meaningfully that a breach of consistency, and hence an error, has occurred in a given case. It is necessary, in short, to explain the frame of reference within which errors occur and are identified as 'errors', and this demands an analysis of the forms and conditions of *social life*.

10. Objective Order and the Criteria of Objective Validity

The main points that have emerged from our discussion of error and objectivity may be summed up as follows. First, to have the concept of error is to understand the possibility of our being in error even if we do not happen to believe that we are. It means to understand the possibility of our being corrected by others. If it were in principle impossible for anyone but myself to know that I am in error, there would be no error.

Secondly, the concept of error is logically linked with the concept of purpose. There are no errors without purposes. It is meaningless to speak of errors occuring within a purely 'causal' context. Clocks do not make errors. Sometimes we speak of computers making 'errors', but this is because we regard them as teleological systems, their operations mimicking in some respects our own goal-directed actions. For similar reasons we speak of animals 'making mistakes' And sometimes it is felt that the concept of error can be appropriately applied in relation to any living organism. But this is a misunderstanding. For, as I have emphasised, the possibility of error demands the possibility of an awareness of error. We cannot, in the strict rational sense, attribute error to someone who is in principle incapable of realising that an error has occured. It is meaningless to say that nature makes mistakes, unless nature can be regarded as a conscious being.

Thirdly, if there are to be public criteria for identifying error, there must be public criteria for verifying purposes, and this presupposes the possibility of other purpose-conscious selves. Moreover, the actual availability of such criteria entails the existence, not just the possibility of other selves. In addition, of course, the criteria for identifying error (and for verifying purposes) necessarily involve references to intersubjectively identifiable public objects, such as physical things. Nevertheless, it is significant that in order to clarify the ontological status of such objects we have to make use of the notion of intersubjective access, and hence, in turn, refer to the idea of different selves.

An analysis of error thus helps to bring to light the full complexity of the subjective/objective distinction. Most important of all, it helps to highlight the connection between objective order and the intersubjective conditions of objective validity. It is clearly insufficient to say simply that objective order is an order with a basis in 'objects'; that it defines the mode in which objects exist and are known as objects: a non-arbitrary order, in short, by contrast to the mere haphazard and subjective 'order of representations'. This, as we recall, was the view held by Kant, who went on to draw the corresponding distinction between what he described as the objectively – meaning at the same time 'universally' – valid 'judgments of experience' (supposedly portraying the objective order) and the merely 'subjectively' valid 'judgments of perception'. But this distinction, combined with Kant's rather narrow view of objects, merely succeeded in obfuscating the whole issue of objective validity. For it can hardly be denied that what Kant called 'judgments of perception', unless expressly prefaced by a qualifying phrase such as 'It seems to me ...' or otherwise contextually presented as expressions of personal opinion, just as much incorporate 'objectivity claims' as any so-called 'judgments of experience'.[1] And it

---

[1] The very examples that Kant uses to illustrate the distinction between 'judgments of perception' and 'judgments of experience' expose the inadequacy of his treatment of objective validity. Thus, according to him, judgments such as 'The room is warm', 'Sugar is sweet', 'When the sun shines on the stone, the stone grows warm', etc. must all be classified as (merely) subjectively validy 'judgments of perception'. Moreover, the first two, he claims, are such that they could *never* become objective. Only the third could be turned into an objective empirical judgment, viz. by 'subsuming' the perceptual connection under the concept of cause and transforming the judgment, accordingly, into 'The sun *warms* the stone'. The latter judgment, Kant claims, is objectively valid because it expresses a state of affairs that obtains among objects, rather than merely reporting a connection between certain perceptions. (See *Prolegomena*, Sections 19 & 20). But as an explanation of objective validity this clearly will not do. There is a perfectly intelligible sense in which all three judgments quoted above can be said to be 'objectively valid'. Formally, at least, none of them are presented merely as an expression of personal opinion, and if they are true within the context within which they are expressed, they are true for everyone in respect of that context. A consequence of Kant's view is that a judgment could be true without being objectively valid, and this seems absurd.

is precisely the *rationale* of such objectivity claims that requires an elucidation.

Accordingly, and in opposition to Kant, I shall argue that all truth-claims, and not just one particular class of such claims, i.e. those explicitly concerned with 'external' objects and relations with such objects, involve objectivity-claims. But although there can be no truth-claims without objectivity-claims, we should be careful not to confuse objective validity with truth, and hence the conditions of objectivity with the conditions of truth. A proposition that satisfies the conditions of objectivity might conceivably be false.

I should emphasise that 'all truth-claims' is meant here to be taken literally. It is intended to include not only truth-claims that are expressed in declarative sentences in direct speech, but also those that refer to 'propositional attitudes' of third persons. Thus to assert that A believes that p, evidently, is to make a truth-claim every bit as much as to assert p. It is to say something about A, viz. that he has a believing-that-p attitude of mind, and this is analogous to any other statements that might be made about A's mental states or attributes.

All such assertions carry objectivity claims, implying that what is being asserted, viz. the relevant state of affairs, can in principle be communicated to, and re-asserted (though not always, or necessarily, in equisignificant sentences) by different speakers, occupying different points of view. Thus if 'A believes that p' is true, and A=B, then 'B believes that p' expresses the same fact. This is a necessary theoretical requirement, but in practice, of course, a substitution of coextensive terms may cause difficulties both outside and within the scope of the 'belief-operator', and it can be carried out successfully only on the basis of certain strictly contextual criteria. The main problems, notoriously, arise within the subsidiary clause governed by the operator. Thus if A believes that m has the property F, and $m=n$, it does not necessarily follow that A believes that n has the property F. If A is a detective, say, he may genuinely believe that m committed the murder of which n, in his (A's) view, is innocent, although A cannot coherently hold both these beliefs while knowing, if he should happen to have such knowledge, or believing, that m and n both designate the same person. I shall return to this presently.

An objectivity-claim as part of an assertion that p implies, in addition, an acceptance of the principle of universal intersubjective corrigibility of p, on the basis of certain specified criteria, in respect of its coherence and appropriateness. But, as was pointed out earlier, the universal intersubjective corrigibility of p in respect of its coherence and appropriateness does not necessarily imply a universal intersubjective accessibility to evidence that makes p true.

Objectivity claims and objective validity

Consider now again statements about mental states and attitudes, involving the use of verbs such as believe, think, desire, hope, expect, intend, look for, etc. Such statements in the ordinary run of things represent a vast bulk of intersubjectively transacted information. Yet it is not always clear how such information should be interpreted, or what kind of inferences can be derived from it. The difficulty, briefly, is in specifying with sufficient precision the logical content of such statements.

The reason for this lies in their 'referential opacity', i.e. the circumstance that coextensive terms cannot be substituted for each other in such statements without the risk of the latter's truth-value being altered as a result of such a substitution. Thus although Oedipus desires to marry the widowed Queen of Thebes, it does not follow that he desires to marry his own mother (psychoanalytic arguments to the contrary). If Oedipus had been fully aware who Jocasta was, he would have acted differently and Sophocles very likely would have had no interesting story to tell. But quite apart from this, Oedipus might have thought that it was desirable to be married to the widowed Queen of Thebes, without any such person ever existing. He might have entertained such a thought even though there was no woman of whom it was true that Oedipus wished to be married to *her*. Or suppose that unbeknown to Oedipus the widowed Queen of Thebes had married someone else, or that she was an impostor. Again the content of Oedipus' thought, viz. that he wished to be married to the widowed Queen of Thebes, would have remained unaffected by this, and it was this content that determined his *action*.

But if 'Oedipus desires to marry the widowed Queen of Thebes' cannot be given an entirely 'referentially transparent' reading, and yet it incorporates an 'objectivity claim', the question is, just how should such a claim be interpreted? The only undeniably non-opaque element of the statement, it would seem, is 'Oedipus'. Yet even 'Oedipus', which lies outside the jurisdiction of the opacity-creating verb ('desires'), is not as instantly or universally transparent as one might wish, for in order to carry out a successful substitution we need certain referential rules which will ensure that the person referred to is the familiar figure from the Greek tragedy, and not some other personage of that name.

Nevertheless there are certain features of the above statement that have a direct bearing on the question of objectivity. Thus although the mere fact the Oedipus desires to marry the widowed Queen of Thebes does not entail actual existence of any such person, evidently Oedipus himself believes that there is someone bearing that description. He assumes that there exists a unique person who is the widowed Queen of Thebes and whom he wishes to marry, and if he is told that Jocasta is that person, he clearly cannot consistently deny that he wishes to marry Jocasta. Jocasta in that case becomes a constituent element of the objective content of his desire, and this confers a degree of transparence to what he says.

A *degree* of transparence, though, not full transparence. For it is plainly not part of his intention to marry Jocasta qua his own mother. Nor is there anything contradictory in Oedipus wishing to marry Jocasta but not his own mother, for being the mother of Oedipus is an accidental property that Jocasta might not have possessed, and it certainly never occurred to him that she did possess it. He therefore has every right to reject any imputation of guilt, even though this brings him little consolation. But although Oedipus is clearly under no obligation to accept every true description of Jocasta as part of the implicit content of his desire, he cannot reasonably reject *all* of them; in particular while addressing himself to the Thebans and trying to communicate with them he cannot reasonably reject all the descriptions under which Jocasta is commonly known in Thebes.

The point is this: that although Oedipus can express his desire to marry the widowed Queen of Thebes while quite genuinely professing ignorance of all her other attributes, he has to accept that there are many other descriptions that are equally applicable to her, and that in the context in which he makes his desire known certain inferences can be legitimately drawn from what he says by those whose knowledge about Jocasta is wider than his own. His desire, once expressed, acquires a social significance and is open to interpretations over which he has no direct control.

Consider another example illustrating a similar point and involving the use of indexical expressions. Suppose Oedipus says: 'I hope that the wedding can take place tomorrow.' The objective content – and hence the nature of permissible paraphrases – of what he says inevitably will depend on the time and context in which he makes his statement. He speaks in the first person singular, but the people of Thebes know very well who the speaker is. He is the man who solved the riddle of the Sphinx, and they are entitled to refer to him under this description, even if Oedipus himself happens to suffer from a temporary amnesia and cannot remember what he did at the crucial time, and why he is being feted. Moreover in the process of intersubjective transmission and exchange of information his 'I' can be contextually replaced with any number of coextensive descriptive phrases, although no such substitutions completely exhaust the meaning of his 'I', or detract from the special epistemological status of the first person singular (see Chapter 7).

The other 'indexical' word in Oedipus' statement is 'tomorrow'. Now 'tomorrow' occurs within the subsidiary clause governed by the verb *hope*, and hence in an 'opaque' position. For example, it cannot be automatically replaced by whatever date tomorrow happens to be, for Oedipus may not associate 'tomorrow' with that date. Yet its meaning within the context of Oedipus' statement clearly is not entirely independent of external circumstances. 'Tomorrow', in the context of its utterance, has an intersubjectively identifiable reference, and Oedipus cannot repeat his statement outside certain clearly defined temporal limits and still claim to have said the same thing. Thus 'tomorrow' will have a different reference tomorrow, irrespective of what he himself may or may not have in mind when he utters the word.

The *objective* content of his message thus may be at variance with its *intended* content, even though he is in this instance merely reporting an attitude of mind, not making a statement about 'external' matters of fact. This raises the question of criteria for identifying the features of statements that are relevant to a consideration of their truth. Obviously it is important to take into account the subjective view of the speaker, his objectives and purposes. At the same time, there is the view, or views, of the speaker's audience; the manifold corporate beliefs and public standards in terms of which an individual's utterances are judged by others. The speaker is using an intersubjective public medium to transmit his messages, and he may or may not succeed to convey what he wishes to convey on a particular occasion, either because of his inadequate command of the language or because of the insufficient knowledge of the circumstances, or for some other reason. In other words, he must accept that the objective content of what he says is not, and can never be wholly under his own control. As to what criteria for evaluating objective content should be applied on what occasion, this (as we shall see presently) may often be a matter of dispute. But the important point of principle is that the speaker cannot alone decide what the objective content of his statement is in a given case.

I have talked so far mainly about the logical or objective content of statements i.e. about the objective aspects of their meaning, and deliberately so, for it is clear that it is impossible to shed light on the problem of objective validity without exploring the question of objective content, even though of course the two topics are not identical and should not be confused with each other. In fact I propose to widen my inquiry further still, along the lines hinted at briefly in the last chapter, and consider the problem of interpretation of actions. This will at once give me an opportunity of emphasising the social genesis and contextual character of criteria for evaluating objective meaning, including linguistic meaning, before resuming the discussion of objective validity. In what follows, I shall use the term 'action' in the general sense of purposive or goal-directed behaviour by agents who can be said to have the concept of purpose.

Subjective and objective meaning of actions

To begin with, it is necessary to distinguish between *doing* x and *believing* oneself to be doing x. It is notoriously possible that someone who believes himself to be doing x is in fact not doing x but something entirely different; or he might be doing x while refusing to believe that he is, in fact, x-ing. As in the case of linguistic utterances, the agent's own intentions are not the only relevant factor in considering the meaning of his actions; and in some cases they might not even be a key factor. Nor is it necessary that the agent should at all times be conscious of the purpose of his action. A very large proportion of our daily activities consists of routine operations in which conscious control plays a minimal part. We gradually develop and come to depend upon certain typical responses to typical situations. This applies not only to the manner in which we carry out our daily tasks, but also in large measure to the way in which we communicate with other people in the process of performing such tasks. Intersubjective signalling of messages depends upon certain patterns of behavioural responses that have solidified into recognisable symbols and have in various degrees become accepted public standards. That they are not always filled, on the part of the agent, with a clear consciousness of their purpose or their social orientation, does not detract from their specific social significance.

Actions acquire their objective meaning in the social context in which they are performed, and the agent's own intentions may or may not coincide with their objective meaning. What is more, the agent's own view of his own action is not necessarily a reliable indication of his true intentions either. It is certainly widely accepted that it is sometimes possible for an informed observer to have a better grasp of what an *agent* is trying to do, as well as what he is actually doing, than that agent himself. The agent concerned may for various reasons be unable to assess the true significance of his own action. He may be the victim of some deep-seated self-delusion. His power of judgment may be impaired, or he may simply lack the requisite concepts or linguistic skill to express himself accurately enough. He may be unaware of certain facts that have a vital bearing upon the meaning of his action. Or he may embark upon a course of action with a none too clear idea of the aims he intends to pursue. For example, he may be drawn into acting in a certain way by the circumstances in which he happens to find himself at the time, without reflecting too much upon the aims, or the consequences, of his own action; and so on.

If none of this were possible, much of the general educational effort would be meaningless. One of the principal aims of education, especially at the elementary level, is to provide its recipient with the necessary moral and intellectual equipment so as to enable him to identify and evaluate more accurately the significance and consequences of his own actions and actions of others in the world in which he lives. He is being taught certain rules, techniques, verbal and non-verbal skills, so that he may organize his own activities into socially identifiable patterns and engage in a fruitful communicative interchange and cooperation with those around him. He is familiarising himself with the existing social conventions and the likely consequences of deviating from those conventions. The almost universal acceptance of the principle of compulsory elementary schooling reflects the measure of our dependence upon social conventions and the institutionalised criteria of meaningfulness.

A particularly striking example of institutionalisation of criteria of socially meaningful actions is provided by mental therapy. The assumption underlying the psychiatric treatment of mental illness is that the patient's own view of himself and the world around him has become distorted to such a degree that he is in need of expert help to enable him to regain his mental balance and reestablish the 'contact with reality' by re-assimilating certain basic ideas and values that in the existing social structure pass for common sense. Accordingly, the therapeutical effort is concentrated towards achieving a change or re-alignment of the patient's own ideas and beliefs, so that he may come to see his own actions and the actions of others in a different light, conforming to certain prevailing standards of normality and reasonableness. (Such a therapy raises thorny moral issues and is notoriously open to political abuse, but I cannot go into these problems now.)

But is all this really sufficient, we may wonder, to warrant the conclusion that in judging the objective meaning of an action the subjective intentions of the agent may be relevant, but are *not* crucially important? Surely, it might be said, this cannot be true. Suppose I offer to help an elderly man to cross a road, and owing to a freak accident he is struck down by a car and dies of his injuries. Then, the circumstances being what they are, the unfortunate result of my action surely cannot be part of its meaning. The old man's death was due to events which were entirely outside my control. My own action can be judged only in the light of my original intention, and my intention was nothing if not honourable.

Nevertheless the onlookers who happened to witness the accident might take a different view. For why did I encourage the old man to cross the road at such a notoriously dangerous spot? Surely I could not have been unaware of the car that at the critical moment was approaching at great speed. Perhaps secretly I wanted the old man to die. The suspicion that this may have been my 'real' intention is likely to gain strength if it should turn out that he was in fact a wealthy relative of mine of whom I expected an inheritance (even though I was not aware of his identity at the time), and after carefully sifting the circumstantial evidence in a court of law a jury may return the verdict 'guilty' despite my strenuous protestations of innocence. The point is that the jury's opinion of my action, in such a case, would depend upon what they thought my intention, in the light of my overt behaviour, is *likely to have been*, rather than on what it actually *was*. My action, in other words, will have been judged in terms of certain teleological models that are contextually accepted as being applicable to normal people like myself, and are associated with certain intersubjectively recognisable patterns of behaviour.

The objective meaning of actions is thus subject to certain contextually accepted public criteria. Such criteria are based on the rules, customs, institutionalised beliefs, etc. that govern social life, and in the light of which an individual's behaviour acquires the status of an intersubjectively identifiable social event. Which behavioural patterns will mean what in which situations will depend largely upon the nature of the existing institutions. Often the same piece of behaviour may mean different things in different social environments. Depending upon which part of the world one finds oneself in, shaking one's head from side to side may mean 'no' or it may mean 'yes'. The point is that it is not possible to shake one's head on a given occasion and claim that one has actually *succeeded* in doing the opposite of what this gesture means in the relevant social context.

We can, of course, claim that our *intended* meaning was different. But intended meanings too are subject to intersubjective tests, and in explaining them we necessarily rely upon certain recognisable social conventions. Nor is it strictly true that an agent's moral responsibility for his own actions can be judged only in the light of his own intentions and not at all in the light of the consequences that his actions may have in the relevant social context. Consequences, it is sometimes argued, are relevant to *legal* not *moral* responsibility. But if I carelessly drop a match on some inflammable material and cause a great deal of damage, and possibly a loss of life as well, I shall most likely be held morally as well as legally responsible for what I did. The point is that as a social agent I am considered to be under a moral obligation to act with foresight and take into account the possible consequences that my actions may have within the community of which I am a member. My actions are interpreted by others in the light of certain public criteria, and although, in a given instance, I may be out of sympathy with such criteria or disapprove of the manner in which they are applied, in so far as I am actively participating in social life and wish to maintain a communicative contact with the other members of the community I must accept that my actions in principle can be validly so interpreted.

Not of course that this means that within a given social context the criteria of interpretation are always readily available or clearly defined. Often, evidently, they are not. Moreover there may be considerable disagreements as to what criteria are appropriate or relevant in what case. Notoriously different groups within one and the same society often rely on different interpretative models in judging various types of social behaviour, which often leads to conflict and strife. In addition, the criteria of interpretation change as the institutional structure of social life develops and changes, and what is thought, at a given time, to be essential or relevant in assessing a type of social action may not be regarded as essential or relevant at another time. All this is unavoidable. What is important is that such objective criteria as may be available are always and necessarily social and contextual. As for the personal attitude of the agent, his own view of his own action may sometimes be considerably at variance with the meaning that contextually attaches to it, but, then, one might argue, the agent's own view of his own action is not necessarily the most reliable guide as to its objective significance in any case.

Objectivity of meaning and objectivity of truth

The distinction, then, has to be drawn between what we merely intend to do in given circumstances, or think we are doing, and what we objectively *succeed* in doing. Similarly, it is necessary to distinguish between what we intend to say, or believe we are saying, on a given occasion, and what we objectively *succeed* in saying. The objective 'result', viz. the objective meaning of an action or utterance, however, can, it seems, be measured only in terms of certain contextually valid public standards.

But now the question arises, can the same principle that applies to meaning be said to apply to truth as well? Can the objective validity of a truth-claim be defined in terms of certain contextually recognised, or at least acceptable, standards of validity? This view immediately gives rise to problems, and in order to see just what these problems are, it is necessary to consider the concept of 'social criteria', or 'social standards', in closer detail.

Social standards embody what might be termed 'corporate attitudes'; by which I mean a wide range of institutionalised or semi-institutionalised beliefs held by social groups of various kinds. I should make it clear at the outset that I propose to use the term 'social group' in a very broad sense to refer to any community or association of human individuals, irrespective of its character or size. I shall not discuss the question how and why such groups come into being, how they are internally constituted and how they operate, change or develop. The factors responsible for the emergence and survival of a group as a group may be economic, political, religious, ethnic, racial, or a combination of any of these. Such factors forge the bonds of common interests that hold the group together and generate in its members a sense of communal identity, and along with it, in varying degrees, the protectionist clan mentality. The feeling of belonging together is strengthened by manifold mutual co-operation in the pursuit of common goals, and such a co-operation inevitably presupposes a degree of social organisation. The larger the group and the more varied the co-operation among its members, the more complex the internal organisational structure of the group will tend to be. Some groups develop into highly organised social-political bodies, with rigid institutions. Others remain loose associations with no rigidly defined institutional framework. Nevertheless any type of social association presupposes an area of shared beliefs, however small, where an individual member of the group can identify with the group as a whole and, in a sense, act as its *spokesman*. The stock of shared beliefs may increase, in which case the bonds that hold the group together will become stronger; or it may diminish, with the group becoming less homogeneous and possibly disintegrating, or giving way to a different type of association. These fluctuations of shared beliefs may be due to various factors, which need not concern us here. What is of intererest in the context of the present discussion is that in some cases such shared beliefs tend to solidify themselves into corporate attitudes and become institutionally enshrined in rituals, common practices and positive law.

Sometimes such attitudes are made explicit in solemn declarations of creed, as in religious or party-political manifestos, beginning with phrases such as 'We believe in (that) ...', 'Our unshakeable conviction is ...', etc. But frequently such 'attitudinal prefixes' are omitted. Sometimes this is done because the 'attitudinal' nature of the statement concerned is sufficiently indicated by the context within which this statement is made. But more often than not, the omission of the prefix indicates that the belief concerned has been added to the stock of what are regarded as 'objective truths', or has been institutionalised to a degree that no longer allows any room for dissent. In internal transactions within the group, as a rule, a corporate belief is rarely presented as a 'belief.' But an outsider may, and of course often does, take a different view. Whereas the members of the group for one reason or another may feel justified in dropping 'attitudinal prefixes' when expressing their corporate beliefs, an outsider is likely to insist that such prefixes should be reinstated. Within the group, understandably enough, there is always a tendency to regard corporately held beliefs as established verities, but, equally understandably, to an uncommitted (let alone hostile) external observer they remain mere beliefs, and he will treat them accordingly.

There are often difficulties, however, in providing an accurate interpretation of corporately held beliefs from an external point of view. Notoriously a group often sees itself differently from the way it appears to outsiders, and the discrepancies between external accounts of its actions and attitudes and the accounts originating from within the group itself may often be considerable, irrespective of possible disagreements concerning 'attitudinal prefixes'. In order to avoid crass misjudgments about such actions and attitudes it is necessary to look at them in the context of the group's own corporate life, its history, its methods of communication, its code of conduct, etc. Even so, a consensus of opinion may prove difficult to achieve, and an 'external' interpretation, however patiently researched and carefully put together, may be rejected by the members of the group as inaccurate or tendentious.

In a sense, the difficulties that are encountered in such cases are much deeper and more insidious than those that one normally has to contend with in trying to interpret actions and attitudes of individuals. While it is possible to argue on good grounds that an external observer can sometimes have a more accurate understanding of an individual's action than that individual himself, a similar claim is much more difficult to sustain in the case of groups, and the larger and more self-sufficient a group is, the more difficult it becomes to justify an attempt to interpret its actions, views and attitudes in terms of an external, i.e. 'non-indigenous', frame of reference. The reason for this lies in the fact that groups tend to evolve their own internal criteria of objective meaning, their own criteria of rationality and objective validity. Corporate beliefs in varying degrees tend to become institutionally entrenched, and to acquire a certain 'immanent rationality' as a result of such entrenchment. The more deeply a belief becomes institutionally entrenched, the more 'rational' and 'natural' it tends to appear; the more often and more readily it is used within the group concerned as a norm and guiding principle in explanations not only of the various activities and attitudes within the group itself, but of social phenomena anywhere, the more firmly it becomes enshrined in the group's *ideology*.

Ideologies and their universalist pretensions

The implications of this can be far-reaching, and I shall give some examples. But, first, let us begin with a definition. Ideologies are systems of ideas and principles that give expression to the values, aspirations and standards of conduct of a social group and help to sustain its corporate identity. They can often vary considerably in the degree of their complexity and the exactitude of their theoretical presentation, and sometimes they are not even made fully explicit in a theoretical form. Nevertheless they supply the basic guidelines in the light of which descriptions of reality, as well as the significance and the rationality of social actions, are evaluated. What is more, such guidelines often tend to be presented as obligatory criteria of 'objective truth'; the more so, the more the ideology concerned has been incorporated into the political structure of a state.

What we are confronted with here in fact is an extreme form of institutionalised belief. The point has been made earlier that within a group sharing a certain belief the 'attitudinal prefixes' tend to be omitted. This is not simply a matter of linguistic economy, but often shows that the belief concerned has acquired the status of something rather more than a mere belief and that the use of 'attitudinal prefixes' in its linguistic formulation is regarded as inappropriate, even undesirable and misleading. What has happened is that the belief in question has become part of the institutional structure of the rules and practices that characterise the group's corporate life, and its institutionalisation alone confers upon it a degree of objectivity. It is also often taken, especially by those who subscribe to it, to represent its *justification*.

The more institutionalised a belief becomes, the stronger the tendency to present it as an 'objective truth'; and, inevitably, the lesser the tolerance of dissension. The belief in the inherent biological and intellectual superiority of the 'Aryan race' was, to begin with, a view shared with varying degrees of clarity and conviction by the members of a minority dedicated to achieving certain immediate political ends. When this minority gained power, this belief became part of the official ideology and was accorded the status of an 'objective truth'. Moreover, once it became institutionalised and backed up by the complex machinery of compulsion of a centralised and powerful state it acquired, within that state, a semblance of rationality. This was not due to any cogent new arguments or independent evidence in its support, but simply and solely to its *institutionalisation*. Dissension became an 'irrational' act; it threatened the stabiiity of the existing, and successfully functioning, institutions and for this reason alone, if no other, it 'had to be suppressed'. Invariably in all such cases, dissension is described not as an offence against the prevailing or officially sanctioned belief qua *belief*, but as contrary to reason itself.

The more widely a belief is shared and the deeper its institutional entrenchment, i.e. the more solidly it is incorporated into the body of rules that govern the life of a society or a social group, the stronger the claims to objective validity and rationality advanced on its behalf. A mediaeval theologian, assured of a wide acceptance of the basic principles of the Christian faith, was able to argue quite convincingly that the Earth was at the centre of the Universe on the grounds that the Earth was the place where God had sent his only son to perform his unique redemptive mission, and that it was inconceivable that such an event should have taken place anywhere except at the centre of all creation. The premiss, or rather the string of premisses, on which this argument rested, represented certain well-entrenched institutionalised beliefs, and given the considerable secular power of the Church as well as its immense spiritual authority, the conclusion not unnaturally seemed to many to make impeccably good sense. It was those who dared to challenge its veracity, and thereby indirectly cast doubt upon the premisses that seemed to be offending against the 'natural light' of reason.

There are two distinct tendencies discernible in such cases: (a) the tendency to treat 'rational' and 'irrational' as evaluative terms, with the concept of rationality being effectively merged with that of (contextually defined) *reasonableness*, and (b) the tendency to conflate the conditions of objective validity with the conditions of truth. These two tendencies are the hall-marks of ideology, and their political implications are obviously far-reaching. Among other things, their effect often has been to inhibit free development of science, or to encourage the use of science for morally doubtful, even sinister, political ends. Galileo's conflict with the Church is probably the best known and most frequently quoted historical example of ideological pressure being exerted upon science, but there are even more sinister recent examples, and in what follows I propose to comment briefly on one particularly characteristic and important case, viz. the notorious Lysenko affair, which culminated in the demands for an 'abolition of genetics'.

The background to this affair was a long-standing scientific controversy in Soviet biology between those who broadly espoused the views on heredity originally put forward by Mendel and Morgan, and relied mainly on the statistical methods in their analysis of hereditary trends – the 'Morgano-Mendelists', as they were called – and the self-professed followers of the Russian nineteenth century agriculturalist and plant-breeder Michurin, led by Lysenko. The 'Morgano-Mendelists' were suspected by Lysenko and others of ideological deviation, and in 1948 Lysenko, having secured official backing for his action, launched a virulent attack on them at a specially convened session of the Lenin Academy of Agricultural Sciences. As a result, many leading biologists, under intense political pressure, were forced to make humiliating public statements retracting their views, and in some cases were summarily dismissed from their posts and exiled into distant provinces.

The central issue, as Lysenko saw it, was simple enough. The 'Michurinist' school headed by him believed that the characteristics that an animal or plant organism acquires in the course of its life can in some degree be passed on to its offspring, and that such characteristics can be reinforced and further developed by exposing successive generations of the relevant animal or plant species to suitable environmental conditions. The organism interacts with its environment in a manner dictated by its needs, and survives through adaptation. The adaptation through 'assimilation of external conditions', Lysenko argued, leads over a number of generations to the formation of relatively enduring hereditary properties. The stability of such properties may be undermined as a result of some drastic change in the environment, and unless the change is of such catastrophic proportions as to prove lethal to the whole species, the surviving specimens will evolve new characteristics to be passed on and progressively reinforced by future generations; until and unless, that is, some other similar environmental change initiates a new evolutionary cycle; and so on. This Lysenko described as the 'materialist', and hence, in his view, the only truly scientific view of evolution. The 'Morgano-Mendelists', on the other hand, were branded by him as 'idealists', and hence, in the official jargon, as 'reactionaries'. Their 'idealism' consisted in their acceptance of the view that genes and chromosomes represented the material basis of heredity and that evolutionary advances occurred as a result of gene mutations which they took to be random events. They argued that such characteristics as an individual organism may acquire during its life cycle do not necessarily affect its genetic make-up and are not necessarily transmitted to its descendants. Transmissible gene mutations occurred either by chance, or could be induced by radiation, or effected by crossing. The central point of disagreement between Lysenko and his 'Michurinists' on the one side, and the 'Morgano-Mendelists', on the other, was that whereas Lysenko and his followers claimed that there existed a direct causal link between environmental conditions and the acquisition of hereditary properties – and consequently that by changing such conditions hereditary properties could be modified in the desired direction – the 'Morgano-Mendelists' reserved their judgment about the environmental roots of heredity and argued that genetic mutations and evolutionary trends in general could more profitably be studied in statistical terms. In other words, they refused to accept Lysenko's – officially sanctioned – deterministic environmental approach, and it was this that precipitated their downfall.

In the context of the present discussion it is immaterial which of the two sides, if indeed either of them, gave the correct answer to the question regarding the transmissibility of acquired properties, or the role of environmental conditions in influencing heredity. What is of interest here is merely that the views of the 'Morgano-Mendelists' were rejected as 'unscientific' on the grounds that they were at variance – or, at any rate, were held by Lysenko and, more ominously, by those who held the reins of political power, to be at variance – with the official ideology. Significantly, Lysenko having delivered his attack publicly proclaimed (ostensibly in an answer to a written question from the floor) that his report had the approval of the Communist Party Central Committee. The result was that no sooner had the conference ended than the Academy of Sciences decided to close down two important scientific laboratories headed by 'Morgano-Mendelists' on the grounds that they were 'unscientific and useless' and issued an official statement declaring that 'Michurinism' was the only genuinely scientific theory because it was 'based on Dialectical Materialism'. All further public debate about the key issues, at least for the time being, was suspended.[2]

The conspicuous feature of the whole affair and one that was fully in keeping with the 'ideological' conception of rationality was the deliberate use of the terms 'scientific' and 'unscientific' in evaluative as well as descriptive terms, implying moral approval and disapproval respectively. 'Michurinism' was commended as 'scientific', whereas the 'Morgano-Mendelism' was dismissed as 'unscientific'. The reason why 'Michurinism' was 'scientific' was that it was consonant with the state doctrine, which was said to represent the 'only correct and scientific view of the world'. Since 'Michurinism' was in harmony with this doctrine, and could even be regarded as a vindication of its basic claims, it was also politically highly useful. By contrast, 'Morgano-Mendelism' was 'unscientific' because it was ideologically deviant; one of its principal 'errors' being its reliance on statistical (or, as Lysenko and his followers insisted on calling them contemptuously 'formal') methods and its refusal to commit itself as to the ontological thesis, espoused by the 'Michurinists', that there existed an unequivocal causal link between external conditions and individual mutations. Since this was seen as in effect encouraging opposition to the basic tenets of the official doctrine, with potentially serious political implications, the term 'unscientific' was at the same time meant to convey the meaning of 'politically and morally reprehensible'.[3] As it happened, it was widely used as a term of abuse, and as a warning.

The conflict was precipitated because the 'Morgano-Mendelists' took the view that science did not need ideological tutelage.

[2] The drastic measures that were subsequently taken in a number of cases to silence the opponents of the officially favoured view were already foreshadowed at the conference itself. One of the speakers, a staunch supporter of Lysenko, joked goulishly: '... unless we strengthen our "external influences" on the minds of our opponents, and create for them the "appropriate environmental conditions", we will not transform them.' See David Joravsky, *The Lysenko Affair*, Cambridge, Mass. 1970, p. 139. An excellent analysis of the Lysenko affair can also be found in Julian Huxley, *Soviet Genetics and World Science*, London 1949.

[3] Another revealing adjective that Lysenko and his followers used in their attacks on the 'Morgano-Mendelists' was 'unpatriotic'. Cf. J. Huxley, op. cit.

Moreover they seemed to imply that science ought not to take sides in ideological disputes at all, whereas the official view was that science not only could not stand aside in such disputes, but that its 'class and party-commitment'[4] in the sense of the official state doctrine was essential to its being a *genuine science*.

Objectivity claims and institutionalised belief

All this raises a number of difficult questions; in particular, what exactly does the objectivity of the propositions of science consist in? What are the criteria of objectivity? To what extent can science preserve, or ought to aim at achieving, ideological or moral neutrality? There is no simple answer to any of these questions. In a sense, it has to be conceded of course that no scientific presentation of facts is entirely free from ideological presuppositions, and it would certainly be foolish to argue that a scientist qua scientist need not concern himself with the wider social implications of his work, or afford to steer clear of moral issues. Strict ideological, or moral, neutrality in science as elsewhere is neither attainable nor wholly desirable. Nevertheless there are important differences in emphasis and attitude. It is one thing for a scientific theory to incorporate, either explicitly or implicitly, a given ideological bias, and quite another for it to claim that the bias in question is universally binding, or that the theory in question owes its status as a genuine scientific theory to its underlying ideological bias.

What the Lysenko case illustrates is a deliberate attempt to impose

[4] The need for an unequivocal 'class and party-commitment' of science in the spirit of Marxism-Leninism was a recurring theme in the media and official pronouncements long before the Lysenko affair came to the boil. In 1932 the official programme for a scientific conference convened to discuss planning of research into genetic selection methods contained the following statement: '... we must address ourselves more resolutely to the question of reconstruction of our science, to the task of re-thinking its methods of work, of introducing the principle of class and party-commitment of science (*klassovost i partiinost nauky*) on the basis of Marxist-Leninist methodology, and of reconsidering the current trends and the inter-relations between our science and the other sciences; all of which has become that much more important as a result of the tendencies in bourgeois science towards fragmentation, mutual isolation and misunderstanding, towards a condition of decay, impotence and nit-picking.' (Quoted in Joravsky, op. cit. p. 68. I have slightly amended the wording of his rather clumsy translation.)

a specific ideological criterion as a universally valid standard. The official ideology was presented as a model of rationality and objectivity, and scientific theories were judged in terms of this model; which meant that to the extent to which they were found to deviate from the model, they were regarded as irrational and arbitrary; and frequently, as in the above instance, proscribed as politically subversive.

Such ideological absurdities, however, help to highlight certain genuine difficulties that are involved in clarifying the concept of objectivity. Let us recall, briefly, the two theses that have been a recurring theme in our discussion so far. First, objectivity claims are not restricted to what Kant called 'objective judgments of experience', but are implicit in all truth claims. Secondly, objectivity claims presuppose the possibility of other selves vetting what is being asserted for coherence and appropriateness on the basis of certain criteria that involve references to things other than experiences. Both these things seem fairly well established. What seems to be in doubt – and the case discussed in the previous section is a reminder of the scale and the importance of the problem – is the precise nature of the relationship between objectivity and universal validity.

Kant, as we saw, treated objectivity as indistinguishable from necessary universal validity; yet clearly they *cannot* be identical concepts. If all objectively valid judgments are necessarily universally valid, it becomes difficult to differentiate between objective validity and truth. All truth-claims, I have argued, involve objectivity claims, but objectivity is not the same as truth. It is conceivable that the objectivity conditions might be satisfied in a given instance without the relevant judgment being true, although no judgment can be true without being objectively valid.

To put it differently, if *p* is true, it is universally true, but 'universally' here does not mean 'unconditionally'. In particular, *p* cannot be true without satisfying the conditions of objective validity. But objective validity, although necessary, is not a sufficient condition of truth. The fact that *p* is objectively valid is not logically incompatible with *p*'s being false. It is here that the distinction between the two concepts lies, although political ideologies, for obvious reasons, try to diminish the importance of this distinction or pretend that it does not exist.

To make an 'objectivity claim' as part of a claim that *p* is to claim in the first instance that *p* satisfies certain conditions of intersubjective acceptability as a valid 'truth candidate'. No proposition that is not in principle inter-subjectively acceptable as a valid truth candidate can be significantly claimed to be true. Conversely, if *p* were true but not in principle intersubjectively acceptable as a valid truth candidate, it would be impossible to make sense of its objective validity, and since truth is interlinked with objective validity (even though they are far from being identical concepts) its truth would be a mystery also.

There is a certain difficulty, however, in coming to terms with the concept of 'intersubjective acceptability'. How do we decide, for example, when or whether the conditions of intersubjective acceptability are actually fulfilled? We have to rely on certain criteria of coherence and appropriateness that are derived from the existing public conventions, customs, rules, practices, etc., and such criteria may vary from context to context. This causes obvious problems. We like to believe that at least some standards of rationality and significance are universal, and here perhaps philosophy itself can serve as an illustration. Does not philosophical analysis itself carry a built-in claim to universal validity? It might even be argued that whatever objective validity the propositions of philosophy do possess flows directly from their universality, and hence that the aspect of intersubjective acceptability has no bearing on their objective validity at all. If the propositions of philosophy are objectively valid, it might be said, they are valid *independently* of whether they are in principle (let alone in actual fact) intersubjectively acceptable.

Yet surely this cannot be so. There is no doubt that philosophy as a metatheory, as a logic of theories, is in something of a special position, for its aim is not just to provide an alternative intellectual frame of reference (which would reduce it to the status of ideology), but to elucidate the logic underlying all frames of reference. Consequently it is not surprising that the clue to the objectivity of philosophical propositions should often be sought in what is assumed to be their inherent 'necessity and universality'. The ultimate aim of philosophy, after all, is to constitute itself as an analytical system, which cuts across all 'possible worlds'. Yet this necessarily remains merely a goal: an ideal which we can never be certain of having attained, and moreover an ideal whose own 'objectivity' depends upon the possibility of its being shared by different selves. The point is that the universalist aspirations of philosophy are based on the assumption that all intelligent beings as a matter of fact are cognitively similar to ourselves. Without this there can be no universal validity, but whether this condition is in fact fulfilled we have no means of knowing.

Part Two

Reality and the Idea of Structure

11. Structural Interdependence of Basic Concepts

The basic concepts in terms of which we can make reality intelligible to ourselves are without exception structural concepts, and can be fully elucidated only by exhibiting their mutual relationships within the logical framework of which they are constituent elements. In Part One I sketched out a general outline of this structure through a discussion of three fundamental and interlocking themes. I began, first, with an examination of the concept of an ontological existent; this, in turn, made it necessary, on the one hand, to address ourselves to the structure of experiences, in order to clarify the sources and the modalities of reference, and, on the other, to explore the concept of objective order and the conditions of objective validity. The order in which I conducted my analysis was not crucial to its outcome. I might have proceeded in the opposite direction, taking the concept of objective order as my starting point, and if I had done this, the same pattern of logical links would have emerged as between the basic topics. None of them can be fully unravelled without recourse to the others. That I addressed myself first to ontological existents was simply for convenience. Preoccupation with things that we assume exist 'out there', independently of their being perceived or thought about by us, is a dominant feature of our daily life and affords a convenient starting point for philosophical reflexion. But despite the pre-eminent position that such things occupy in our daily concerns, there is no philosophical justification for regarding the concept of an ontological existent as the fundamental, rather than merely one among a number of equally fundamental philosophical categories, although philosophers have often succumbed to the contrary, and to the ordinary common sense more attractive and plausible view.

To the three interlocking themes discussed in Part One, there correspond three interconnected groups of basic concepts. The concept of an ontological existent is the focal category within one such group, but there is no hierarchical order of philosophical importance as between different groups, nor do these groups have a very rigid boundaries between them. Long chains of concepts issuing from different topic areas criss-cross and intertwine, and such order of logical priorities as we may find necessary to follow is dictated more by the angle of our approach than by the subject matter.

Obviously the task of sorting out the various regional categorial structures and their complex intra-systematic relationships is a long-term philosophical enterprise. All that can be done here is to sketch out the bare essentials of the framework of concepts that emerges from a discussion of ontological existents as conducted in Part One of this treatise. The concepts that this discussion brought into focus were those of identity, individuality, unity of biographical time, error and plurality. In what follows, I propose, in a summary fashion, to comment upon each of these concepts in turn, with a view to bringing out a little more clearly their structural interconnectedness.

Identity

Nothing can feature as a topic of discourse unless on successive occasions it can be referred to as 'the same A', with 'A' representing a descriptive expression of some sort. This, as was pointed out, is part of what 'topic' means, not a claim about how things are 'in themselves' (or 'unconditionally'). There is nothing that can be intelligibly said about how things are independently of how they can be said to be. The identity condition, however, says nothing about the criteria under which something can be recognised as the same on two separate occasions. Before we can even begin to define such criteria we must assume that it is in principle possible to refer to the topic in question as 'the same'.

Identity thus is not a 'property' that a topic conceivably might 'lack', but a condition of the possibility of anything being a topic at all. It is, to characterise it in the spirit of the general approach outlined in Part One, an *a priori modality*; a structural category that can be elucidated only through a contextual structural analysis of the whole cluster of interrelated concepts of which it is a constituent element.

The point is not only that identity is not a property (in any ordinary sense of that word), but that it cannot very well be classified as a relation either. In formal logic it is usually treated as a relation, and assigned the characteristics of reflexiveness, symmetry and transitivity. But if it is a relation, what exactly are its terms? No sooner is this question raised than we are assailed by all sorts of philosophical difficulties that show themselves to be remarkably resistant to analytical treatment. A good illustration of this in modern philosophy is provided by Frege's discussion of identity. Frege notoriously agonized over whether identity should be regarded as a relation between objects or between names (or signs) of objects, and having at first defended the latter position he subsequently had second thoughts, and it is usually assumed – although he himself never said so unequivocally – that he in effect decided in favour of the former view.[1] Wittgenstein, on the other hand, realising that either view leads to almost insoluble difficulties, rejected the idea of identity as a relation altogether. Since, however, the conception of identity as a property was just as unacceptable, his characteristic 'solution' was to try to axe identity out of logical discourse. The identity sign, he claimed, was not needed in a logically perfect language anyway. Identity propositions of the A = A variety were pseudo-propositions. As for the non-trivial identity propositions of the A = B type, they could in principle be paraphrased into non-relational propositions to the effect that A, and A alone, had the given property (no question of identity being that property, of course).

My own view is that Frege's and Wittgenstein's inability to cope

[1] Cf. his *On Sense and Reference* (in *Translations from the Philosophical Writings of Gottlob Frege*, by P. Geach and Max Black, 1960.) According to some commentators, he never really strayed from the former view in practice, even though in his *Begriffsschrift* he ostensibly took the opposite line, arguing that in identity propositions names appear *in propria persona*, i.e. stand for themselves, and hence that what is involved in such propositions is a relation between two names that have the same 'content' (*Inhalt*). Cf. Roger White, *Wittgenstein on Identity*, Proceedings of the Aristotelian Society, Vol. 78, 1978. Some other commentators, on the other hand, argue that it was on the contrary the *Begriffsschrift* view, i.e. that identity is a relation between names, which remained the dominant theme in his thinking, and that his occasional vacillations merely indicate that he was 'confused about the grounds of objection to the theory'. See Gregory Currie, *Frege: An Introduction to his Philosophy*, The Harvester Press 1982, pp. 108-12. Anxious to discover some continuity in Frege's position, these commentators, in my view, underestimate or deliberately underplay his profound perplexity about the whole problem.

with identity can be traced back to Frege's theory of concepts, and the *de facto* attempt to reduce all questions about concepts to questions about syntactical properties of certain predicables. I shall have to say more about this in a moment. First, it is necessary to make some preliminary clarifications.

There are identity propositions that relate to meanings and those that relate to non-meanings. Both meanings and non-meanings subdivide into a variety of different classes, and the comparable divisions are to be expected among identity propositions. The nature of the topic in a given case determines the nature of the identity proposition, which, at the same time, serves as a substitution rule, whereby the expressions flanking the identity sign may be substituted for each other in appropriate contexts.

If confusion is to be avoided, it is essential, first of all, to draw a clear distinction between the identity of topics talked about, and the equivalence, or interchangeability, of linguistic symbols. There are at least three different aspects under which symbols may be treated as equivalent (and hence interchangeable), two of which relate to non-meanings. First, they may express the same state of affairs; secondly, they may designate the same individual, or the same class of individuals; thirdly, they may carry the same meaning. In the first case, we have the equivalence of certain sentences with regard to what can be truly or falsely asserted by means of those sentences; in the second case, we have either the equivalence between singular expressions with respect to their reference, or the equivalence between general terms (or predicates) with regard to the latter's extension – I shall make no fundamental distinction between the two; finally, in the third case, we have the equivalence between expressions with respect to their meaning. Accordingly, we may distinguish between the equivalence *salva veritate*, the equivalence *salva designatione seu extensione* (to which I shall generally refer as the 'equivalence by equipollence') and, finally, the equivalence *salva significatione*.

One example falling into the first category is the truth-functional equivalence between 'If the speed limit is abolished, the number of accidents will increase' and 'Either the speed limit will not be abolished or the number of accidents will increase', which follows from the definition of truth-functional implication. Another is that between 'All men are mortal' and its equivalent obvert 'No men are immortal'. It is clearly impossible coherently to assert either of these sentences while at the same time rejecting the other; to claim that one of them is true is effectively to commit oneself to accepting the truth of both.

Consider next the equivalence by equipollence. If two singular terms have the same reference, I shall say that they are'equipollent'. Thus '2' and 'the square root of the first prime' are equipollent; so are 'the Morning Star' and 'the Evening Star'; so are also 'the Capital of England' and 'the largest city in Europe'. It is immaterial, for the present, whether the object in question is real or imaginary. Thus the singular expressions 'the finest soldier in Agamemnon's army', 'the man who killed Hector' and 'Patroclus' best friend' may all be regarded as equipollent irrespective of whether Achilles existed or not. The same applies to the expressions 'the omniscient being' and 'the omnipotent being', and 'the substance which Descartes said pervades all physical universe' and 'the substance whose existence was called in question by Michelson's experiment'. It should be noted, however, that although equipollent these expressions are by no means universally interchangeable. They are interchangeable only so long as the differences between their respective meanings do not interfere with the truth-value of the statement concerned. But often, of course, they do, as in statements about belief. London is the capital of England and it is also the largest city in Europe, but there is nothing inconsistent between believing one of these statements while disbelieving, or wishing to dispute, the other.

Similar conditions apply in respect of interchangeability of general terms. Two general terms are equipollent if they have the same extension. Thus 'equilateral triangle' and 'equiangular triangle' are co-extensive in the sense that each of them is true of exactly the same objects as the other. But although equipollent they have very different meaning contents and can be substituted for each other only in referentially transparent contexts where such differences are not vitally important.

Problems of substitution, notoriously, can arise with a wide range of statements, not just those expressive of the so-called 'propositional attitudes' (such as belief-statements). Given the meaning of 'son' and 'parent', in a human context, 'All sons have parents' is analytic, and hence necessarily true. But although the class of sons (in humans) happens to coincide with that of androgenic featherless bipeds, we cannot, on the strength of this, replace 'all sons' with 'all androgenic featherles bipeds' without altering the modal character of the original statement. That 'All androgenic featherless bipeds have parents' may be fact, but it is not a necessary fact. Or, to take another example (which has become something of a favourite among logicians) that 9 is greater than 7 is a necessary, and, as most philosophers seem to agree, Kant's arguments notwithstanding, an analytic, proposition. But although the number of planets happens to be 9, 'the number of planets' and '9' are not interchangeable, for a substitution yields 'The number of planets is greater than 7', which is neither necessary nor analytic.

What this shows is that there can be no unrestricted substitution of equipollent terms. A substitution can be successfully carried out only under certain clearly specified contextual conditions. Furthermore the failure of substitutivity in the so-called 'modal' contexts in particular reveals a discrepancy between terms which do and those which don't characterise their objects in an 'essential' way, and the need for some rule for sorting out one kind from the other. Thus to take the last example given above, the replacement of 'the number of planets' for '9' changes the modal character of the proposition because there is no essential link between the number of planets and the number nine (or any other number, for that matter). If, instead, we had used the phrase 'three threes', or 'the square root of 81', no logical disaster would have ensued, even though the meaning-content of the proposition would not have remained exactly the same.

Finally, consider the equivalence by equisignificance. It is often urged that there are no real synonyms. If this means that no two expressions in any natural language are such that they are always interchangeable without a loss of meaning, this is almost certainly true. But it does not rule out the possibility of contextual interchangeability of expressions *salva significatione*. We do after all have a notion of sameness of meaning (although, as was shown in Chapter 2, this does not qualify meanings as potential existents). Thus we understand the contrast between the *same meaning/not the same meaning*; we understand, that is, what is intended by such phrases, although the precise criteria of synonymy may prove impossible to define. There is an objective and a subjective/performative aspect to meaning, and I am now of course referring to the former, i.e. to meanings qua explicitly posited thought-modalities.

The point is that the intelligibility of phrases such as 'designates the same object as' or 'means the same as' does not depend on the possibility, in a given case, of defining the precise criteria under which such phrases can be justifiably used. The conditions of identification often change in any case, and such rules of substitution as can be formulated are of necessity contextual. This applies both to equivalence by equipollence and equivalence by equisignificance. Symbols that are interchangeable in one context may not be interchangeable in a different context. In England the rules of current usage permit us to make the inferential step from 'A is wearing a mackintosh' to 'A is wearing a raincoat', and vice versa, although this may puzzle an American English speaker. And there is of course the additional difficulty presented by the non-equivalence as between 'A *thinks* he is wearing a mackintosh' and 'A *thinks* he is wearing a raincoat' (and similar such statements) irrespective of the synonymy rules anywhere.

However, I am here concerned not so much with the criteria of interchangeability of linguistic symbols as with the identity assumptions that make the idea of symbol substitution intelligible. These assumptions, as already indicated in Part One, demand a complex structural analysis, and cannot be analysed simply in the context of identity propositions, in accordance with the principles of the 'functional' theory of concepts.

The 'functional' theory, as we saw earlier (Chapter 1), involves an attempt at a wholesale transformation of concepts into 'predicables'. The idea, basically is that concepts should be treated as propositional machines and analysed 'at work', as it were. This necessitates a distinction between concepts, on the one hand, and objects, as the 'raw material', on the other. Concepts are essentially 'unsaturated'. They supply propositional matrices with empty slots, which if filled in with appropriate constants or 'object-terms', i.e. with appropriate proper names or naming phrases, yield true or false propositions. Some propositional matrices have only one, others more than one, slot reserved for constants. Expressed differently, there are one-place, and more-than-one-place, or polyadic predicates.

But how much light does such an approach in fact shed upon the concept of identity? What kind of propositional matrix does identity represent, and what, if anything, can this tell us about the nature of the concept? Is identity to be classified as a polyadic predicate, or is it essentially a monadic predicate? Is it a 'property', or a 'relation'? Or, if neither description quite fits (as Wittgenstein rightly suspected), what kind of concept is it, and how should it be elucidated?

Difficulties begin already with the distinction between A=A and A=B. 'The capital of England is the capital of England' is trivial and always true. 'The capital of England is London' involves the use of different object-terms; it is ampliative and might conceivably be false. Consider A=A first. It is not immediately clear what kind of syntactical structure this does represent. It all depends, it seems, on how we separate the ingredients involved, and there are two ways of doing this. We may draw a dividing line after the first A, and treat the equals sign as a 'mere sign of predication', with the second occurrence of A being part of what is now a monadic predicate. Or we might draw dividing lines on either side of the equals sign, in which case we get what is technically a two-place predicate, a relation. Suppose we do the latter. What can this tell us about the nature of the concept? If identity is a relation, what are its terms? Is it a relation between signs, or things signified? It clearly cannot be the latter. Each and every thing is identical with itself; i.e. each thing is exactly what it is; and what else might it possibly be? But A evidently is not what it is in virtue of being related to itself. Nor is A=A strictly a relation between signs, for if it is, then it is no longer trivial, for the two A's might conceivably refer to different things, which would make the proposition false, and this of course is not what is intended.

The point is that although technically A=A may be treated as a two-place predicate, this does not reveal a great deal about the concept of identity unless it is made clear what goes into the respective object-slots, and this gives rise to some considerable problems. But suppose we take the other available approach and treat the equals sign in A=A as a 'mere sign of predication', and hence analogously to cases in which a property is assigned to an object. Then we shall end up with the monadic predicate 'identical with A' (or 'no other than A', or 'indistinguishable from A'), which is the matrix of a class of individual concepts, viz. 'identical with *a*', 'identical with *b*', 'identical with *c*', etc. These concepts, however, are akin to names. They are certainly a very special type of concepts, for although they look grammatically incomplete, they can hardly be described as logically 'unsaturated', in the sense of being divorced from their objects. So far from being 'divorced' from their objects, they are nothing without them. And this, of course, is very different from what is claimed about concepts by the 'functional' theory.

So how exactly should A=A be interpreted? The formula clearly cannot mean that the two sign-tokens are indistinguishable from each other, for they quite palpably are; if not by their shape, then certainly by their positions relative to the 'equals' sign. Does the formula, then, simply mean that the two sign-tokens belong to the same species of signs? Evidently it intends to say more than this. It proclaims the identity of any topic, individual specimens as well as species. It might seem that the most convenient way to read the formula would be to say that the signs flanking the 'equals' sign are signs of the same x (whatever this x might be). But the difficulty with such a reading is that it does not distinguish between $A=A$ and $A=B$, if the latter is true. We thus have a genuine puzzle on our hands, and it is clear that if we are to get anywhere, we shall have to modify our approach radically. A mere 'syntactical' analysis raises more questions than it is capable of answering. In particular, it does not enable us to say with a sufficient degree of clarity what kind of concept we are in fact dealing with. In the end, all it allows us to establish, it seems, is what $A=A$ does *not* represent. It does not represent a relation in any ordinary sense of the word, and it does not represent what normally passes for property-ascription. So how should it be interpreted? I think it should be emphasised, to begin with, that the predicate 'identical with A' is essentially an adverb, and accordingly should be read 'A-identically', or simply 'A-ly'. But nothing is A-ly that is not A. A-ly is what makes A the thing it is. It is like saying 'Socrates is Socrates-ly'; but being Socrates-ly can hardly be correctly described as one of the 'properties' of Socrates. What 'A is A-ly' conveys, if anything, is not a 'property' of A, but the general mode in which topics appear as objects of thought. Every topic exists in its own peculiar manner, and if it is thinkable once, then it is thinkable, qua that particular topic, any number of times.

Consider now statements of $A=B$ type. The capital of England is the largest city in Europe. The man on the bridge is the captain. These statements are informative and falsifiable. So what kind of 'identity' is being asserted here? If $A=B$ is a relation, what kind of relation does it represent; what are its terms? Are they objects, or object-signs (symbols)? If $A=B$ is a relation between objects, then, if true, it is a relation of a single object with itself, and hence – one might argue – no different from $A=A$. But this cannot be the case with the above examples. If, on the other hand, it is to be understood as a relation between object-signs, it can mean one of two things: either that A and B are equisignificant or that they are (merely) equipollent. In other words, we shall have two different functions (two different polyadic predicates), viz. 'means the same as' and 'refers to (or designates) the same object as'. Only the second seems relevant in the case of the above examples. Thus 'the capital of England' has the same designation, but is non-synonymous with 'the largest city in Europe'. And the same applies to 'the man on the bridge' and 'the captain'. The respective expressions in the two cases refer to the same object *in two different modes.*

Yet we can hardly paraphrase the above statements – as is here implied it should be possible – into statements about object-signs without to some extent changing their meaning. To say that the object-sign (the expression) 'the capital of England' has the same reference as 'the largest city in Europe' is clearly *not* quite the same as to say 'the capital of England is the largest city in Europe'. In the latter statement, we are saying something about the object, not about the object-signs; in other words, we are *using* the object-signs, not 'mentioning' them. That two object-signs have the same reference can be purely a matter of convention, or arbitrary decision. Certainly to say that 'the capital of England' and 'the largest city in Europe' are equipollent is not to say why they are equipollent, objectively speaking; although our second statement above, purporting to be about the actual object, not any object-signs – if true – may provide an answer why.

The point is, as Frege realised, that if identity is interpreted as a relation between signs, we are confronted with the problem of explaining the difference in cognitive value as between A=A and A=B. Statements of A=B type can genuinely add to our knowledge about the world. But they can do this only to the extent to which they reflect an *objective order;* i.e. inasmuch as the relation is not 'arbitrary', but is grounded in objects themselves. The cognitive interest that A=B possesses, in a given case, stems from the fact that what is being talked about are *objects* not *signs* of objects.

So the problem seems to be this. Identity cannot be interpreted as a relation between names or object-signs, because what we are talking about in non-trivial cases are objects not object signs. Yet, as already explained, we cannot really treat identity as a relation between objects either. It is, I believe, in an attempt to break this impasse that Wittgenstein argued that the idea of identity as a relation, a two-place predicate, should be given up altogether. What his view amounted to, as was pointed out earlier, was that A=B can be given a non-relational paraphrase, and thereby all the difficulties associated with the idea of identity as a relation avoided once and for all. A=B becomes 'A is an F and only A satisfies the function F', or 'A is an F and there is at most one F'. Notice that these are in effect reductivist paraphrases, involving a suggestion that we can get by without making use of the notion of identity at all.

Wittgenstein is thus attacking the relational view of identity by adopting what is in effect a reductivist stance, and in this he is of course mistaken. No wonder he had to proscribe A=A, everything is identical with itself, etc. as 'pseudo-propositions'. But the notion of self-identity communicated in these propositions cannot of course be swept from the philosophical horizon by means of a clever paraphrase. Nor does the treatment he suggests work in the case of A=B, for the uniqueness condition on which his paraphrase depends, if closely examined, can be seen to *presuppose* the notions of both identity and difference; it does not help to 'explain' them.

All of which points to one conclusion only, namely that an attempt to analyse identity in terms of predicates – one-place or more-than-one-place – in accordance with the canons of the 'functional' theory of concepts does not, and cannot, fully do justice to its meaning. Identity is an a priori category, not a 'predicable'. The 'functional' theory presupposes a strict separation of concepts from objects, but identity defies such a separation, if only because it has to do with the manner in which objects come to be known as objects. In other words, identity is a modal concept ('modal' a wide sense, not to be confused with the narrow technical sense of 'modal', as the latter term is used in logic), demanding a complex structural analysis. This means that in order fully to elucidate its meaning it is necessary to explore the logical links that bind this concept with certain other basic concepts into a structural whole. Indeed an analysis of identity, sufficiently thoroughly pursued, cannot fail to reveal this conceptual structure. As we saw earlier, the concept that such an analysis brings into the focus first is that of *individuality*.

Individuality

A topic, by definition, is such that on different occasions it can be referred to as 'the same', but not all topics qualify as possible existents, and on occasion what seems to be the topic talked about is found, on closer examination, not to have been the real topic at all.

The minimal criterion for distinguishing apparent from real topics, as we saw, is provided by the principle of Contradiction. An intended topic is not the real topic if it is inherently contradictory, so that no coherent notion of it can be formed. Often this is not immediately obvious and it is only after a long and painstaking analysis that we discover that the topic talked about on a given occasion was not what at first was thought it was, but something different.

But now the question arises, what is it that individuates a given topic, i.e. what makes it distinguishable from any other topic that may be 'talked about'. This question has a direct bearing on the problem of the distinction between topics that do and those that do not qualify as potential ontological existents. The most elementary and at the same time the most general principle of individuation, as we saw earlier, is based on the principle of the Excluded Middle. This principle stipulates that it should be possible at any given time, in each context, or 'universe of discourse', in which a given topic is discussed, to assign to this topic one and only one out of each pair of contradictory predicates. A topic is thus fully determined within its own context. Unless this is assumed, we cannot make unambiguous references to any topic. In particular, we cannot, without making this assumption, think coherently of a topic as an ontological existent, and hence as a bearer of a non-arbitrary set of properties. In short, the most general (or 'logical') 'principle of individuation' referred to above as well as ensuring the identity of a topic qua topic represents a minimal condition under which a topic qualifies as a potential existent in the *modus per se*. But notice that this is only a minimal, not a sufficient, condition.

What we have to consider is the distinction between qualitative and numerical identity, or the distinction between qualitative sameness and existential uniqueness. The statement that a topic is such that on different occasions it can be referred to as 'the same' merely invites the question: 'the same' in what sense? We take it for granted that a meaningful distinction can be drawn between the qualitative sameness of species and the numerical sameness of particulars. Yet what is it that makes this distinction intelligible? What is the justification for drawing it?

It is vital, as we saw, to exercise maximal critical caution in handling these questions, for it is easy to be misled into looking for some short-cut, simple solutions, which all too often turn out to be metaphysical blind alleys. Thus the tendency, frequently, is to take the view that the problem of clarifying the idea of particularity and the distinction between particular and species-identity reduces to the problem of deciding what kind of entities exist in the ontologically fundamental sense. All that is needed, it is thought, is to establish the identity of basic existents.

Accordingly, the main effort is concentrated on defining an ontological 'principle of individuation'. But, as has been shown, the meaningfulness of the idea of particularity does not depend upon the possibility of defining unequivocal criteria of identification of ontologically basic particulars. There are different theories of 'basic particulars' and it is not only that none of them has a better claim to truth than any of the others, but that, moreover, in formulating their respective 'principles of individuation' they all implicitly rely upon the intelligibility of the very ideas which they ostensibly purport to explain. Which is a clear indication that there is something wrong with the way the whole problem is being approached. The point is that rather than trying to settle what objects do exist in an ontologically fundamental sense, we should concentrate on exploring the structural interrelationships between certain fundamental concepts that we have to rely on in describing what we assume – in whatever context – to exist in the modus *per se*.

Any meaningful reference to existents of any kind whatever presupposes an understanding of the distinction between species-identity and particular-identity. The decision as to which objects to adopt as basic is always and inescapably a contextual decision and depends on considerations of practicality and convenience; but whatever ontological choice is made, the above distinction remains in force. This granted, the inevitable question arises, where is the understanding of this distinction rooted?, and this question, in turn, brings another fundamental concept into focus: that of the unity of biographical time.

Unity of biographical time

The structural links here may not seem very obvious. Yet very little reflective effort is needed to discover that they do exist, and moreover that the structural 'lines of intelligibility' necessarily lead from the ideas of qualitative sameness and existential uniqueness to the idea of the unity of biographical time.

We are moving now from the topic of objects qua ontological items into the area of witnessing experience, but the move can hardly be described as 'epistemological' in the traditional sense, although clearly certain ideas that are central to epistemology now gain prominence. The emphasis remains firmly on structure and inter-structural intelligibility. The distinction between qualitative sameness and existential uniqueness, it has been stressed, cannot be explained in terms of the conditions under which objects are individuated, the simple reason being that the very attempt to define such conditions presupposes an elementary understanding of this distinction. There can be no absolutely unequivocal criteria of existential individuation, and consequently no possibility of explaining or 'justifying' this distinction in terms of such criteria. What is more, there can be no 'justification' of any category or categorial distinction except within the general conceptual framework within which they exhibit their interdependence through the 'lines of intelligibility' that branch out of each one of them and hold them together within the same system of concepts. Their 'justification' consists in an elucidation of their analytical *interconnectedness*. This is also the only way of fully expounding their *meaning*. None of this implies, needless to say, that the question of 'applicability' of categories is unimportant, and that, for example, the possibility of individuating references to actual particulars is irrelevant to the meaning of the above distinction. What is being claimed is simply that such references can be made fully intelligible only against the background of a general system of ideas of which this distinction is a necessary constituent feature.

Returning now to the idea of particularity, we saw that an attempt to elucidate the conditions of the intelligibility of this idea inevitably leads one into the field of experiences; or more accurately: modes of experiencing (or 'modes of consciousness'). It is futile to try to provide an elucidation in terms of the 'criteria of re-identification'. Rather one has to explore the wider context in which references to numerically identical existents, and indeed the very ideas of numerical uniqueness and difference, make sense, and this means, in the first instance, studying the structure of experiences and the manner in which experiences link up in biographical chains. In short, the topic to which we have to address ourselves is that of *time*.

Experiences are temporal events which by their very nature occur biographically. They are part of biographical time series; and this, at the same time, accounts for their existential uniqueness; for it is precisely because they occur biographically, i.e. because they are part of a one-directional process in time, that they occur only once. Their non-repeatability is ensured by the experienced unity of the time-series of which they are constituent elements; i.e. by what I have called the 'unity of biographical time'.

The unity of biographical time is an experiential modality, not an ontological object. I should re-emphasise that whenever I speak of biographical time I speak of it under the aspect of *lived* time. It is only qua lived or experienced time that biographical time provides a clue to existential uniqueness. A biography qua experienced unity of biographical time is unrepeatable. It is nonsensical to assume the possibility of an experienced 'duplicate' unity of biographical time. If there existed an exact duplicate of my own biography, there is no way in which I could experience the two biographies as numerically distinct. If they could be experienced as numerically distinct, their experienced times would not wholly overlap, and hence would not be identical in any case.

But surely, it might be said, it is possible that a given biography might be exactly repeated in a parallel universe; or the universe as a whole might be endlessly repeated in a cyclic fashion. It is not inconceivable that our universe might be just one of an infinite number of carbon copy specimens of the same general kind.

The answer to this is that either these universes could in principle be sorted out from each other within a more embracing frame of reference, in which case they would not be identical with what we call 'the universe', for there would be things (other universes, frames of references, etc.) existing *external* to them; or else they would be indiscernible.

From the point of view of my own experienced unity of biographical time, then, I am existentially unique, absolutely unrepeatable. I cannot significantly refer to myself in the plural[2] (although it is not logically contradictory to think that physically I could consist of several different bodies occupying different places at different times). In short, if 'self' is defined in the sense of the experienced unity of biographical time, then there cannot be a plurality of identical selves.

---

[2] The first person plural sometimes used by popes and kings is merely a way of emphasising the role of the speaker as the chief spokesman of an institution whose corporate identity he himself personifies by virtue of the office he holds.

Indeed, it is incoherent to suppose that there might be.

But if there can be no plurality of identical selves, why, we may ask, should there be *different* selves? Why should there be a plurality of selves at all? What makes the very idea of different selves intelligible? One possible reply to this, as we saw earlier, might be that unless we are able to conceive of the possibility of different selves, we cannot think of the self *in specie*, for every species is in principle exemplifiable by more than one specimen. However, the difficulty here is that if selves cannot be distinguished from each other except through possible experiences as posited by me, they might not be independent of myself after all. They might be merely features of my own biography. What justification do I have for assuming that they are not just my own imaginings?

The ability that I have to conceive of experiences different from those that I actually have is a precondition of significantly claiming any experiences as mine, i.e. as part of my own biography. It is also, as we saw earlier, a precondition of understanding the meaning of fiction. It cannot, however, on its own, enable me to clarify the idea of genuinely different *selves*. For this, another concept is needed: that of error.

Error

What we need, in effect, is a distinction between a subjective and an objective order. But the intelligibility of this distinction is inseparable from, and depends upon the intelligibility of the idea of error. The idea of error, however, is further analytically interlinked with the concept of purpose and the idea of an 'external' world of public objects.

If I wish to go to London but find myself driving along the road to Manchester, I am in error because my action is incongruent with its purpose. I err in saying that three and three make seven because my intention is to state an arithmetical fact. I was mistaken predicting rain this morning, because I intended my forecast to be taken seriously; i.e. I was not simply quoting a sentence from a story, mimicking somebody else's speech, or simply teasing my audience. What is more, while it is quite possible to be in error on a given occasion without realising, or believing, that one is, it makes no clear sense to attribute error to anyone who is in principle incapable of realising that an error has in fact occurred, or is incapable of reflecting on and drawing inferences from error.

Error, then, in the sense in which I have been using the word, represents an incongruity between an action and its stated or implied purpose; and purposes of actions clearly cannot be determined independently of the intentions or desires, or the implicit intentions or desires, of the agent, or agents, concerned.

Nevertheless the criteria for deciding whether there exists an incongruity in a given case, or what kind of incongruity it is, cannot be entirely 'subjective'. No subject of knowledge is in a position to claim that it is in principle impossible for anyone but himself to decide whether an error has occurred on a given occasion. At the same time, the 'publicity' of the criteria depends upon such criteria involving references to publicly accessible things: i.e. to ontological items of one kind or another. It follows that we need the concept of ontological existent as well as that of purpose if we are to make clear sense of the concept of error, and that – given their analytical links – all three are involved in the concept of objective order.

An answer to 'What makes objective order possible?', then, is inevitably a complex one. Kant, as we saw, treated this question as part of what he regarded as the larger epistemological question, namely 'What makes knowledge of objects possible?' To clarify the conditions of objective order is to clarify the conditions of objective validity of propositions purporting to describe such order, and in order to clarify the conditions of objective validity of such propositions (or knowledge-claims expressed in them) it is necessary to clarify the conditions that make knowledge of *objects* possible. What is more, Kant, as we saw, deliberately equates objective validity with necessary universal validity. To him, if p is objectively valid, it is necessarily universally valid, and vice versa.

But this evidently cannot apply to the propositions of science, for such objective validity as attaches to these propositions is always and inevitably context-relative. So where should we look for universal validity? In the end, Kant was able to offer only the categories and principles of his own 'transcendental' theory of science as the most likely candidates for universal validity. In point of fact, his central thesis was that their universal (and hence their objective) validity flowed directly from their *epistemological necessity*.

But the difficulty here, of course, is that if it should turn out that such categories and principles are not as necessary as they are assumed to be, their objective validity would go by the board too. As it happened, Kant was unable to produce a satisfactory proof of their 'necessity'.

The point is that what we need in the first instance in order to make sense of objective validity is not necessity but the idea of error. It is because I make mistakes that I become aware of the possibility of an order different from the order of my own experiences; and hence the possibility of different criteria of validity too. At the same time, such criteria of correctness and error as one is able to define, as has been pointed out, demands the possibility of 'external' public objects and, with it, the possibility of different points of view occupied by different selves.

Plurality

In other words, the concept of error is inseparable from the idea of *plurality*. What still remains to be clarified, however, is the relation between the idea of different 'selves' (qua experienced unities of biographioal time) and the idea of a plurality of non-selves, i.e. ontological, publicly accessible items posited in the modus *per se*. For it might be argued that whereas an assumption of the possibility of different 'selves' may indeed be necessary, the need for a plurality of such public items is not so obvious. Why is it not sufficient to postulate just one such item with a plurality of different attributes?

In order to answer this question it is necessary to take a closer look at what is involved in assuming a plurality of 'selves'. (It should be stressed again that 'selves' here are to be understood primarily in the sense of experienced unities of biographical time.) An analysis of this assumption reveals a structural interdependence of the two aspects of the idea of plurality.

Consider again the salient points in our discussion of error. Error, it has been argued, is explicable in terms of a conflict that enables us to understand the possibility of an objective as distinct from a subjective order. The criteria of error are necessarily public; I cannot be the sole judge of whether an error has occurred in a given instance. The use of criteria presupposes the possibility of an inspection by other 'witnesses', other 'selves'. But if there are to be different 'selves', their positions relative to each other can be determined only via the external relations between public objects. The possibility of discriminating between different selves depends upon the possibility of external relations, and the possibility of external relations is linked up with the possibility of a plurality of such public items.

It follows (a) that the plurality of 'selves' is linked with the plurality of public objects and (b) that we cannot consistently both accept the plurality of 'selves' and maintain (as Leibniz did, for example) that there are no genuine 'external' or 'irreducible' relations, i.e. that all relations are explicable exclusively in terms of 'intrinsic properties of substances'.

It will be noticed that here I have reversed the strategy employed in the chapter on pluralism. There I linked the possibility of pluralism with the idea of 'external' relations. The idea of 'external' relations, it was found, demanded an analysis of such concepts as objective order, error and the plurality of 'selves'. I have now tried to show that the idea of a plurality of 'selves', for its part, demands a plurality of certain ontological public items, and hence that the intelligibility of each of these ideas depends upon the intelligibility of both.

Conclusion

In sum, an analytic survey of the basic concepts confirms that such concepts are linked up with each other through the manifold structural 'lines of intelligibility' and that together they form a logical unity. None of them can be separated from the others without a vital aspect of its meaning becoming obscured, even though this may not seem obvious at first glance. At the same time, these concepts are not simply constructions of the mind, the component parts of a categorial model of our own design whose function is to enable us to sort out the tangled web of experience. Rather they are the very sinews that hold reality together and such 'unity of understanding' as we are capable of achieving is made possible precisely by their structural inter-connectedness.

However, it is necessary to make the sense in which I have been using the word 'structure' more precise by comparing it with some other uses of this word, and in particular by commenting on the general differences between structures, objects and functions.

12. Structures, Objects and Functions

'Structure', in the most general sense, means the manner in which a given whole is constituted; the mode in which the component parts of the whole hang together. Most frequently this word is used to refer to the internal organisation of an object or substance which have already been identified in some other way. When we speak of 'the structure of x', in general we assume a degree of familiarity with x, or at least the possibility of (contextually) identifying x in terms other than through its internal constitution. I am familiar – in the everyday, pragmatic sense of 'familiar' – with a great many things in my near and not so near surroundings of whose internal constitution I am wholly ignorant. For example, I know their location, what they look like, their functional characteristics. As for their internal constitution, their 'structure', it often takes a great deal of ingenuity and effort to identify it and bring it to light, and sometimes, despite all efforts, it continues to elude us.

'Structure' is thus most frequently associated with 'internal' as opposed to 'external', and by definition more accessible, features of things or substances. Moreover it is generally accepted that an object *contextually* can be sufficiently individuated without any reference being made to this object's internal features. 'The cigar-shaped object I am holding in my right hand' refers unmistakably to my pen, although nothing has been said about its internal constitution. (I am not now concerned with the conditions of intelligibility of such references, or whether such references can be regarded as sufficiently individuative in a *metaphysical* sense.) Similar things are true of kinds of stuff or substances. We all know how to describe water even if we do not happen to know its chemical make-up. Furthermore, it is normally taken for granted that while two people may agree, within a given context, as to the identity of a given individual object or type of substance, they may nevertheless hold widely diverging views about their internal structure – although where types of stuff are concerned it is usually accepted that an objective identification, in the final

230

analysis, depends upon an identification of their chemical composition.

The point is that questions about structure are normally preceded by certain identifying references in terms of extra-structural characteristics. We begin, for example, by noting certain dispositional properties and then try to discover the underlying structural characteristics with which such properties might be connected. Chemists investigate the molecular structure of a substance whose typical reactions in certain contexts are already familiar to them; or they wish to know the atomic structure of an element which they have already identified by its chemical properties. Etc.

In all such cases, the interest in structure is motivated mainly by causal considerations. The aim is to find out why a given object or a type of substance behaves or reacts as it does; why does it have the peculiar properties it has. The answer to this, it is felt, must lie in its internal constitution. In order to explain its properties, we must find out how it is *built*.

Perceptual structures

But the concept of structure has also a more direct application. Psychologists like to emphasise that sense-perception necessarily involves a degree of 'sensory organisation'. What we perceive, it is argued, are certain structured sensory units, and it is the perception of such sensory units that underlies all acts of identification of enduring discrete things. Moreover perceptual differentiation is a direct result of sensory organisation. This framed drawing on the wall opposite consists of a large number of tiny squiggles and curved discontinuous lines, but I perceive it as a whole clearly distinguishable from its background; moreover I see it as a drawing and not just as a random group of pencil marks on a sheet of white paper. The stream of sounds now reaching my ear has a certain configuration that makes it clearly recognisable as a tune, rather than as a series of discrete and unconnected events. Etc. Whereas in the cases mentioned previously, 'structure' was associated with certain internal and not immediately perceptible features of objects and substances, here this word is linked with the very nature of our perceptual experience.

Perceptual structures can vary considerably in the degree of their stability. Some exhibit a high degree of fixity and cohesion, while others are rather loose and transient. Often a complex unitary structure on closer inspection dissolves into a number of less complex but more cohesive units, for example when a feature in a landscape, seen from a distance as a single compact figure, gradually melts away as we approach it, unfolding into a number of separate and unrelated objects. Conversely, certain sensory configurations that are at first perceived as discrete independent units, if closely examined, show themselves to be parts of more complex structural wholes. What we see or do not see in given circumstances depends in large measure upon our previous experience and our theoretical assumptions. Furthermore our exploratory activity directed at objects of perception often leads to radical structural rearrangements. Certain objects forfeit their previous relative independence and become part of larger wholes, while certain others gain a relative independence; some disappear from view, others emerge into existence.

In all this, the experience of structural unity of certain perceptual configurations remains a key factor. As our view of structural relationships changes, our perception of objects often changes too. Sometimes this may lead to extensive reclassifications of objects and the corresponding changes in identification criteria and procedures. However, such changes and their consequences do not concern us now. What interests us is merely the fact that it is in virtue of certain structural characteristics that an object is perceptually experienced as an object, and hence that the concept of structure enters directly into the concept of a perceived object.[1]

Linguistic structures

Finally, consider the use of 'structure' in a linguistic context. Here the determining factor is not perceptual unity but the principles of syntactical and semantic cohesion, even though in a given case the perceptual unity may be a feature of the experience.

THIS PEN HAS A GOLD NIB. What is written here consists of

---

[1] The term often used to refer to the structural homogeneity of perceived sensory units is *Gestalt* (shape). *Gestalt* is said to be an irreducible, primitive quality. We see a figure as a figure in virtue of its *Gestalt*. It is argued that this is where the roots should be sought of the idea that we have of solid discrete things. Cf. Wolfgang Köhler, *Gestalt Psychology*, 1947, Ch. VI.

certain signs ordered in small groups along a straight line. All signs are of uniform size, unlike those in the surrounding print. In addition, the closeness of the individual groups to each other contributes to the perceptual compactness of the sequence. The sequence stands out on the page and is visually registered as a separate and distinguishable aggregate of signs even before we understand its meaning. However, its perceptual unity can easily be destroyed. If the signs were exactly the same size as the other signs on this page, or if the sentence were to be divided and a portion of it printed in the next line below it, or on the following page, its perceptual unity would be lost, but not its syntactical unity. Its unity as a sentence is ensured primarily (though not exclusively) by its syntactical structure.

Conversely, it is possible to destroy the syntactical unity of the sentence without thereby upsetting the perceptual cohesion of the sequence of signs. If I wrote instead 'NIB A PEN GOLD HAS THIS', this too would be perceivable as a distinct group, but it would no longer be a sentence.

However, linguistic structures notoriously give rise to special problems. 'This pen has a gold nib' looks similar to 'This man has a bicycle' and they both seem syntactically indistinguishable from 'This man has a toothache'. (I revert now to mixed capital and low-case letters, since the considerations of perceptual unity are no longer relevant.) Yet such similarities as do exist between them cannot obscure the important differences. Thus the sense of 'having' in 'This pen has a gold nib' is clearly not quite the same as in 'This man has a bicycle'. To say that a person has a bicycle means that he is in charge of a bicycle or that he owns one. But it would be hardly appropriate to describe the pen as the 'owner' of a gold nib. And the third example illustrates yet another sense of 'having'. For whereas I can give away, or be dispossessed of my bicycle, and the nib could be transferred to another pen, I cannot give away, or be dispossessed of my toothache. My toothache is not 'transferable'. It belongs to me only; it can never become someone else's toothache.

Despite their overtly identical syntax, then, these sentences have different internal grammar and must be analysed in different ways. Nor do they represent the only possible uses of the verb 'to have'. Consider one more example. 'The current shortage of oil has an adverse effect on the economy'. In this sentence the word 'has' has an unmistakable causal meaning. But in addition, there are other factors that might complicate still further its logical substructure. Thus depending upon the context, it might be argued that gramatical appearances to the contrary it is the economy rather than the current shortage of oil that is really being 'talked about'.

One way of highlighting the difference between surface grammar and sub-surface structures is by taking the extreme case where all intelligible sense breaks down and words are held together purely by certain formal rules. For example, 'This reversibility has a triangular nonsense' is constructed in exactly the same fashion as 'This pen has a gold nib'. The corresponding words in the two examples are all of the same grammatical type and occur in the same order, viz. noun-phrase – verb – adjective – noun. But something has gone badly wrong with the sentence, for although it shows certain unifying syntactical features, it cannot be regarded as well-formed in respect of its semantic composition.

A distinction, then, has to be made between the surface structure and the logical substructure of a sentence. The similarities in surface structure often conceal extensive differences in logical substructure. These differences can be rendered manifest by paraphrasing the sentences concerned, with a view to making their logical grammar explicit. Sometimes, depending upon the degree of logical complexity involved, this may result in constructions which deviate considerably from the natural ways of speaking and are in any case much too long and unwieldy. This can as a rule be remedied to some extent, and the underlying semantics of the sentence made easier to identify, by an appropriate use of symbols. But whether symbols are used or not, the general aim remains always to bring into the open the internal logical features of linguistic expressions that often lie buried behind their 'surface grammar'.

Structures as complexes of simpler elements

I have briefly outlined three different uses of the concept of structure: its 'ontological' use in respect of things and substances; its use in the psychology of perception; and its use in logico-linguistic analysis. The sense in which I am myself using this concept is at once different and more comprehensive than any of these, in that it includes certain vital epistemological elements which they all lack. Thus I shall be concerned with the type of structure that includes the conditions that make structural configurations qua epistemic objects possible. Accordingly, the general emphasis in my analysis will be not on structures *of* objects, or on structures *as* objects, but rather on structures of which objects are a feature.

In order to clarify what is at stake here, it will be convenient to begin by briefly recollecting some traditional mechanistic interpretations of structures, which have exercised a powerful influence on the philosophy of language from Leibniz onwards. The central idea in such interpretations is that structures represent complexes of elements simpler than themselves, and can – theoretically speaking – be dismantled and re-assembled, or 'made happen' again, at any number of different places and different times. This idea is deeply engrained in our normal way of thinking. Thus we are naturally inclined to think of the world as being populated with certain discrete substantival items, and of structured, complex, objects as arrangements or configurations of such items. From this natural bias there is a relatively short step to the metaphysical thesis that the basic existents are unstructured simples.

There are clearly powerful common sense considerations that encourage such a view. Consider the following example. If men drive a shaft through a mountain and call it a 'tunnel', they have not created a new entity, although the manner in which they refer to it is not dissimilar to the manner in which they refer to substantival things. Thus when they talk about the tunnel they speak of 'its' location, 'its' dimension, 'its' ventilation, 'its' height from the sea level, etc. Moreover the tunnel clearly cannot be adequately described entirely in terms of the attributes of the mountain as a mountain. For one thing, it is not a natural feature of the mountain; it was made by men for a certain purpose and its function is an essential part of its description. Accordingly, we speak of 'road tunnels', 'railway tunnels', 'water tunnels', etc. Once completed, such a tunnel is frequently ceremoniously opened and named in a similar manner in which ships or bridges are named. Nevertheless no one pretends that what is thus being named is an existent of the same order as the mountain itself. If the tunnel has certain perceptually distinctive features, this is not in virtue of any 'intrinsic' properties, but solely in virtue of the structural characteristics of the setting of which it is a part. Remove the surrounding rock and the tunnel will cease to exist.

Analogously, it seems, with structural configurations of all kinds. Remove the constituent elements of such a configuration, or change their relations to each other by rearranging them in a different order, and the original configuration vanishes without trace. New configurations are brought into existence all the time as a result of such rearrangements. Frequently such rearrangements are effected by deliberate human intervention, a large number occur naturally. But irrespective of how they are brought about (it might be argued) structural configurations, on account of their complexity alone, do not qualify as fundamental ontological existents.

Mechanistic view of structures

The mechanistic bias and the idea that the basic constituents of reality are unstructured, simple objects, thus seem to go naturally together. The gist of the 'simplicity argument', as we saw, was that the ultimate constituents of complexes cannot themselves be complex, for if they were complex, they could not be 'ultimate'.

But the problem that immediately arises, is: how can such ultimate constituent of complexes be identified; what can we know about them? No sooner these questions are asked, than it becomes clear that the mechanistic bias is incompatible with the assumption that such constituents are physical entities. For consider what is being asserted. It is asserted that complexes depend for their existence upon their constituent elements, but that the opposite is not true. In other words, the relationship between a complex and its elements is not one of close organic interdependence but represents a much looser type of association. While the nature of the complex is completely determined by the nature and the arrangement of its elements, the nature of the elements is not necessarily affected by their presence in the complex. Once such a view of complexes is adopted, the conclusion that the basic elements are simple follows naturally. However, it also follows that the basic constituents of the world cannot be physical objects, for physical objects are without exception complex. This is why some philosophers – largely, it should be stressed, under the influence of the mechanistic idea of structure – have defended the view that the fundamental building blocks of reality are in fact spiritual.

But the mechanistic conception of structures, as I already pointed out, has also had a powerful influence on the analysis of language and has encouraged what I shall call the 'clockwork view' of propositions. Propositions are seen accordingly as mechanisms of different degrees of complexity, whose ability to convey meaning is a function of their internal constitution. The idea is that a proposition shows a meaning as a clock shows time. In either case we have to look inside the mechanism in order to explain how the mechanism works, and this involves examining carefully its constituent parts and the order in which they are arranged. Within a mechanical set-up individual parts are not organically linked with each other, and consequently replacements can be made of individual parts by other similar parts without thereby causing any disturbance to the normal functioning of the system as a whole. In a similar way, it is assumed that within a propositional context – at least in non-opaque, or 'referentially transparent', cases – replacements can be made of certain expressions by certain other expressions without thereby necessarily altering either the logical content or the truth-value of the proposition concerned. It is further assumed that complex propositions can in principle be paraphrased and reduced to concatenations of 'basic propositions' which are all *logically independent* of each other and are held together merely as a result of a series of happy logical accidents.[2]

Perfect universal language

In a sense, it is this very same mechanistic bias that lies behind the idea of a perfect universal language. The assumption made by the advocates of this idea is that the logical (or 'objective') content of assertions can be considered in abstraction from the actual conditions of their utterance. It is maintained that the possibility of unequivocal definitions of concepts depends on this. Ambiguities and imprecision affecting ordinary language are often due not only to the laxity with which concepts are frequently used, but also to the particular circumstances and the manner in which words are employed in speaker-hearer situations. In order to regain precision, it is argued, we must focus attention exclusively on the logical content

---

[2] Wittgenstein's *Tractatus Logico-Philosophicus*, in particular represents an uninspired version of the old mechanistic bias in a new idiom. Facts are seen here as 'pictured' in propositions, basic facts in basic propositions. Basic facts are configurations of simple objects which, it is said, 'hang in each other like links in a chain'. 'Every statement about complexes,' Wittgenstein says, 'can be analysed into a statement about their constituent parts, and into those propositions which completely describe the complexes.' *Tractatus*, 2.0201.

of what is said, and if we do so, we shall find that this content can be expressed in an entirely objective and impersonal way and subjected to an appropriately objective impersonal analysis.

As an expression of the desire for precision, the idea of a formalised universal language has the appearance of a thoroughly worthy objective. Nor do some early presentations of this idea, at first sight, seem in any way objectionable. Leibniz for example, explains his idea of a *characteristica universalis* (or 'universal analytic', as he also called it) thus: '*Ars characteristica* is the art of constructing and ordering language signs (characters) in such a way that they accurately represent thoughts, or that their relations reflect the relations existing between thoughts. An expression is an aggregate of signs which represent what is being expressed. The law of expression is this: that an expression must consist of the signs of just those objects the ideas of which make up the corresponding thought.'³ Nothing wrong with this, surely. Leibniz's goal, accordingly, was to devise a logical instrument which would make it possible to dissect analytically all processes of reasoning and to reconstruct all arguments in a rigorous, algorithmic fashion. Already as a very young man, he tells us, he struck upon the idea that a kind of 'alphabet of human thoughts' might be worked out and that 'everything can be discovered and judged by a comparison of the letters of this alphabet and an analysis of the words made from them'.⁴ This idea remained a dominant factor in all his later philosophical preoccupations.

Yet despite its attractions, this idea is philosophically profoundly misleading. It is misleading because it suggests that thoughts could be divorced from acts of thinking and that thus separated from their living context they could be taken apart and re-assembled in the manner reminiscent of a meccano set. Nor is this the only drawback of Leibniz's project. If inspected more closely, the whole project

---

³ 'Ars characteristica est ars ita formandi atque ordinandi characteres, ut referant cogitationes seu ut eam inter se habeant relationem, quam cogitationes inter se habent. Expressio est aggregatum characterum rem quae exprimitur repraesantium. Lex expressionum haec sunt: ut ex quarum rerum ideis componitur rei exprimendae idea, ex illarum rerum characteribus componatur rei expressio.' See E. Bodemann, *Die Leibnizhandschriften der Königlichen öffentlichen Bibliothek zu Hannover*, 1895, p. 80.

⁴ G.W. Leibniz, *Philosophical Papers and Letters*, edited by Leroy E. Loemker, Dordrecht 1969, p. 222.

shows itself to be excessively reductivistic. Evidence for this can be found in some notes that Leibniz made in 1678 on the topic of 'rational grammar', indicating that a radical pruning of what he regarded as the logically dispensable features of ordinary language would have to be carried out. What emerges from these notes, in fact, is a reductivist programme of far-reaching proportions. The distinction between adjective and substantive, he maintains, is not of great moment for a rational language. Everything in discourse can be analysed into the substantive *ens* or *res*, the copula, adjectives and formal particles. Furthermore, we can dispense with the distinctions of gender; also with declensions and conjugations (and hence with tense). Abstract general terms like 'beauty' too are dispensable and should be avoided as far as possible. Etc.[5] What Leibniz wants to say, in short, is that the logical content of assertions can be adequately reproduced *without* such grammatical features, and this, of course, merely indicates that he has a very restricted view of logical content.

Frege's formalised language of pure thought

Another, more recent, example is Frege's 'formalised language of pure thought', i.e. his *Begriffsschrift*. Like Leibniz, Frege is similarly anxious to show that all ambiguities and vaguenesses can be eradicated from language by suitably restructuring ordinary modes of expression and pruning them of all logically inessential features. Only that which pertains to the logical (he calls it 'conceptual') content should be preserved: viz. that which determines what can be validly inferred from a given judgment. Accordingly, in his formalised language of pure thought – to quote his own words – 'only that part of judgments which affects *possible inferences* is taken into consideration. Whatever is needed for a valid inference is fully expressed; what is not needed is for the most part not indicated either; *no scope is left for conjecture*. In this' – he goes on – 'I follow absolutely the example of the formalised language of mathematics'.[6]

The phrase 'that part of judgment which affects possible inferences' sounds comprehensive enough; in fact, it is usually interpreted in a

[5] See *Opuscules et Fragments inedit de Leibniz*, edited by Louis Couturat, rep. Hildesheim 1961, pp. 286-90.
[6] See *Translations from the Philosophical Writings of Gottlob Frege*, edited by P. Geach and Max Black, Oxford 1960, p. 3.

fairly restricted sense. If judgments are considered in the context of a speaker-hearer situation, taking into account the circumstances and the manner of their utterance as well as their grammatical structure, obviously there will be many features that are relevant to possible inferences that (contextually) might be drawn from them. Words are usually accompanied by a variety of gestures and facial expressions, and are modulated, emphasised, or deliberately slurred over, carrying a whole spectrum of meanings. It makes a great deal of difference whether a judgment is spoken in a normal tone of voice, or whether it is uttered through tears, or laughter, or whether it is sung! The point is that the content of what is said cannot be entirely dissociated from the performative aspects of utterance, and this necessarily introduces a degree of imprecision into the communicative process. But in Frege's reformed language 'no scope is left for conjecture'. The clockwork image, evidently, is never far away. The logical content of judgments can be laid out in such a way that its internal mechanism becomes universally accessible and universally intelligible. Anyone can see how the mechanism works, anyone can operate it, anyone can take it to parts and repair it, if need be. There is nothing that could be kept away from an 'outsider'. He knows as much, and often more, about what is being asserted than the judging subject himself. The subjective aspects of judgment-making are dismissed as strictly irrelevant to the logical content.

Now it is, of course, quite clear that the 'logical content' must be accessible to other language users, and moreover that the intersubjective intelligibility of judgments is a precondition of their objectivity. But the 'clockwork theory' of language neglects the contextual epistemological conditions (and limitations) of such intelligibility. The idea of a formalised universal language is born of the misconceived notion of language as an instrument that could be analysed independently of the conditions of its use. This leads to an adoption of a radical policy of paraphrasing and pruning of what are regarded as peripheral and inessential features of language, sometimes with disastrous results. In the name of 'objectivity', attempts are made to axe all egocentric elements out of discourse. Only the impersonal timeless logical content, it is claimed, is strictly relevant to truth, and it is truth, after all, that remains our ultimate goal. Frege notoriously combined his pursuit of 'objectivity' with an attack on psychologism in logic. Psychologism, be argued, involved a fundamental misconception about the nature of logic because it involved a fundamental misconception about truth. It confused the idea of something being true with the idea of something being held to be true. But 'being true' – he warns – 'is different from being taken to be true, whether by one or many or everybody, and in no case is to be reduced to it. There is no contradiction in the idea of something being true which everybody takes to be false. I understand by 'laws of logic' not psychological laws involved in taking-something-to-be-true (*Gesetze des Fürwahrhaltens*), but laws of truth. If it is true that I am writing this in my study on the 13th of July 1893, while the wind howls outside, then this remains true even if all men should subsequently take it to be false. If being true is thus independent of being acknowledged by somebody or other, then the laws of truth are not psychological laws: they are boundary stones set in an eternal foundation, which our thought can overflow, but never displace. It is because of this that they represent the standards that our thought must abide by if it wishes to attain to truth.'[7]

But this illustrates an altogether misconceived notion of objectivity. Frege is rejecting psychologism, but at the price of importing into logic the metaphysical notion of 'truth in itself'.[8] But there is no such thing as 'truth in itself'. Small wonder he wants to eliminate all subjective elements involved in judgment-making from the 'logical content'. He wants a language that is uncontaminated by any 'subjectivistic' features. But the process of paraphrasing involved in an attempt to attain this goal cannot be carried out without a considerable loss of meaning and it is necessary to explain why such a loss does not matter so much. As it happens, it does matter; and, as I shall argue later (see Chapter14), it is a grave misconception to assume that the subjective features of meaning as distinct from the 'logical content' are irrelevant to truth.

But quite apart from this, an identification of the logical content is itself dependent upon certain epistemological assumptions. This equally applies to the distinction, referred to earlier, between surface structure and subsurface grammar, which would hardly be intelligible without certain epistemological considerations. The

[7] See Gottlob Frege, *The Basic Laws of Arithmetic*, tr. and ed. Montgomery Furth, Berkeley & Los Angeles 1964, p. 13. (I have made a few changes in Mr Furth's translation.)

[8] Cf. ibid., p. 23: 'If we want to emerge from the subjective at all, we must conceive of knowledge as an activity that does not create what is known but *grasps what is already there*' (my italics).

clockwork theory of language, on the other hand, involves an attempt
to separate the logical from the 'epistemological' features of meaning,
and creates additional problems by treating the 'logical content', in
effect, as a complex mechanism consisting of certain logically simple
elements. The assumption, as we saw, is that such a mechanism can
in principle be disassembled and restructured by rearranging its
constituent elements; the idea being that there is no organic
relationship between individual elements, or between individual
elements and the structure as a whole.

This approach naturally tends to lead to an adoption of an
ontology of 'simple objects'. (Leibniz, for his part, tried to offset the
mechanistic implications of his mathematically inspired theory of
universal language by postulating the existence of organically
self-developing monads.) The metaphysical counterpart to the
ontology of 'simple objects' is the ontology of complexes as *organic*
structures. However, my aim here is not to try to settle the
metaphysical dispute as to whether the ultimate constituents of
reality are really simple or complex – a dispute which in any case
arises from a misunderstanding of the very concept of reality – but to
clarify the various conceptions of structures with a view to throwing
my own concept of reality as structure into clearer relief. The above
analogy merely draws attention to a narrow and inadequate view of
linguistic structures and shows that a different approach is needed in
order to deal with the problems that such structures present.

Structured or complex objects in the modus per se

Before saying more about this, however, it is necessary to add one or
two more observations about structures qua structured objects
posited in the modus *per se*. We take it for granted that most objects
that we observe in our environment are structured, complex objects –
the question of how and where we draw the line between
'mechanistic' and 'organic' structures may be left to one side for the
present. We make individuating references to such objects in various
ways from various points of view. Moreover we automatically assume
that they can be described in terms other than those of their internal
constitution. Indeed it is necessary that it should be possible so to
describe them if it is to be possible to think of them consistently in
the modus *per se*. i.e. as ontological objects. (It should be
remembered that the term *per se*, in the sense in which I here use it,

does not imply existence in a metaphysical or 'unconditional' sense. I distinguish between the contextual *per se* and the metaphysical 'in itself'. No ontological object can be intelligibly claimed to exist unconditionally 'in itself'.) If, on the other hand, we speak of the world as a structure, we face a different kind of situation. Here there can be no description other than in terms of internal or intra-structural relationships. But then, for this very reason, the world as a whole cannot be regarded as an ontological *object*.

In order to make this a little clearer consider the following example. Take an object fairly close at hand, say this TV set. It is a fairly complicated piece of electronic machinery, consisting of many different parts each of which has a clearly defined function within the context of the whole. They are all put together with the one specific purpose, viz. to produce the desired effect on the screen, and it is because of this that when looking at its works I see it as a homogeneous unit and not as a random assemblage of various unrelated pieces of electronic equipment.

Now it will be said that such a thing as a TV set is perceptually experienced as a distinct object even if its function is not immediately apparent. I need not have seen television ever, nor need I know how a TV set works in order to be able to distinguish it from the other objects in the room. I can identify it just as easily as I can identify this book, or that chair by the window. As I walk into the room I am immediately struck by its distinctive shape against the background of the greyly coloured wall. Moreover I can describe it to other people in a way which they would readily understand and which would enable them to locate it without much difficulty. In all this I am making certain ontological assumptions. I am assuming that the object I see is a solid, can be reached from different directions and identified from different points of view, can be moved to a different place, used as a stand to put flowers on, etc. I am placing it in a functional context and relating it to my own interests and needs.

Moreover, in positing an object qua 'out here' and not just as a transient feature of our own perceptual field we are necessarily placing it, to begin with, within a purely 'functional' context: Questions about internal structure, as was already emphasised earlier, arise only after a description in functional (or perhaps dispositional) terms has already been given, or is assumed possible. If the object in question happens to be a physical particular, the assumption is that, within a given framework of communication, the initial identifying reference to such an object can be made by indicating contextually its location relative to ourselves. The intention in such a case is to convey, within the context of adopted conventions, where the relevant object can be *found*. (It should be emphasised that here we are not concerned with the problem as to whether the latter actually provides an adequate 'criterion of individuation' – this was discussed in Chapter 3 – but merely noting that preliminary identifying references to physical particulars are phrased in terms of place-occupancy within the horizon of our potential activity.)

The conclusion, then, that must be drawn is that no structured object qua ontological existent can be described adequately in terms of its internal structure alone. This does not mean that structured objects, for this reason, do not qualify as 'basic ontological existents', i.e. that only unstructured 'simples' can be assumed to exist in such a way. What it means is only that in order that structures qua structured objects should qualify as possible existents *per se* we must be able to identify them, contextually, in terms other than those of their own internal constitution. They must be assignable certain other properties: properties that relate them to other objects and to our own interests and needs. If I experience this TV set as an object 'out there', then not purely on account of its external shape but because I see it as a TV set or as a stand to put flowers on, or simply as an obstacle that needs to be moved out of the way.

There are many different classes of objects, and spatio-temporal particulars are just one such class. What I have called structured objects include all complex objects, material or otherwise, those occupying a single place in physical space or several. They all are such as necessarily lend themselves to a description in terms other than their internal structural characteristics.

Linguistic structures — a concluding comment

Let us now return to linguistic structures. As we saw, the 'clockwork theory' operates with much too restrictive an idea of logical content and is confronted, as a result, with the problem of explaining the discrepancy between the 'logical content' so conceived and *meaning* (in a wide sense). The key assumption of this theory is that the logical content of ordinary language statements can – and, indeed, where a high degree of precision is required, should – be paraphrased into statements of a logically reformed language. Unfortunately such paraphrases, in varying degrees, involve a loss of meaning, and the problem accordingly becomes one of explaining just why the original statement and its paraphrase do not mean the same, even though they have the same logical content.

This is a problem for which an exponent of the idea of a universal standard language has no solution, and which he usually tends to avoid, or pretends that philosophically it is of no great consequence. Yet it is of paramount philosophical importance. No aspect of meaning can be deliberately left out or neglected without this resulting in a damage to truth. An attempt to regiment ordinary modes of expression by forcing them into pre-ordained canonical forms, with a view to 'disambiguating' them and making them universally transparent, echoes the pious illusion of traditional metaphysics about the possibility of an accurate description of the world from an 'uninvolved', God's eye point of view, and once this illusion is set aside – as Kant urged it should be – the idea of such a wholesale linguistic regimentation must be set aside too. This does not mean, naturally, that all paraphrases are in principle undesirable. On the contrary, they are often both desirable and useful. More than this: it is *necessary* that it should be possible, within a given context, to paraphrase, within limits, the contents of a given statement from different points of view. But this is something very different from a reductivist paraphrase demanded by the 'clockwork theory'. Nor can the demands of objectivity be used to justify a policy of wholesale reductivism for, as is clear from our discussion in the preceding chapters, the principles of objectivity are quite compatible with an 'anti-reductivist' stance.

But the above problem has much wider philosophical implications, in that it raises a question-mark about the whole idea of a purely 'linguistic' treatment of meaning. It is not only that there is no a-historical linguistic standard in terms of which the content of linguistic utterances can be accurately gauged and rendered fully explicit, but – as even analytical philosophers have long begun to realise – there are strict limits to what any linguistic analysis can accomplish without presupposing certain extra-linguistic 'epistemological' conditions of understanding. Language, as has often been said, conveys, and is intelligible only as, a form of life. It is not merely a question of explaining the 'rules of the game', as in the game of chess. Even the game of chess, strictly speaking, cannot be explained to someone who has no conception of a competitive game, or lacks all grasp of emotions associated with executing a good move, with winning or losing.

An analysis of linguistic meaning thus demands a careful dissection of the context in which language is used, and such a dissection reveals a structure of diverse but inter-related elements all of which have a bearing on the meaning of the utterance. Those who dreamed of an ideal universal language believed that language could be turned into an impersonal and atemporal mechanism immediately transparent to anyone – stranger and native alike – who cared to learn its basic rules. But language cannot be considered in isolation from language users, for the simple reason that it is they and they only who infuse it with meaning.

Objects and beyond

What I have just said about linguistic meaning explains at the same time why meanings cannot qualify as 'ontological objects', even though they function as legitimate topics of discourse and are moreover contextually referred to as 'identical' or 'different' in linguistic exchanges as between different language users. There is a subjective as well as an objective aspect to meaning, and in order to clarify the relationship between these two aspects a new structural analysis is needed that goes beyond the horizon of mere objects and functions and explores the phenomenon of meaning in its totality. In a sense, our structural analysis of basic concepts provides a foundation for just such an exploration. It also shows why the world cannot be appropriately described as an object, or even as a totality of objects (whether they are interpreted as things, events or whatever). Rather the world *contains* objects, in addition to certain other features which are not object-like at all.

13. The Incoherence of Metaphysical Realism

One of the consequences of the structural approach that I have been pursuing is that no clear meaning can be attached to claims purporting to be about an 'out there' supposedly existing independently of the conditions or the manner in which it may be thought or talked about. In what follows, I want to bring additional arguments to show why independence in this sense is strictly an incoherent concept.[1]

---

[1] The present chapter is based on a paper I read to the Jowett Society in Oxford in February 1976. I have profited from the perceptive comments made on that paper at the time by Timothy Williamson, as well as from the subsequent comments on the earlier drafts of this chapter by numerous friends and colleagues. I thank them all. I would just like to refer briefly to some observations made recently in a letter to me by Hilary Putnam, which sum up what seems to be the main reaction to the kind of argument that I am advancing. Putnam concedes that what I have to say is both 'correct and worth saying', but thinks nevertheless that the argument, as it stands, is not quite sufficient to demolish the metaphysical realist position; the reason (according to him) being that the metaphysical realist 'denies at the outset' that there is a close connection between the possibility of (coherently) asserting a sentence and the existence of a truth claim. The realist's justification for taking this view, Putnam continues, is 'his entire picture, including the idea of a "correspondence theory of truth". In order to shake his faith in this picture is not not enough to point out that certain sentences, e.g. "Nothing exists except empty space-time", cannot be used to make an assertion. The realist will simply reply that they have truth conditions nonetheless, and that in fact it is the truth conditions that *explain* why this sentence cannot be used to make an assertion.' My reply to this is as follows. I am quite willing to accept that (unless Putnam's example is a straightforward contradiction) truth conditions may exist for such sentences, even though what they express conflicts with our present beliefs. What is more, as I go on to show in the present chapter, the same applies to some sentences which give rise to an 'assertoric inconsistency'. Thus 'I am dead', strictly, cannot be consistently asserted, but it is not void of meaning,

I might begin by drawing a distinction between 'independent of thought', 'external to thought' and 'quasi-external to thought'. If anything whatever is independent of thought, it is necessarily external to thought, in the sense of existing without necessarily being thought of at any given time; i.e. it is external to any specific act of thinking. But if something is external to any specific act of thinking, it does not necessarily follow that it is independent of all thought, i.e. that it can be meaningfully claimed to exist irrespective of whether it is ever thought or talked about in any manner whatsoever.

Ontological existents, in the sense in which I have been using the term, are external to thought, but they are not independent of thought. They exist in the modus '*per se*' and '*per se*' is a structural category, not a metaphysical one, like the Kantian 'in itself'. It signifies an intra-structural state and is dependent upon a whole cluster of mutually inter-related categories. Outside the structure, I shall argue, it has no application.

With regard now to the distinction between 'external to thought' and 'quasi-external to thought', the former of these two terms applies to ontological existents in this sense: that an ontological existent is to be conceived as the subject of a non-arbitrary set of predicates in any context in which such an existent features as a topic. The latter term, by contrast, applies to topics which though posited as transcendent to individual acts of thinking, are nevertheless recognised as constructions of the mind (for example, characters or places in literature or mythology).

I shall, therefore, concentrate in the following on analysing the logic of the assertion:

> *(1) There is something that exists*
> *independently of whether it is thought or talked about;*

which, in accordance with the explanation given above, represents the position of metaphysical realism, and has to be distinguished from 'critical' or 'contextual' realism (or what I have had occasion

and hence not void of truth-value either. It is not void of meaning, because there are coextensive sentences, expressing the same state of affairs, which *can* be consistently asserted. This, however, is *not* the case with the metaphysical realist thesis, whose 'objective content' cannot be consistently asserted in any possible universe. It is precisely this fact that calls into question its meaningfulness.

earlier on to refer to briefly as the 'realist thesis'). 'Independently', of course, has to be taken in an all-embracing sense, and hence as including the independence of the thought of being independent of thought or being talked about. The idea, in short, is that the relevant existent or existents must be capable of existing *without* being thought or talked about in any manner whatsoever. Evidently this cannot be 'verified', if only because any singular proposition that might act as its 'verifier' cannot be asserted without such an assertion providing a counterinstance to what is being asserted. What is more, I shall argue that (1), in the general form in which it is phrased, gives rise to certain inconsistencies and cannot be made clear sense of. But if so, then the metaphysical realist view[2] will have to be rejected as philosophically untenable.

A preliminary note on all-designators

First, I wish to introduce the notion of what I shall call an 'all-designator'. 'All', 'everything', 'something', 'nothing', are notorious trouble-spots in philosophy and have engendered a vast amount of controversy. In a sense 'All S are P' is straightforward enough. Everyone understands what is meant by 'All men are mortal'. Yet there are at least three different ways of reading this statement. If 'All men are mortal' is interpreted as part of an analysis of the concept man, and hence in the sense of strict entailment, it can be reproduced by saying 'necessarily, for any *x*, if *x* is a man, *x* is mortal', and of course there need not be any men. 'All' thus disappears in the paraphrase, being supplanted by the 'universal quantifier' If 'All men are mortal' is understood as an ad hoc hypothesis, then again 'all' is not needed and can be got rid of by aplying a similar procedure. The statement then reads: 'Probably (or possibly), for any *x*, if *x* is a man, *x* is mortal'. This too is compatible with there being no men. A third possibility is to regard 'All men are mortal', as referring to, and being contingently true of, the actual men, namely those that *actually exist*; deliberately leaving aside all considerations of 'possible' men, on the grounds that what does not actually exist literally cannot have the property of mortality; or any

---

[2] One example of what I here call 'metaphysical realism' is provided by traditional materialism. In fact, if the argument to be put forward in this chapter is correct, then the materialist thesis is strictly unintelligible rather than significant but false.

property, for that matter. In short, the statement is now taken to mean that all the existing – in the tenseless sense of 'existing' – men are, as a matter of fact, mortal. Can 'all' in this case too be paraphrased out as in the other two cases?

Or, to phrase the question differently: Does the 'universal quantifier' provide a reliable key to all 'all-statements'? Notoriously one of the reasons that led to the introduction of quantifiers was the desire to eliminate all suggestion that 'all', 'everything', 'something', 'nothing', might contextually assume the role of referential symbols and play the role of genuine subjects in a sentence, not unlike demonstrative pronouns. Accordingly, 'All men are mortal' became 'For any *x*, if *x* is a man, *x* is mortal'. This latter formula, on the face of it at least, works reasonably well in the first two cases quoted above. All that is required, it seems, is to preface it with the appropriate modal operator, viz. 'necessarily' or 'possibly'. But in the last case, i.e. under the assumption that 'All men are mortal' is in fact true (though not 'necessarily' true) of the actual men, a paraphrase, if it is going to work at all, will have to include, at the very least, an *existential proposition*. Thus we shall have to say 'There are men (or rather 'men actually exist'), and nothing is a man and is not-mortal', or something of that sort. Yet, as will be shown presently, it is doubtful whether even such a paraphrase is entirely adequate, i.e. whether it enables us to dispense with the 'all-designator'.

In order to avoid getting into disputes about the 'unrestricted', or 'unqualified', quantification, let us begin with a somewhat simpler example. Suppose it is asserted:

(A) All the men in this room are mortal.

Let us now write this as a conjunction of two sentences, as follows:

(B) Some things in this room are men & if anything is a man in this room it is mortal.

The question that we have to ask now, is, does (B) represent an adequate paraphrase of (A)? Or, to put it differently, does (B) prove that (A) is not a subject/predicate proposition, with an 'all-designator' ('All the men in this room') acting as a genuine subject-term? Schematically, what is being asserted in (B) is that some F's are G's, and if anything is a G, it is also an H. Now the conventional wisdom is that this really is a complex statement about the relevant concepts; and if so, it turns out that in (A) we are really not talking about any man or men in the room at all; which seems counterintuitive, to say the least.

But what does it mean to say that (B) is a statement about certain concepts anyway? In order to make sense of (B), it must be possible in principle to cash it in terms of statements about the relevant objects. Suppose we reproduce the first conjuct of (B) thus: 'Either a is a thing in this room and is a man, or b is a thing in this room and is a man, or ... etc.' and its second conjuct as a series of implications, viz. 'If a is a man in this room, then a is mortal; and if b is a man in this room, then b is mortal; and ...', with $\{a ... n\}$ being the set of all things in this room, or, if preferred, the set of all (suitably defined) spatial regions, or whatever, then the additional assumption needed to make the analysis work is that $\{a ... n\}$ is a finite set; in other words, there must be a point where we can say 'And these are all the things there are in the room', or ' ...all the spatial regions', etc.; and such statements themselves involve the use of all-designators as well as confronting us all over again with the problem of clarifying the meaning of existential claims. What is more, an analysis along these lines cannot be adequate for our purposes anyway, for what is talked about in (A) are the men in this room, not 'all the things' in this room, etc.

The point is that in order to provide a reasonably satisfactory paraphrase of (A) something else is needed that is so conspicuously absent from (B), namely the concept of *set inclusion*. For suppose that we deliberately omit all mention of set inclusion. Suppose that in the spirit of (B) we confine ourselves to saying simply 'Some members of $\{a ... n\}$ are men in this room, and if anything is a man in this room, it is mortal'. This clearly will not do, for (A) demands that we say not only 'Some members of $\{a ... n\}$ are F, and ...', but 'All the F's are members of $\{a ... n\}$, and ...'. These two sentences are far from being logically equivalent. In particular, the truth of the former, if the former is indeed true, does not imply the truth of the latter. If I might illustrate the point with a different example, there is evidently no convertibility as between, say, 'Some men are philosophers' and 'All philosophers are men'.

I conclude, therefore, that a paraphrase like (B) does not fully do justice to the actual content of (A), and does not help to eliminate the need for 'all-designators'.

Proof that the metaphysical realist claim gives rise to an assertoric inconsistency

Let us now return to the metaphysical realist claim, viz. that there is something that exists independently of whether it is thought or talked about. If such things do exists, then of course it makes no difference whether anyone ever says anything about them; either about all of them collectively, or individually. They might be thought, or talked about, as a matter of fact, but need not be. As it happens, we normally assume that only a very tiny number of such things get talked about at any one time, and by far the largest proportion do not get talked about at all. Let us now suppose that Jones makes a statement to this effect, viz. that there are things which are independent of thought but that no one says or asserts anything about them; I shall settle for 'asserts' to simplify the matter. Using symbols, with *Ind* meaning 'independent of thought', *ass* standing for 'asserts that', p representing any person and F any property, Jones's statement might be expressed thus:

$$\text{(i) } (\text{E}x) \ [\text{Ind } x \ \& \ (p)(\text{F}){\sim}p \text{ ass } \text{F}x]$$

An analysis of (i) will show that Jones cannot consistently assert what he does assert; and if Jones cannot do this, then evidently no one can.

It should be emphasised at the outset that the inconsistency here talked about is not a 'propositional' inconsistency in the usual sense, i.e. the conflict between two or more logically incompatible propositions within the context of a theory or argument, but what I shall call the *assertoric inconsistency*, i.e. the inconsistency arising from an act of assertion implicitly cancelling what is being granted in its content.

However, in order to prove that an assertion of (i) does give rise to such an inconsistency, two assumptions are necessary. First, it is necessary to assume that if Jones asserts p, and p entails q, then Jones by implication asserts q as well as p. I shall call this 'Rule (a)'. The immediate objection to this is likely to be that 'asserts' is an intensional or 'opacity-inducing' verb, i.e. that there is no certainty that anyone who asserts p is aware, let alone willing to accept what p entails. But I shall assume that Jones is a perfectly rational being who is unhesitatingly prepared to assent to whatever is logically entailed by what he asserts. The Rule (a), therefore, might also be called the 'principle of rationality'.

In addition, it is necessary to assume that the following holds:

$$(Ex)Fx \quad \longrightarrow \quad F(\hat{x}\, Fx)$$

which might be called the 'axiom of universal designation', and should be read as follows: If there are F-things (whatever F might be), then all the F-things are F-like. If men exist, then all the men are man-like. This may seem so trivial as to be hardly worth stating. Yet, as we shall see presently, its implications are far from trivial. The role of the capped variable $\hat{x}$ in the above axiomatic entailment formula is to indicate an 'all-designator'. The bracketed expression $(\hat{x}\, Fx)$ refers, or purports to refer, to the existing F-things in an exhaustive manner, and to those things only. What the 'axiom' conveys is that any existential proposition $(Ex)Fx$ is capable of generating an all-designator referring to the things of the indicated sort. Accordingly, and in the spirit of Rule (a), I postulate:

$$A \text{ ass } (Ex)Fx \quad \longrightarrow \quad A \text{ ass } (Ex)[\, Fx \,\&\, F(\hat{x}\, Fx)\,]$$

i.e. if A asserts that there are F's, then he asserts both that there are F's and that all the F's are F-like. For my present purposes, I shall refer to this as 'Rule (b)'.

If these two rules are granted, it is clear that the proposition (i) above cannot be asserted without equivocation. Thus if Jones asserts (i), viz. 'There are Ind-things but no one says anything about them ever , then by Rule (a) it follows that Jones himself does not say anything about them either. Now if independence of thought is to be taken seriously, this should be taken to mean that he is literally not saying anything about them either collectively or individually. But it cannot mean 'collectively' without giving rise to an assertoric inconsistency.

In order to show this, let us consider the following corollary of (i):

(ii) Jones ass (Ex) [Ind x & $(F)\sim$Jones ass Fx]

By Rules (a) and (b), this in turn yields:

(iii) Jones ass (Ex) [Ind x & Ind($\hat{x}$ Ind x)]

and (assuming that the Ind-things are referred to collectively throughout):

(iv) Jones ass (Ex) [Ind x & (F)∼Jones ass F($\hat{x}$ Ind x)]

Finally, by Rule (a) and (iv):

(v) Jones ass (Ex) [Ind x & ∼ Jones ass Ind($\hat{x}$ Ind x)]

viz. Jones asserts both that there are Ind-things and that he (Jones) does not assert that the Ind-things are Ind-like, which is in conflict with what he asserts at (iii). In consequence, he is going to be in some difficulty explaining what he is in fact asserting. For, as has been shown, he is confronted with the fact that in asserting (i) he is by implication saying that while all the Ind-things are Ind-like, they are nevertheless such that no one, including himself, asserts anything about them, not even that they are Ind-like. In short, he is guilty of an assertoric inconsistency.

But let us now suppose that (i) means merely that the Ind-things are not talked about *individually*. In other words, suppose that what Jones asserts is simply that no one, including Jones, asserts anything about any *specific* Ind-thing, even though we might be asserting something about them 'collectively'. (Notice, incidentally, that this implies a somewhat weaker version of realism.) Does such an interpretation help to eliminate the problem of assertoric inconsistency?

It does not really. The reason, as will be shown presently, can again be traced to the all-designator which unavoidably crops up in an analytic paraphrase of (i).

Let us begin by positing a particular Ind-thing *a*. Then, on the present interpretation, Jones, by merely asserting the existence of Ind-things, is not saying anything about *a*, not even that it is Ind-like. In other words – given, of course, the 'principle of rationality' which overrides all opacity considerations – the inference that can be drawn from (i), is:

Jones ass (Ex) [Ind x & (Ind a →   ∼Jones ass Ind a)]

Yet, as we saw earlier, to assert that there are Ind-things is to assert by implication that all the Ind-things are Ind-like; and if so, then

Jones has no choice but to concede that if a is one of the Ind-things, then a is Ind-like too. Or, in symbols again:

$$\text{Jones ass (E}x) \, [\text{Ind } a \, \& \, (a \, \varepsilon \, \hat{x}\text{Ind } x \quad \longrightarrow \quad \text{Jones ass Ind } a)]$$

which – assuming that the sentence '$a \, \varepsilon \, \hat{x}$Ind x', expressing a class membership of a, can be replaced by the predicative statement 'Ind a', on the grounds that while not synonymous they are nevertheless strictly *coextensive* – yields the following inference:

$$\text{Jones ass (E}x)\,[\text{Ind } x \, \& \, (\text{Ind } a \quad \longrightarrow \quad \text{Jones ass Ind } a \, \& \sim \text{Jones ass Ind } a)]$$

i.e. Jones asserts that there are Ind-things and that if a is an Ind-thing, he both does and does not assert that a is an Ind-thing. In short, he is getting himself entangled again in an assertoric inconsistency.

Assertoric inconsistency and incoherence

Consider now some objections that might be raised against the above argument. First, it might be objected that there is really no need to postulate the existence of unthought-of, unspoken-of, things in order to make the metaphysical realist point. All that is needed is to postulate the existence of things that are *capable* of existing without being an object of thought. If we confine ourselves to talking in terms of 'capacities', it might be said, the problem of 'assertoric inconsistency' no longer arises.

This is not strictly true. Suppose that I make a statement about a specific thing, claiming that this thing is capable of existing without ever being an object of thought, and hence a topic for anyone, including the thought of being capable of so existing. Suppose I say of this chair in front of me: 'This chair can exist without ever being thought or spoken of by me or anyone else in any manner whatsoever.' Then, evidently, what I say is true only provided the proposition 'This chair is never thought or spoken of by anyone in any manner whatsoever' expresses a *possible* state of affairs. But it is easy to see that the latter proposition cannot be asserted without being falsified by being asserted. In short, we are still confronted with the problem of 'assertoric inconsistency'.

But, surely, it will be said, this alone does not render the original proposition *meaningless*. We should be careful not to conflate inconsistency with incoherence. A proposition, when asserted, may result in an assertoric inconsistency without its objective content thereby becoming unintelligible. I cannot assert 'I am not now thinking of this chair', while being fully aware of what I am saying, without literally refuting what I am asserting; yet no one has any difficulty in understanding what I mean. Similarly, it is in principle impossible to claim self-consistently 'No one is now saying anything'; yet this surely is a perfectly meaningful sentence. But if so, this is proof enough that there is nothing logically amiss with the idea that the possibility of a certain state of affairs does not necessarily depend on the relevant proposition being self-consistently assertable. In other words, a concept may have instances even though it may be such as to give rise to an assertoric inconsistency each time it is applied.

What reply should we give to this? To begin with, the claim that the above examples, and any other similarly constructed sentences, make clear sense, ought to be treated with caution. If such sentences are taken in isolation from the context, they are anything but transparent. 'I am not now thinking of this chair' is unlikely to be taken seriously unless it was clear from the context, or was explicitly stated by the speaker, in what respect the chair is not being referred to or thought about. Similarly the kind of response that the statement 'No one is now saying anything' is likely to elicit is 'What exactly do you mean? Saying anything about what?' In short, the speaker would be expected to complete his statement by providing some kind of explanation. As it stands, the statement is self-defeating, and the intention behind it is obscure.

Now it will no doubt be said that after all it is not difficult to imagine the possibility of no one at this moment uttering anything at all. Yet why this is not difficult? In actually saying 'No one is now saying anything' we are in effect making sure that the possibility in question is not available. What is more, owing to the ambiguity of 'now', which could apply to any time, or stretch of time, it is not even clear that the relevant possibility is in principle actualisable. What can be said unambiguously is 'No one is saying anything at 3.30 p.m.'; placing, that is, one's statement within an objective frame of reference. If it is found that the statement is made at 3.30 p.m., the statement is false, but not meaningless, for it is perfectly conceivable that at 3.30 p.m. no one utters a single word. What is not possible is to claim coherently that at the time of making the statement no one is saying anything at all.

So the main problem centres on the question: What can be coherently said to be possible? If 'No one is now saying anything' can be accepted as expressing a possible state of affairs, and hence as meaningful, it is only because it can be disambiguated and made free from assertoric inconsistency by being replaced with 'No one is saying anything at 3.30 p.m.', which contextually qualifies as a coextensive sentence, expressing the same state of affairs. If it was not possible to provide a truth-functionally equivalent (though not necessarily synonymous) paraphrase of such a statement, one would have every right to question the meaningfulness of the truth-claim involved.

Consider one more example. I cannot say 'I am dead' without commiting an assertoric inconsistency. But what I say is false, not meaningless, inasmuch as the same state of affairs can be reproduced *without* assertoric inconsistency by saying 'Edo Pivcevic is dead', or even 'The man with the Roman nose is dead' (all of which, contextually, may be regarded as coextensive sentences). What cannot be similarly reproduced without assertoric inconsistency is 'I am not I', which is not just false but incoherent.

Accordingly, I wish to advance the following general principle:

> *If* p *is to be possible, then it must be possible*
> *to assert* p *or at least a sentence which is coextensive,*
> *though not necessarily synonymous, with* p,
> *without providing a counter-instance to what is being*
> *asserted by virtue of asserting it.*

If this principle is accepted, it is clear that Jones's assertion that there are things that are independent of thought such that no one ever says anything about such things does not satisfy the stated condition, for there is no truth-functionally equivalent paraphrase available which would not yield the same kind of inconsistency. So the conclusion must be that the relevant truth claim does not make clear sense.

Possibility and assertibility – a final comment

Another objection that might be raised against the above argument is that it does not distinguish clearly between 'asserting *p*' and 'asserting the possibility that *p*' Surely, it might be said, it is one thing to assert (a) 'There is something independent of thought but no one ever thinks or claims that there is something independent of thought', and quite another to assert the *possibility* of (a). To assert (a) produces an assertoric inconsistency, but to assert the possibility of (a) does not give rise to any inconsistency and is perfectly intelligible and acceptable.

But the problem with this objection is that it takes for granted, does not explain why, the claim that

It is possible that there is something independent of thought, although no one ever thinks so;

and the claim that

It is not possible for anyone consistently to assert that there is something independent of thought although no one thinks so,

are *both* significant and mutually compatible; and it is this very assumption that needs to be explained and justified. The key issue before us is this: how can we significantly claim that a proposition which cannot be self-consistently asserted *in any possible universe* might nevertheless be true? What does 'true' mean in such an instance? It is precisely the meaningfulness of truth claims such as these that the above argument calls into question.

What I have argued, briefly, is this: that if *p* in all its truth-functionally equivalent variants produces an assertoric inconsistency, we have a right to question its coherence. The implication of the argument is that the objective content of propositions is not something that can be considered in complete isolation from the conditions of their assertibility; i.e. that the consideration of assertibility is a necessary constituent part of an analysis of significance of any truth claim qua truth claim. If the metaphysical realist thesis appears a philosophically attractive and plausible proposition, this is largely due to a failure to appreciate the importance of this fact.

14. The Structure of Truth

I now proceed to a more detailed consideration of the concept of truth. As is already clear from what has been said so far, there can be no 'simple' definition of truth, and what is more 'definition', strictly, is quite the wrong word to use. It is closer to the mark to speak of a description of the conditions that characterise the 'occurrence' of truth. Truth, I shall argue, is an ontological event in which we ourselves are participants, and which can be adequately described only in terms of structure. It represents the fulfilment of the conditions implicit in relevant truth claims; conditions that reveal a pattern of certain basic and inter-related ideas. In the present chapter, I propose to examine these ideas and their mutual connections. The view that will be rejected is that truth might be explicable as some kind of property of an independently identifiable object x, like being red, for example; or having blond hair; or being a cause of y; or that it represents some sort of irreducible relation of 'correspondence' between two otherwise mutually independent terms. Least of all is truth object-like, although it has been argued by some philosophers that truth is a special kind of object which acts as the reference of true propositions.[1]

What I wish to maintain, briefly, is that an analysis of truth is inseparable from, and should be approached via an analysis of truth-claims, or via an analysis of assertions. To say that p is true is to express the view that the conditions implicit in the relevant truth-claim are satisfied, such that p forms part of the occurence of truth. The conditions implicit in the given truth-claim need not of course be satisfied. Very frequently they are not satisfied. None the less without truth-claims, strictly, there is no truth. There is no 'metaphysically pre-existing truth', just as there are no 'metaphysically pre-existing' facts. This, needless to say, does not mean

---

[1] Frege notoriously defended this view and used both 'das Wahre' and 'das Falsche' as object-terms.

that truth is being 'invented' by ourselves; it only means that truth cannot take place without the involvement in it of cognitive agents who are intellectually endowed similarly to ourselves.

Accordingly, the question I shall concern myself with, will be: What is involved in making a truth-claim? To put it differently: I shall be inquiring into what it means to assert p, rather than into what it means for the asserted proposition 'to be' true, because the latter question suggests that it is meaningful to attribute truth to propositions independently of possible truth-claims, which I regard as mistaken.

As for truth-claims, I shall maintain that a truth-claim unfolds under analysis into a threefold thesis, viz.

(a) p

(b) p can be seen to be the case.

(c) The statement that p is objectively valid, i.e. it is an objectively valid record of the case p.

These three conditions are all closely interlinked. Together they represent what I shall call the 'structure of truth'.

Truth-claims and the predicate true

It should be made clear at once that while rejecting the view that truth reduces to a property of an independently identifiable object x, I do not wish to suggest that the predicative use of 'true' is in some way inappropriate or ungrammatical. It would be absurd to suggest this. At the same time, it is important to recognise that the predicative use of 'true' does not provide a sufficient ground for interpreting truth as a property *tout court*, even if the concept of an object is understood to include linguistic items. Truth is neither an object, nor a property of objects, but an event, of which the given proposition, or propositions are a *feature*. It is useful to remind oneself that the adverb 'truly' can perform a similar function to 'true' as part of a grammatical predicate.[2] It is equally helpful to note that 'true'

---

[2] The adverb 'truly' usually occurs conjointly with an adjective or a past participle, which it serves to emphasize, but not always. The archaic form of 'truly' is 'verily', and 'Verily, verily ...' is used in the Authorized Version of the Bible as a rendering of 'Amen, amen ...' with which Jesus frequently prefaces his sayings (*amên, amên, legô humin*). The point Jesus wants to make is

often can easily be replaced with a substantive. Thus we say 'What A says is true', and also 'What A says is the truth', or 'He spoke the truth'. Witnesses in court swear to speak 'the truth, the whole truth, and nothing but the truth'. This elasticity of common usage which allows one to express the same thought now with the adjecive now with the noun frequently tends to be ignored in discussions about truth. Yet this in itself is a sufficient warning against any over simple 'attributive' analysis of the concept.

Might we not then regard 'true', while not as 'ungrammatical' (if properly interpreted), nevertheless as theoretically dispensable? What difference, if any, would it make to the concept of truth if this word was not available? Perhaps no 'truth-predicates' are really necessary, and could be dropped from a logically reformed language altogether?

The argument in favour of this view, as we saw earlier (Chapter 1), is usually presented along the following lines. If p is the case, then p, and to say that p is 'true' is no different from reiterating p. It is not to attribute to p a property which it conceivably might not have; for p is either a fact or it is not a fact. It cannot be both fact and not fact, nor can it be fact at one time and not fact at another time and still remain the same p. If we were to allow such a possibility, we would have to allow the possibility of facts existing independently of how they might be expressed in language, and this is unintelligible.

To use the predicate 'true' (it is argued) is not to add to, or detract from, or alter anything in the content of what is said. If A says 'It is true that Socrates is mortal', A does not give any more information about the relevant fact than by saying simply 'Socrates is mortal'. If 'It is true that …' serves any purpose at all, it is merely to emphasise the claim that one is making, or to signalise that we are indeed making an assertion and not asking a question or making a jocular

---

that he is a realiable and true witness of God. (Cf. *Theological Dictionary of the new Testament*, edited by Gerhard Kittel, vol. 1, p. 336f.) Incidentally, *The New English Bible* reproduces 'Amen, amen …' with the phrase 'In truth, in very truth …', while *The Jerusalem Bible* renders 'Amen, amen', together with 'lego humin', as 'I tell you most solemnly …', which surely is an oversimplification. The emphasis in the incantation is on the reliability of the messenger, as well as on the veracity and the importance of the message.

But back to 'truly', it is not very difficult to imagine other possibilities of it being used without an adjective or a past participle. Thus the construction 'He spoke truly', although awkward, is not unintelligible.

remark. But if so, we might just as well say 'honestly' or 'seriously', or use some other cognate expression to indicate our intention. Such expressions may or may not achieve their purpose on a given occasion, but whether they do is entirely immaterial to the substance of the statement concerned. If what we say is true, it is true irrespective of whether anyone describes it as such. The predicate 'true', while it may conceivably have an emotional significance, is logically unnecessary.

Similarly for 'false' For to say '*p* is false' is merely to assert the contradictory of *p*. If it is false that Socrates is alive today, Socrates is not alive today. If *p* is false, not-*p* is the case. But then 'false' can be dispensed with just as easily as 'true' can. Both words merely evince certain emotional attitudes; they do not provide any factual information that cannot be provided by simply stating the relevant facts.

It should be noted that this argument, if valid, proves merely that it is not logically necessary that truth-claims should be made explicit via 'truth-predicates'; it does not show that the topic of truth-claims can be left out of philosophical considerations altogether; that it more properly belongs in the province of psychology rather than philosophy.

As a matter of fact, we do need 'truth-predicates'. We need them precisely as a means of advertising, either our own truth-claims, or our views on other people's truth-claims. According to the 'redundancy theory', to describe what A says as 'true' is not to say anything that cannot be said by saying 'A states that *p*, and *p*'. But this clearly does not eliminate the need for the predicate 'true' if I am anxious to stress not just that A happens to state that *p*, and (as it happens) *p*, but that it is indeed true to say that *p*, i.e. if I am anxious to comment on A's truth-claim qua truth-claim. Sometimes we do this by saying 'A says that *p*, and he is right where 'right' acts as some sort of surrogate truth-predicate. What I am suggesting is that this 'right' is part of the actual metalinguistic comment on what A says, not, as the adherent of the 'redundancy theory' would presumably argue, merely an inference from A says that *p*, and *p*.

All this is equally valid for false. To describe someone's statement as 'false' is not exactly on a par with asserting its negation, although obviously we could not consistently do the former while refusing to do the latter. Thus I do not wish merely to state – in reply, say, to someone else's contrary claim – that this paper is white. I wish to dissent from his assertion by emphasising that it is false to say that this paper is not white. In other words, I wish to emphasise the falsity of his claim, rather than just make a straighforward statement about the facts as I see them.

There is of course another, more familiar objection against the view that truth-predicates are 'logically redundant'. Briefly, it runs like this. The redundancy view, in effect, presupposes that the truth-value of what is stated or asserted on any given occasion is independent of the circumstances in which it is stated or asserted. But what is stated or asserted need not necessarily have a truth-value. If it *does* have a truth-value, i.e. if it is true or false, then it is only under certain clearly specifiable conditions, and if such conditions are not satisfied, the question of truth or falsehood does not arise. If an actor on the stage says 'It's a fine day', it is pointless to wonder whether what he say is really true. By the same token, in different circumstances, querying a similar statement may be far from pointless; and if so, truth-predicates evidently won't be 'redundant'.

The main target of attack, in short, is the assumption that truth and falsehood are somehow built into the propositions themselves; that propositions are *per se* true or *per se* false. But surely it is actual statements, it is argued, and the circumstances in which statements are made, not any mysterious propositions *per se*, that are relevant to truth. To give yet another example, 'Socrates loves Xantippe' may well have been true at one time and false at another, but if the statement was made during Socrates early childhood, say, long before he knew anything of Xantippe or the delights of marital love, the proper reply would be that the question of truth or falsity did not arise. And the same reply would have to be given if Socrates did not exist.

However, the above objection is perhaps less weighty than it at first might appear, for it is conceivable that in certain circumstances it may be possible to devise a suitable paraphrase, which, if asserted, cannot fail to produce a truth-value. In some cases there will of course be disagreements as to what qualifies as a suitable or adequate paraphrase. This raises a number of separate issues which I do not wish to pursue at the moment, for they are not of crucial importance to my argument. What is important to emphasise in the context of the present discussion is simply this: that the question of truth and falsehood arises only in conjunction with actual or possible assertions, or, in the more general idiom that I have adopted, in conjunction with truth-claims. No paraphrase is capable of acquiring a truth value except as a possible instrument of a truth-claim. And this means that it is the structure of truth-claims that one has to focus on in order to clarify the nature of truth.

As for the words 'true' and 'false', contextually they are surely indispensable. At the same time, their predicative use does not make truth and falsehood into 'properties'. To call a statement 'true' is not to ascribe truth to an object as one might ascribe the property red to an apple.[3] Rather, I wish to argue, it is to claim – or to assent to a claim – that the objective content of what is asserted in given case forms, or, within certain conditions, is capable of forming, part of a 'truth event'. It is like saying of a play that it forms, or is capable of forming, an integral part of a performance.

Truth-claims and the case p

Nevertheless the reductivist instincts, which we saw at work in the 'redundancy theory', are difficult to lay to rest. Thus the immediate objection, phrased in terms of the above analogy, is likely to be that the merits of a play have nothing to do with performance in any case. Whether the play is good or bad, this surely can be significantly discussed irrespective of whether the play is ever performed, or even performable. And similarly for truth. It is propositions and what they express that matters, not how and under what circumstances the propositions are mouthed. In the beginning of this chapter truth was linked with the fulfilment of a triadic pattern of the conditions that emerged from an analysis of truth claims. But why, it will be asked, is it not sufficient to say that the truth of a given statement consists simply in things being as is said they are? If 'Socrates is mortal' is true, Socrates is mortal; and if it is true that Socrates loves Xantippe, most assuredly Socrates loves Xantippe. What we are saying when calling a statement 'true' is neither more nor less than that things are as stated, or that the relevant state of affairs *obtains*

---

[3] As Frege quite rightly emphasised, truth cannot be analysed in predicative terms. The relation of the thought [as expressed in a sentence] to the True may not be compared with that of subject to predicate', he wrote. (See *Translations from the Philosophical Writings of Gottlob Frege*, 1960, p. 64.) The trouble was only that, having decided that truth cannot be treated predicatively, he wrongly concluded that here we have a special kind of object, the true, and not a concept at all; which of course only exposed the grievous inadequacy of his theory of concepts.

in reality.

All this sounds self-evident, and so banal, in fact, that it seems churlish to wish to question its meaning. Yet its apparent banality hides a tangle of problems. The idea that the truth of what is said consists in things in reality being as they are said to be may look straighforward enough; in fact, it is one of the murkiest.

For what does the phrase 'things being as they are said to be' really mean? To begin with, we cannnot know how things are independently of how they are said to be. For if there is such knowledge, it cannot be made sense of in words. If the question is, what it is that 'makes' that which is stated on a given occasion 'true', another statement will have to be given in reply. This, in turn, will lead to yet more statements, until we reach a point where there is nothing further left to be said, except to repeat what has been said before.

So in what terms precisely, if any, can truth be talked about? Superficially, it might seem that the puzzle evaporates if we imagine a situation involving two different speakers. Thus, it might be said, it is perfectly possible for A to know how things are independently of how B claims them to be; and if so, there is nothing strange or unintelligible in A characterising B's statement as 'true'; or, which comes to the same thing, saying that things are exactly as B says they are. However, this does not quite remove the main difficulty, for A is, in effect, merely adjudicating B's statement in the light of the statements that he himself would be prepared to make.

There is a strong temptation at this point to reiterate the familiar common sense position. Surely, it might be said, what we are verbalising, or attempting to verbalise, are certain facts, and facts exist independently of the linguistic reports that are made, or might be made, about them. If it makes sense to describe statements as 'true' or 'false' it is only because there are facts that make them so. Facts are chunks of reality that may or may not be reflected adequately in linguistic reports; or they may not be reported at all. None of this makes any difference as far as their existence is concerned.

The difficulty with such reasoning is of course that it assumes that the idea of 'facts existing independently of the linguistic reports that are made, or might be made, about them' makes clear sense, whereas there is nothing that is more obscure. What we should be asking ourselves instead is: What makes meaningful references to extra-linguistic facts possible? What are the conditions of intelligibility of such references? No sooner such questions are asked, however, than it becomes evident that to talk about facts is really to talk about the contents of actual or possible statements of fact. To refer to Socrates being mortal is to refer to what the statement 'Socrates is mortal' states. Instead of 'fact', therefore, we might equally well talk of 'case p'.

But now the question arises about the precise implications of assuming p to be the case. Surely if it is absurd to talk of facts existing independently of how they might be expressed in language, it seems equally absurd to suppose that p subsists as an item in a universal (and presumably ever-expanding) library of truths, independently of whether it can be 'read out' or seen to be the case by any 'reader'. For how could we make the idea of such a self-subsisting truth item, or state of affairs, intelligible? If no facts exist unconditionally 'in themselves' no propositional 'truth-bearers' can exist unconditionally 'in themselves' either. To make a truth-claim in respect of p is to claim that p is the case, and if p is the case, it is so for a potential witness, or not at all.

Truth-claims and seeing that p is the case

Truth, then, does not reduce literally to 'true propositions'; it presupposes an experience of truth. Truth is *alêtheia*: it manifests itself through evidential experience. A complete description of the world would still fall short of the complete truth unless the relevant evidential experience was possible. As against this, it is sometimes urged that the possibility of an evidential experience is merely a condition of verifiability of truth claims, not part of the *meaning* of truth. But this is a misunderstanding; for in order to be able to elucidate the meaning of truth it is necessary to analyse the logic underlying truth claims, and to make a truth claim in respect of p is not just to claim that p, but also to claim by implication that p can be seen to be the case. It would be incoherent to make a truth claim in respect of p, while at the same time disputing the possibility of anyone (including the proverbial God) ever being able to say on the basis of own evidential experience 'That's how things are'. Similarly it would be just as nonsensical to claim that p can be seen to be the case, while actually denying that p. The assumption that p and the assumption that p can (in principle) be seen to be the case, are both equally essential features of a significant truth claim.

The reason why there is often a reluctance to accept that there exists a logical link between verifiability and truth is that the positivists have vulgarised the concept of verifiability by interpreting it exclusively in terms of sense experience. But as philosophers have long argued, there are different types of cognitive insight, and it is not only singular propositions, but general propositions too, that can be genuine candidates for knowledge; with what is sometimes called the 'logical intuition', in addition to 'empirical' intuition, providing an access to truth. Moreover it is necessary not only that evidential experiences should be 'possible', but that we should have had some such experiences already; for if no evidential experiences had ever occured, there would be no means of explaining what sort of claim is being made; indeed there would be no occasion for making any truth-claims at all. If significant truth-claims presuppose the possibility of evidential experience of one sort or another, it is because such claims originally are inspired by such experiences (which, at the same time, supply a degree of their 'legitimation').

None of this, needless to say, makes truth.claims as expressed in statements of fact logically equivalent to reports of certain evidential experiences – or, as they are also occasionally called *truth*-experiences – either one's own or anyone else's. My claim that there are penguins in Antarctica is not a report of a personal experience, for I have never been there. But nor am I reporting the evidential experience of the witness from whose first-hand account I have derived this information. I am making a direct truth-claim, not giving an oblique description of someone else's experience, although the evidential experience of the witness, in this instance, is the ultimate basis of my claim.

But surely, it might be objected, it is not always possible to draw a meaningful distinction between a report of a (subjective) evidential experience and an (objective) truth-claim. Suppose I feel cold and merely wish to report the fact. Then what I claim to be true coincides with what I experience, and the above distinction is vacuous.

This is not so, because in so far as I make a truth claim when I say 'I am cold', I am saying not merely that this is how I experience the sensation, but that this is what my sensation, in fact, is. To make a truth-claim is not to say (or, at any rate, not merely to say) 'This is how things look to me' but 'This is how things are', quite irrespective of whether the truth-claim in question refers to the speaker's own mental state, or states, or is concerned with external objects accessible to inter-subjective inspection.

At the same time, it is clear that this does not in the least alter the fact that in asserting p, i.e. in making the appropriate truth-claim, we are by implication claiming the possibility of an experience of seeing that p is the case. The point is that the assumption of the (logical) possibility of a 'so it is' experience is built into every truth-claim qua truth-claim. Moreover, as I have pointed out before, truth-claims, as a rule, presuppose that certain relevant evidential experiences have already occured. Characteristically, those who make fraudulent truth-claims have to pretend that they are basing their claims upon such experiences, either their own or other people's, if they wish to be taken seriously. Their pretence is designed not merely to persuade other people of the truth of what they are saying, but to emphasise that they are indeed making a genuine truth-claim, not making a joke, or reciting a piece of poetry.

To conclude: I have argued that truth-claims make sense only against the background of certain evidential experiences. They presuppose such experiences and imply the possibility of such experiences. They should not, however, be confused with reports of such experiences. In making a truth-claim we are not simply reporting an evidential experience, nor are we merely postulating the possibility of such an experience, although without assuming the possibility of such experiences we cannot meaningfully speak of truth.

Objective validity of statements expressing truth-claims

It now remains to consider the third and last basic ingredient of truth-claims. As I pointed out earlier, a truth-claim in respect of p implies not merely that p is the case, and can moreover be seen to be the case, but also that a statement to the effect that p has an objective validity. (I am of course assuming that the same truth-claim can be made via different but coextensive statements.) No coherent idea can be formed of a truth-claim that does not carry this implication.

But what exactly is involved in claiming objective validity for a statement that p? Briefly, it is to claim that the statement in question satisfies at least four conditions. First it must be intelligible at points of view that are biographically distinct from one's own. The principle involved here is one of inter-subjective communicability of the 'objective content'. No p in respect of which a truth-claim can appropriately be made is an exclusively 'private property'. In particular, to assert p is to publicise it, to acknowledge the possibility of others sharing the information that p. Secondly, it means that what the given statement states can be reiterated by different speakers from different and biographically unrelated points of view. Thirdly, it means that the statement in question can be subjected to certain inter-subjective tests, with a view to determining whether its constituent words have been appropriately used. The necessary public accessibility of the rules of appropriateness follows from the familiar argument against the idea of a private language, which was discussed in Chapter 8. Fourthly, it means that the statement in question is such that it must be possible, in principle, to construct an indefinite number of other statements that are coextensive with it, but involve the use of different descriptive expressions for the same object, or objects, places, times, etc. A corollary of this is that whoever asserts that Plato's teacher was not afraid of dying, must in principle be prepared to accept that the philosopher who drank hemlock was not afraid of dying, if it was demonstrated to him that the same man was involved in both cases.

Of the four conditions enumerated above, the one concerning communicability is the most crucial. What is stated or asserted on a given occasion must in principle be intelligible at points of view other one's own, i.e. it must in principle be inter-subjectively transmissible. The inter-subjective transmissibility of the objective content is a pre-condition of coherence of any truth-claim qua truth-claim.

However, the exaggerated emphasis that is sometimes placed on the 'objective content', and, connected with this, the failure to appreciate the complexity of the concept of truth, has sometimes led to an equally exaggerated emphasis being placed on what is described as the 'subjectivity aspect' of truth. Thus it is not unusual to find in philosophical writings statements to the effect that truth, in the most fundamental sense, is to be found only within one's own interiority. In the final analysis, it is argued, truth is a 'lived truth'; it is 'irreducibly existential', something to be felt and lived, not publicly transacted. 'Truth', claimed Kierkegaard, 'is subjectivity.'[4] But even Kierkegaard, of course, wrote long books in an attempt to persuade others of the fact.

What is 'subjective', and inescapably so, are evidential

[4] See *Concluding Unscientific Postscript*, vol. 1, Pt. II/2, Ch. 2.

experiences. But we cannot talk intelligibly even about the relevance of evidential experiences to truth, without implicitly conceding the intersubjective communicability of that which is claimed to be experienced as true. Furthermore, as was emphasised earlier on, to make any sort of truth-claim is to acknowledge by implication the right of others to subject our truth-claim to rigorous tests on the basis of certain public, or publicly accessible, criteria. It is also to concede that neither we nor any other person, for that matter, can be the sole judge as to whether all the requisite truth-conditions have been fulfilled in a given case.

The main point about objectivity is this: that any statement carrying a truth-claim can be suitably paraphrased at points of view occupied by different subjects of experiences without necessarily ceasing to refer to the same state of affairs. This remains so, irrespective of whether what is being talked about is external things or personal experiences. 'I am cold' is no less a statement of fact than 'There are dark spots on the Sun', or 'The philosopher who drank hemlock was not afraid of dying', and similarly aspires to objective validity.

Some difficulties in paraphrasing first-person statements

My chief concern in the above has been to elucidate the logical implications of a truth-claim. I have not been concerned with the question of the conditions under which true statements can be made about other people's experiences, important though this question undoubtedly is. It is not at all easy to decide whether the evidence on which we base our statement in a given case is in fact adequate. There may be abundant behavioural evidence to support the statement 'A is cold', and yet the statement may conceivably be false, for the person concerned may be merely cleverly feigning the experience. However, these are practical problems which do not concern us here. What is relevant to the present discussion is that it must in principle be possible for a statement expressing a truth-claim to be paraphrased from different and biographically unrelated points of view. It is a condition of intelligibility of truth-claims that such paraphrases should be possible.

Nevertheless there remains the problem of the loss of meaning that occurs in such paraphrases. Obviously the freer the paraphrase the more it will differ in its meaning content from the original. But then, it might be asked, on what grounds can we claim in a given case that what is stated in two differently worded statements is in fact 'the same'? As we saw earlier (cf. Chapter 7), even such an apparently innocent and contextually perspicuous transposition as from 'I am cold', as said by A, to 'A is cold', as said by B, involves an important change of significance, for the way A views himself is not identical with the way he is viewed by an external observer such as B. And this being so, it is not entirely clear what it means to say that the same case p can be re-expressed at different and biographically unrelated points of view. What right do we have to insist that it is a necessary condition of making a significant truth-claim that it should be possible to repeat what is actually stated by *any* number of speakers?

Before answering, we must emphasise two things. First, the difficulty over repeatability is confined to statements in the first person singular. There is no difficulty in repeating at any number of biographically unrelated points of view statements like 'There are dark spots on the Sun' or 'The philosopher who drank hemlock was not afraid of dying', or any statement made in the first person *plural*, for that matter. It is only if the statement begins with 'I', or the inflected verb pointing back to the speaker, that it cannot be repeated literally by others. Secondly, it is necessary to distinguish between literally uttering the same p and merely making a statement that is coextensive with p. If two utterances literally reproduce the same p, they are necessarily coextensive, but they may be coextensive without necessarily being equisignificant.

Let us now restate the problem in the light of what has just been said. How can a statement that someone makes in the first person singular be reproduced by someone else such that it still conveys the same p? A clue to an answer (as I pointed out earlier) may be found in the way personal pronouns are used in communication. We cannot use the word 'I' meaningfully without by implication accepting that one can be addressed by others as 'you', or 'he', or 'she'. If A says 'I am cold' and B turns to him and asks 'Who? You?', then (provided in both cases the words have been used in their customary meanings) A cannot coherently answer the question negatively. And if A can be referred to as 'you', he can be referred to in any number of other ways as well, although inevitably the further away we move from personal (or demonstrative) pronouns, the greater the possibility of ambiguity and misunderstanding, and hence the greater the risk of the referential symbol failing to find its intended target. Thus there is nothing incoherent, for example, in A answering negatively the question 'Do you mean that the man wearing a moustache is cold?', even though he does happen to wear a moustache, for there may be any number of moustachioed persons in the room.

This is not to say, of course, that a replacement of 'I' with a descriptive phrase necessarily results in an alteration of the state of affairs expressed, merely that it might. The important point is that a second- and third-person paraphrase must in principle be possible. Whenever I make a statement in the first person, I am logically commited to accepting the possibility of what I say being paraphrased into an other-person mode from points of view which I myself do not occupy, without the paraphrase necessarily misrepresenting what I am trying to convey; and it is here that an answer to the above problem must be sought.

Nevertheless there is still the distinction to be drawn between what I say and my saying it. The person who repeats or paraphrases what I say may reproduce the same p but he does so in a different speech act. And he does not, and in the nature of things cannot, have the same experience. It is important not to lose sight of this, for truth as an event, as I have tried to argue, has a subjective as well as an objective aspect to it, and is not concerned solely with the 'impersonal content' of truth-claims.

What matters, in other words, is not merely what is stated or claimed to be true, but how and when it is stated, and by whom. Two statements, notoriously, can be identical word for word, yet they may differ in their 'episodic meaning', depending upon who is doing the uttering, and when. It follows that there can be no question of the 'impersonal content' of what is stated or asserted on any given occasion being the sole bearer of truth. The chief source of confusion lies in what seems to be an irresistible urge to simplify what is manifestly a complex concept, and to over-emphasise either the impersonal 'transmissible' content, or, by contrast, the 'ineffable' aspect of evidential experiences; thereby obscuring the structural inter-relatedness of these two features within what is essentially one and the same event.

The structure theory of truth

I have sought to clarify the concept of truth by analysing the logic of truth-claims. There is indeed little that can be usefully, or even intelligibly, said about truth without studying the logic of truth-claims. If, however, attention is focused upon truth-claims, it soon becomes evident that truth can no longer be treated as a 'property' of propositions. Predicates such as 'true', 'correct', etc. properly apply to truth-claims, and an analysis of truth-claims shows that truth is not simply propositional, but includes certain experiential elements through which it becomes 'truth for us'. Truth, in short, reveals itself as an event in which the cognitive subject actively participates through his own actions and cognitive experience.

As a final objection, the opponent of this view is likely to say that it is all very well to talk about the structure of truth-claims, but what is really at issue is what justifies a truth-claim; and surely what justifies a truth-claim is that the relevant proposition is true, i.e. that things are exactly as they are said to be.

But propositions, as I have argued, are not true 'in themselves'. They are promisory notes that have to be 'cashed' in terms of evidential experience. It is a misconception to refer to a proposition as 'possibly true', irrespective of whether it can in principle be seen to be true. Mathematical conjectures are sometimes referred to in this way; but if anything is said in such cases, it is only that it is not self-contradictory to make a truth-claim in respect of the conjecture concerned, and whoever actually makes such a claim commits himself to accepting the conditions that make such claims meaningful.

As to whether these conditions are fulfilled in a given instance, this can only be decided, if a decision is required, on the basis of some other claims that have been previously accepted or recognised as 'correct'. In the final analysis, truth is *its own criterion and witness*, and falsehood is a kind of error.

It follows that truth cannot be defined in terms of 'correspondence', least of all in terms of correspondence with 'external' and 'pre-existent' facts. Admittedly in making a truth-claim we do posit a state of affairs 'external' to the act of making such a claim. After all, the same truth-claim can be made by different persons at different times. But this does not mean either that the state of affairs thus posited does (or can) exist *independently* of what can be said about it or that truth is possible *without* truth-claims. Rather the reverse, a truth-claim, with all its implicit demands fulfilled, is an integral part of the *occurrence* of truth.

Attempts that are occasionally made to reformulate the correspondence theory, with a view to freeing it from the damaging misconception about facts as some kind of ready-made external models that are logically independent of their propositional pictures usually do not go far enough, and generally do little to clarify the meaning of 'correspondence'. In addition, there is a complete failure to appreciate the relevance of a consideration of the objectivity aspect of truth-claims, as well as of the possibility of evidential experiences, to the meaning of truth.

But if the correspondence theory does not provide a satisfactory clarification of truth, neither does the so-called 'coherence theory' (I should make it clear that I am here referring to the *propositional* coherence theory). Truth, in terms of the coherence theory, is a totality of true propositions, with every true propositions depending for its truth upon every other true proposition; all of them together forming a coherent (though not necessarily 'analytical') system. Now, while it may well be that all 'true propositions' are mutually interlinked in certain essential aspects, this does not in the least help to explain the meaning of truth, unless we know its meaning already, and to know its meaning, as I hope the preceding analysis has shown, is also to know that truth does not reduce to 'true propositions'.

15. Reason and Reality

It remains now to try and gather together the results of the various arguments that have been advanced in the preceding pages and draw some general conclusions. What these results show might be briefly summed up as follows. To elucidate the concept of reality is to construct a theory of reality, and such a theory must at the same time supply an account of the conditions in the light of which its own significance and veracity might be judged. What is more, such conditions are not 'external' to the theory, but are an integral part of it. For the world that such a theory is designed to fit is not a naturalistic machine 'out there', but a self-referential system that 'talks about itself'. It 'thematises' itself through the epistemic activity of certain cognitive agents. There is no reality *independently* of such an epistemic activity. The point is not simply that such a reality does not exist, but that it cannot be coherently conceived; i.e. the epistemic activity through which reality presents itself as a topic is part of what 'reality' means.

Nevertheless the 'naturalistic' conception of reality is deeply ingrained on our ordinary modes of thinking, and even those among philosophers who profess to reject it often implicitly succumb to its charms. It is a strangely attractive notion; yet it is full of pitfalls and contradictions, and is essentially reductivist and intellectually destructive. There is, as I hope the arguments presented in this book help to show, only one way of avoiding this ontological version of the 'naturalistic fallacy', viz. by adopting a radically *structural approach*. The significance of this will become clearer if we look briefly at some historically familiar types of theories and examine their underlying principles.

Historically, the problem of 'making reality intelligible to ourselves' most frequently has been approached from three different perspectives. One style of approach, which might be called 'ontologico-metaphysical', involves attempts to interpret reality in terms of certain ontological items (substances, centres of forces, events or whatever) and their attributes (properties and relations). This approach for a long time was a main point of contact between philosophy and natural science. Scientists have traditionally sought to provide an explanation of natural phenomena in terms of interactions and specific arrangements of a limited number of types of basic elements (particles and/or forces). Philosophers, for their part, have often been engaged in a similar type of enterprise, but on a much more ambitious scale, looking for what is *necessarily* not just empirically basic.

A second style of approach, which (echoing the spirit though not the letter of Kant's method) might be called 'criticist', involves attempts to pin down the conditions of intelligibility of existence claims. The main argument here is that the mere non-contradictoriness of such claims, though necessary, is not automatically also a sufficient condition of their meaningfulness, and hence does not provide a clue to their intelligibility either. To make an existence claim, or any truth-claim, for that matter, it is argued, is to suppose by implication that what is being claimed could in principle be *known* to someone to be true. The question of meaningfulness thus largely reduces to the question about the sources and the conditions of knowledge – although there are often widely differing conceptions as to what precisely knowledge consist in, and what kinds of knowledge there are.

A third style of approach, which might in a broad sense be called 'sociological', involves a transference of the main emphasis to objectivity, with 'objective knowledge' and 'objective truth' being treated as essentially interchangeable concepts, and the conditions of objectivity being interpreted in terms of the conditions of *inter-subjective validity*. It is taken for granted that there is a plurality of interacting and inter-communicating subjects, sharing a framework of common institutions; in short, the existence is presupposed of a social setting, and such explanations of the conditions of objectivity as are provided are couched in terms of the categories descriptive of the modes and conditions of social life.

These three styles of approach address themselves effectively to three separate questions, which in each case determine the general direction of philosophical investigation: one such question is, What does actually exist? A second is, What makes an existence claim intelligible? and a third is, What makes an existence claim, indeed any claim whatever, objectively valid? Underlying these questions, I wish to argue, there is a pattern of certain structurally inter-related ideas, although their structural links tend to be obscured by the manner in which individual questions are answered in the various philosophical theories. Thus the tendency all too often is to subject these questions to a narrow one-dimensional treatment, ignoring the complexity of the issues they raise. There is no serious attempt critically to monitor the presuppositions implicit in one's own reasoning and in general there is a lack of determination to press the philosophical investigation sufficiently far. In consequence, the choice (or implied choice) of a given question as basic usually leads to others being suitably altered and subordinated to it, giving rise to reductivist and naturalistic distortions and resulting in a severance of all meaningful communicative contact between the respective points of view.

Reality in three dimensions

But this is neither unavoidable nor philosophically acceptable, as can be easily seen by taking a closer look at the above questions. I propose now to comment briefly on their differences and their underlying structural interconnectedness; this will at the same time give me an opportunity of rehearsing some of the main points of the tripartite argument presented in Part One, Chapters 2-10, as well as providing some useful additional points of reference in the light of which this argument might be judged.

Consider the first question first, viz. What does actually exist? Given the way this question is phrased, there are evidently certain limits to what can qualify as an appropriate or significant (though not necessarily correct) reply. Thus it is possible to answer it appropriately with a noun or a noun phrase, or with a chain of nouns or noun phrases, or perhaps with an indefinite pronoun followed by a qualifying adjective or verb, but not, say, with an adjective, or a verb, or an adverb, on their own. Accordingly, it would be formally quite in order, although perhaps defective on other grounds, to answer it by saying simply 'Men', or 'Apples and pears and chairs', or 'Dragons', or 'Water', or even 'Something green'; but it would be formally incorrect and meaningless to answer it by saying 'Excellent', or 'Speaks', or 'Slowly'. The question aims at ontological existents and demands that an answer be given in terms of expressions that purport to refer to such existents.

The underlying assumption, however, is that within the limits of such formal constraints the world presents a cognitively accessible and essentially perspicuous system. There is no section or aspect of reality that is in principle impenetrable to cognition. Furthermore the implication seems to be that the knowledge relating to the forms and conditions of knowing, i.e. the knowledge of *how* we know what we know, should be treated merely as a sub-department of what we know, and not as its central or most important sub-department either.[1]

By contrast, the 'criticist' question focuses attention on the problem of intelligibility. The analytical interest now shifts from ontological existents to the presuppositions underlying the claims that may be meaningfully made about such existents. What is demanded, in effect, is a radical critique of meaning; and the suggestion, usually, is that such a critique can be supplied only via a thoroughgoing critique of knowledge. On the face of it, such a critique as well as irreparably undermining the 'ontologico-metaphysical' approach exposes the essential irrationality of what is our natural bias. For we normally assume that what exists exists irrespective of whether it is actually known, or even can be known, to anyone. That there is such a thing as knowledge or beings endowed with the faculty of knowledge, we normally assume, is a contingent fact no different in its ontological status from the fact that there are stones or trees.

From the 'criticist' standpoint, however, this is not really a rationally sustainable position, and the first question will have to be appropriately altered before it can receive an intelligible reply. The natural alliance betweeen metaphysics and unenlightened common sense, it seems, cannot survive the barrage of well-aimed 'criticist'

---

[1] This view which is normally associated with classical metaphysics has also been espoused by some modern 'analytical' philosophers. Consider the following statement by Russell: 'I reverse the process which has been common in philosophy since Kant. It has been common among philosophers to begin with how we know and proceed afterwards to what we know. I think this a mistake, because knowing how we know is one small department of knowing what we know. I think it a mistake for another reason: it tends to give to knowing a cosmic importance which it by no means deserves, and thus prepares the philosophical student for the belief that mind has some kind of supremacy over non-mental universe, or even that the non-mental universe is nothing but a nightmare dreamt by mind in its unphilosophical moments.' See B. Russell, *My Philosophical Development*, 1959, p. 16.

arguments, and, if we are to make any progress, the 'ontologico-metaphysical' approach will have give way to an approach based exclusively on an analysis of knowledge. However, a closer look reveals this to be a superficial and misleading view.

What a 'criticist' analysis shows is this: that a condition of intelligibly asserting p, i.e. asserting that something actually is the case, is the intelligibility of the idea of someone being in a position to know that p. We cannot coherently maintain that p is the case and at the same time deny that p could ever be known to anyone. But it does not follow from this that p is the case, if it is, solely because it can be known to someone. In asserting that x actually exist, i.e. that it is part of the actual world, we are committing ourselves by implication to accepting that legitimate knowledge claims can in principle be made in respect of certain propositions about x, or perhaps about the world qua 'x-containing'. We cannot coherently both claim that x actually exists and reject such a commitment. Conversely we cannot maintain that certain propositions about x (in a genuine sense of 'aboutness') can be known and at the same time deny that x actually exists. But this does not mean that x actually exists simply because certain knowledge claims in respect of it can be legitimately made. For what does make such knowledge claims legitimate? How are we meaningfully to distinguish between legitimate and illegitimate knowledge claims if we are not allowed to make assumptions about the existence or non-existence of the object, or objects, of knowledge in evaluating such claims?

The point is that the assumption of a possible knowledge that p, though necessary, is not a sufficient condition of the intelligibility of a truth-claim that p. But if so, the 'verificationist' epistemological arguments do not, and cannot, completely invalidate the 'ontologico-metaphysical' question. Nor, of course, does the latter question make the 'criticist' question redundant. The two questions neither exclude each other, nor can they be 'subsumed' under each other. Rather they are structurally interlinked, in that each of them draws attention to the presuppositions of possible replies to the other.[2]

Moreover, not only are they linked with each other; they are also both linked with the third. For to claim that p is the case, or that it can be known it is, is at the same time to make an objectivity claim

---

[2] The metaphysical realism I argued against in Chapter 13 does not recognise this structural interdependence.

on behalf of *p*. It is impossible coherently to make either of the first two claims without implicitly making the latter claim as well. And, as we saw earlier, the condition of objectivity have to do primarily with the conditions that make a given proposition intersubjectively acceptable as a valid truth candidate. For in claiming, or implying, the objective validity of *p*, we are at the same time claiming by implication that *p* conforms to certain public criteria of coherence and appropriateness, and hence can be tested for error by third persons on the basis of such criteria. In other words, to make a significant objectivity claim as part of a truth claim that *p* is at the same time to accept by implication the principle of universal inter-subjective corrigibility of *p* – although it must be emphasied that the universal intersubjective corrigibility of *p* with regard to its coherence and appropriateness does not necessarily imply a universal intersubjective accessibility to evidence that makes *p* true. Objectivity attaches not to the evidence but to the propositions in which the evidence is reported or talked about.

As an illustration, consider the following example. If I accidentally knock over a teacup – part of an expensive set – when sitting down for tea, say, and then announce to my dismayed hostess, 'The handle has come off. I am sorry', I am stating two very different facts. She can verify the first easily enough, but she conceivably may remain dubious about the second, however grief-stricken and contrite I might look, for she may suspect that I am not really enjoying the party and am moreover secretly determined to annoy her. Her suspicion may be unreasonable in the circumstances but it cannot be dismissed as incoherent, for she cannot know how I feel with the same degree of evidence as I can myself. Yet both my statements are true, and in making them I am at the same time making an *objectivity claim* on behalf of both. I am implying – indeed in this case I am quite anxious – that they both should be 'inter-subjectively accepted', although they might not be. The point, briefly, is this: if they are true, as I claim they are, they are true not just for me but universally. But although true universally, they are not not true 'unconditionally'. Above all, they must satisfy certain *objectivity conditions*; i.e. they are subject to certain criteria in terms of which their meaning, their coherence and their formal appropriateness can be inter-subjectively judged, and such criteria are always contextual and presuppose an institutionalised framework of social life.

It follows that the questions underlying the three styles of approach, for all their differences, are not really logically independent of each other, although the impression often conveyed by the answers that they are given in various theories is as if they were. The misconceptions and distortions found in such answers arise mainly from an insufficient self-critical awareness of the presuppositions that underly the principles upon which such answers rest. It is the superficiality and inadequacy of the foundational analysis that encourages rash generalisations and makes the differences between the respective styles of approach appear even greater than they are. It also obscures the fact that what is needed if progress is to be made towards achieving the goal of making reality intelligible to ourselves, is a completely different method; a method designed systematically to expose and expound the structural relationships wherever such relationships might be found, beginning with a systematic analysis of certain basic concepts, such as identity, individuality, error, etc., which are part of the categorial equipment of any theory. Such concepts, I have argued, are without exception structural concepts, whose meaning cannot be adequately elucidated except through an exploration of their structural *interconnectedness*. This process of structural analysis is a continuing one, yielding an ever widening network of structurally inter-related ideas. I cannot claim to have done more than indicate its general direction.

Structures and their features

If this approach is accepted, however, it becomes clear why a description of the world, strictly, cannot be couched in terms of the schema of 'objects and attributes'. The concept of an object qua ontological item is itself a structural concept which can be fully made sense of only in the context of certain other ideas which are all structurally interdependent. The basic concept now has to be the concept of structure, and structures themselves are not ontological objects. A structure may be an object of thought, but it cannot be an ontological existent in its own right. This, as we saw earlier on, is reflected in the way we generally talk about structures. When we refer to structures we usually think of types of configuration or arrangement of certain potentially repeatedly instantiable (physical or non-physical) compounds. Water in place A has exactly the same molecular structure as water in place B. Moreover chemists can reproduce the same kind of stuff in the laboratory by 'mimicking' its molecular composition. Sentences with the same syntactical structure can be reproduced on different occasions by different language users. Structures are repeatable patterns, capable of being exemplified in different places at different times by different things, different quantities of a given kind of stuff, different events. They have no ontological status independently of such things, stuffs or events. Structures qua structures are legitimate topics of discourse: objects of thought, certainly, but not ontological entities in their own right.

But neither can structures be properly categorised as 'attributes' of certain ontological items. When the mathematician speaks of the 'Euclidean space' or the 'four-dimensional space-time continuum', he is not talking about certain special attributes of some independently identifiable entities; he is talking about certain mathematical structures qua structures straight and simple. Similarly the syntactical structure of a sentence cannot be properly described as an 'attribute' of that sentence; to call it an attribute of the sentence would, in a sense, be like saying that being Socrates is an attribute of Socrates. The chemical structure of the air we breath is not just another of its 'attributes', it is what the air we breath chemically is. Of course, this is not to deny that frequently in referring to structures of entities or types of stuff we assume that such entities or types of stuff have been, or can be (contextually) identified in terms other than their internal constitution. But it is the structure of x (whatever x might be) that characterises this x 'intrinsically'. And the structure of x in such a case cannot be described as an attribute of an extra-structural substance x.

An attempt to define structures in terms of attributes of 'substances' almost inevitably turns into an attempt to show that the basic existents are unstructured simples and that all complex objects are merely configurations of such simples; and, consequently, that all attributes, in the final analysis, are reducible to 'extrinsic' attributes of such simples; in effect, to relations that are essentially external to the related terms.

But structure, in the sense in which I have been using the term, is not a mechanistic system of simples and external relations (certainly linguistic structures are not of this sort). References to structures cannot be translated simply into references to their elements and the latter's extrinsic attributes. Structures have their own peculiar identity. They cannot be categorised either as ontological objects or 'attributes' of such objects. Rather they are what might be termed 'complex qualities'; not attributes but species of situations of which objects and attributes are often the most conspicuous features.

But if structure is to be our basic category, if objects and attributes are to be interpreted in terms of structure rather than the other way round, clearly this calls for a radical reconsideration of the apparatus of concepts and ideas in terms of which we normally describe the world around us. It also raises certain fundamental issues concerning the relationship between the structure of language and the structure of the world.

On the face of it, the ontological differentiation between objects and attributes is suggested by the very structure of the subject/predicate statements. We use certain symbols in a referring function as subjects, and certain other symbols in an attributive and descriptive function as predicates. Not all grammatical subjects, of course, designate genuine existents, but this does not undermine the validity of the distinction, and the main problem, it seems, becomes simply one of deciding what the 'genuine' or 'logical' subject is in a given case. Thus 'Jones smokes', 'Smoking is harmful to health' and 'That smoking is harmful to health is supported by sound empirical evidence' all have a similar syntactical structure, with 'Jones', 'Smoking' and 'That smoking is harmful to health' occupying subject positions; but not all of these expressions can be regarded as genuine 'object-terms'; and while there can be no doubt that they are all valid *grammatical* subjects, they cannot (it is argued) all be regarded as representing the 'logical' subjects of the statements concerned.

The search for ontological objects thus usually goes hand in hand with an attempt to identify the 'logical subjects' of statements. But there are strict limits to what can be accomplished by any such project. If the aim is to establish what does exist in a metaphysically basic sense, and, correspondingly, what does qualify as an irreducible object-term (sometimes referred to as the 'logically proper name'), all this is clearly a futile philosophical exercise. The criteria of 'basicness' can be only contextually defined, viz. relative to certain initially adopted premises; which means that there are always likely to be differing theories as to what can or cannot function as a genuine 'logical subject' in a given case, and there will be no possibility of resolving such differences in a definitive fashion from a 'neutral' point of view.

But quite apart from this, our reliance on subject/predicate statements does not necessarily commit us to an ontology of objects and attributes, and the identification of 'logical subjects' with 'genuine object-terms' is a mistake. A grammatical subject may or may not designate an ontological object, but the point is that it does not have to designate such an object in order to qualify as a 'genuine' subject. Structures can function as legitimate subjects of subject/predicate statements, but structures are not ontological objects, nor can statements about structures in any way be reduced to statements about such objects.

What is more, as I have argued, the very idea of an ontological object is subsidiary to the idea of structure and cannot be made sense of except in 'structural terms', i.e. in conjunction with a number of other ideas relating to the epistemic conditions and inter-subjective praxis, with which it is logically interlinked. And if so, any attempt to construct an ontological model of reality in terms of objects and attributes (or even events, 'naturalistically' conceived as happenings 'out there', and their characteristics) is philosophically doomed from the start. What we should be concentrating on, rather, is explicating the structure of actuality assumptions underlying such models, and if we do this, we shall find that meaningful references to ontological objects can be made only in the context of certain epistemic situations which belong to a completely diferent logical type and cannot, in turn, themselves be analysed in terms of certain ontological objects and their attributes.

How should existential propositions be interpreted

So the conclusion, once again, must be that the world is not just a 'totality of objects', or naturalistically conceived events, but is rather an arrangement whereby such objects, events, etc. present themselves as ontological existents to cognitive agents under certain concrete historical conditions. This inevitably has important implications for an interpretation of existential propositions. Existential propositions, I argued earlier on, involve certain claims about the world qua such an arrangement, viz. that such an arrangement has, or does not have, certain specific features. Let us now try to make this a little clearer by reconsidering the traditional slogan that existence is 'not a predicate', or rather not a *first-level* predicate, or predicate of objects.

This slogan goes back to Kant's criticism of the ontological proof. Kant rejected the proof on the grounds that no concept is such that its instantiation is analytically guaranteed. It is futile, he argued, to try to demonstrate the existence of a supreme being by trying to show that the assumption of its non-existence generates a contradiction. No existential judgments can be proved from concepts alone. All existential judgments are 'synthetic', which means that they require an independent proof. Nor does the mere non-contradictoriness of the concept necessarily ensure the *possibility* of the relevant object, or objects. While a concept may ostensibly make perfectly good sense, the question as to whether anything does, or even *can*, fall under it cannot be decided 'unless the objective reality of the synthesis through which the concept is generated has been specifically proved; and such proof ... rests on principles of possible experience, and not on the principle of analysis (the law of contradiction)'.[3]

The faulty reasoning embodied in the 'ontological proof', as Kant sees it, reveals a confusion of logical with ontological necessity, or the 'necessity of judgments' with the 'necessity of things'. However, Kant gives a somewhat unusual interpretation of necessary judgments. Thus that a triangle has three angles, according to him, is not to be regarded as 'absolutely' necessary, but should rather be interpreted in this sense: viz. that under the condition that there is a triangle, or that a triangle is actually given – *unter der Bedingung, dass ein Triangel da is (gegeben ist)* – three angles will necessarily be found in it'. In other words, there are no unconditionally necessary judgments. The necessity of a necessary judgment does not make clear sense except in relation to the posited object, or objects. What is more, it is only in respect of the posited object, or objects, that a negation of a necessary judgement produces a contradiction. If, in a given case, the existence of the object is rejected, then, on Kant's view, the question of contradiction, strictly, does not, indeed cannot, arise.

In a sense, it is a logical separation of concepts from objects implicit in his argument, and his strict insistence that all existential judgments are 'synthetic', that led Kant to adopt this position. His attitude was that no concept is such that it imposes upon us an existential commitment in virtue of its meaning. But in this, I shall

---

[3] *Critique of Pure Reason*, A596/B624; footnote.

argue, he was mistaken.

Reverting now to the slogan 'Existence is not a predicate', it is fairly obvious why the idea that existence might be treated as a genuine predicate of objects was obnoxious to Kant. Having decided that all existential judgments are 'synthetic', he was committed to the view that they can be meaningfully denied. But if 'Socrates' is used as a proper name, then 'Socrates exists' is vacuous, and 'Socrates does not exist' self-defeating. We *posit* Socrates as an existent, do not attribute the 'property' of existence to him. Similarly with 'God exists'. So far from being the conceptual truth that the advocates of the ontological proof claimed it was, this sentence (it seems) is just an example of faulty grammar. If 'God' is used as a proper name, the sentence presupposes what is being overtly asserted, and again the possibility is precluded of a meaningful denial. A more appropriate way of putting things, it seems, would be to say 'Something like God (or: A God-like being) exists', where 'God' is used predicatively, i.e. as a 'concept-word'. This, I suspect, may have been at the back of Kant's mind when, having cited the controversial sentence *Gott ist*, he immediately went on to suggest an alternative paraphrase: *oder*, he added, *es ist ein Gott*. The latter version contains the words *ein Gott*, which clearly stand for the concept. This version is more satisfactory from his point of view in that it seems to show with greater clarity that nothing new (no new 'predicate') is being added to the 'content' of the concept. All that is being said, it seems, is that the concept of God is instantiated, which is a synthetic proposition that conceivably might be false.

The theory of existence as a predicate, not of objects, but of other predicates, or *second*-level predicate, and the parallel development of quantification as a means of expressing, or rendering explicit, existential claims, due to Frege and Russell, clearly owes a great deal to this Kantian analysis. The main message of their theory was the essentially Kant-inspired view that existential propositions are necessarily general propositions involving variables, and that singular existential propositions should be disqualified and banished from meaningful discourse on the grounds that they are ill-formed.

But this surely is much too simple a view of the problem presented by such propositions. To begin with, as was shown earlier on (see Chapter 1), 'exists', and especially 'actually exists', can be attached to names and naming phrases without this resulting in meaningless or uninformative sentences. No one has the slightest difficulty in understanding what is meant by 'Socrates actually existed'. He might not have done. When people ask 'Did King Arthur actually exist?', they expect a yes or no answer, even though a definitive answer may never be possible. The point is that if their curiosity is to be satisfied, it will have to be satisfied with an existential statement, and unless they are relatively simple souls, they will expect to be given a singular existential statement in reply, or some form of words that amounts to the same thing.

It is not difficult to see why. Notice – *pace* Kant – that what is being asked is not 'Did someone like King Arthur actually exist?' but 'Did King Arthur actually exist?' The question is about the posited unique individual King Arthur, not about any old individual who conceivably might have had the kind of properties that King Arthur was supposed to have. In other words, it is not about a type of individual, but about a particular specimen. It won't do, therefore, to answer the question by saying simply that there is a specific property, or a specific series of properties, namely those that people associate with Arthur, and which at one time were in fact instantiated. We shall have to say, at the very least, that they were *uniquely* instantiated.

However, the problem immediately arises how to clarify this 'uniquely'. As I argued earlier (Chapter 3), there is no 'objective' principle of individuation that might enable us to differentiate with absolute certainty as between qualitatively identical individuals inhabiting duplicate universes. Moreover, there can be no property, or set of properties, that is *intrinsically* such as may be said to individuate an object qua ontological existent in an absolute sense. And if so, then there is no way in which a question that aims at a numerically unique individual could be adequately – in a strict logical sense of 'adequately' – answered in terms of properties, and characteristics of properties.

But suppose we form an individual concept, say 'Arthur-ly', and decree that this concept must on no account apply to more than one individual. Surely, it will be said, we can then phrase our reply in terms of the characteristics of that concept. All that we need say is that the concept Arthurly is instantiated, or, if preferred, that someone is uniquely Arthur-ly (or that no one is). There is no need to add anything else.

Does this mean that whoever says that King Arthur actually existed, or that he was a fictional character, is talking about a concept after all? My answer to this is that if Frege's 'functional' theory of concepts is adopted, this cannot be the case. On Frege's view, no concept is such that it necessarily applies to one individual only, although it may do so as a matter fact. If the range of a concept is necessarily confined to a single individual, such a concept is indistinguishable from a proper name (and hence cannot be treated as a concept). Thus 'Moon of the Earth' applies to only one object, but does not do so necessarily. If it represents an 'individual concept' it does so in virtue of the fact that the Earth has only one moon, and would cease to do so if the Earth tomorrow acquired another natural satellite. This, however, cannot apply to 'Arthur-ly'. If there is a possibility of 'Arthur-ly' being applicable to more than one individual, this concept cannot help us reproduce the meaning of the original assertion, for the intention is to say not that as matter of fact the extension of the concept 'Arthur-ly' comprised only one object, but that the unique individual King Arthur actually existed.

It follows that there can be no question of completely eliminating singular existential propositions, or proscribing them as 'ungrammatical'. They require not elimination, but a suitable interpretation that recognises their special status. The central issue, in short, is not whether we should tolerate such propositions, but how we come by the idea of individuality that enables us to ask meaningfully whether a posited, numerically unique individual actually exists; even though such criteria as might be available are inevitably contextual, and in an important sense incomplete. I have discussed this question in Part One, Section B; especially Chapter 7.

Now superficially it might seem that if we adopt this view, we really have no choice but to revert to the 'pre-Kantian' position, and accept that existence can be treated literally as a property of objects, a 'first-level' predicate. This impression, however, is wrong; for, as I emphasised before, in the final analysis it is the world that gets 'talked about' in such propositions. To assert that A actually exists is to say that the world is so arranged that it features A; and to deny the existence of A is to say that the world is so arranged that it does not feature A, or that it would be arranged or structured differently if it did feature A. Similarly to assert the existence of F-like things is merely to say that the world is F-like in at least one instance; and to deny their existence is to say that the world would be arranged differently if it did contain F-like instances. In short, we are essentially talking about *the world*, and the world itself is not an object, but (if I may be allowed for once to borrow the term which has come to play such a central role in modern physics, with all due reservations regarding its use in a purely 'naturalistic' context) a 'field', of which objects are one of the constituent features. An object exists as an object only as part of a *structured whole*.

Reality and fiction

The interpretation of existential claims that I have just outlined provides at the same time a clue for an explication of all truth claims. The thesis that I wish to put forward, allowing for the ambiguities of language, might be expressed thus: an assertion that *p* has the basic form 'The world is in a *p*-state', or, phrased more conveniently perhaps, 'The world is S-ly', with 'S-ly' representing the relevant adverb. In other words, the ultimate subject of all assertions (provided, of course, care is taken not to confuse 'subject' with 'substance') is the world as a whole.

The world is a field, a complex epistemic-ontological event, and moreover an event whose occurrence is part of its concept. This echoes, in a sense, the 'ontological proof', and in view of the trenchant criticism that this 'proof' has been subjected to by Kant and others, it seems at first sight an odd, even absurd, claim to make. For why should we have to accept that anything whatever occurs 'necessarily'? Surely it is not essential for a concept to have exemplifying instances in order that it might be intelligible. We know very well what dragons are, even though there are no dragons. It is not a condition of meaningfulness of a concept that it should be non-empty.

Yet it is by no means universally the case that concepts do not demand the existence of their exemplifying instances. The concept of the ego would hardly be intelligible if there were no selves. The concept of truth demands that something at least be true. We could not coherently both claim that we understand what truth is and that no truth claim is even fulfilled. It is not difficult to find many other similar examples. In all such cases the requirement that there should be exemplifying instances is part of the meaning of the concept.

The concept of the world has the additional characteristic that it is uniquely instantiated, and necessarily so. Moreover to understand what 'world' means is at the same time to grasp that such an understanding can be had only from 'within' the world. It is to understand, in other words, why the world cannot be treated as an ontological item 'out there', and hence why questions that may be validly asked in relation to objects are here inappropriate and meaningless. All this has considerable implications. Thus it not only disposes of the 'universal doubt' as a legitimate philosophical device for gaining a secure foothold for a 'rational reconstruction' of the world; it also exposes the meaninglessness of asking, Why is there a world at all? It has frequently been claimed by philosophers that the question 'Why is there something rather than nothing?' is the most central philosophical question and represents the foundation and *raison d'être* of all metaphysics. But it is one of the consequences of the structural approach that I have been outlining that this question *cannot be meaningfully asked*. We can ask 'Why are there trees rather than something else?' but not 'Why does anything exist at all?' or 'Why the world and not nothingness?' The existence of the world follows from its concept and the idea of 'nothingness' is strictly speaking *unintelligible*.

This, inevitably, demands a reconsideration of the whole concept of fiction. We began our analysis of the concept of reality with a discussion of the distinction between fact and fiction. Such understanding as we have of the concept of reality, it seems, is inseparable, and flows directly from our understanding of this distinction. Yet unless we wish to be forced into an intolerable metaphysical impasse, it seems equally sensible to ask, How must the world be structured for such a distinction to be significant? What are the conditions that make an understanding of this distinction possible? We use 'actually exists' contrastingly with 'fictional'; but an investigation of the conditions of intelligibility of these two predicates reveals a deeper sense of reality which is not contrastingly tied to the concept of fiction. More fundamental than the contrast between the predicates is the concept of reality as a context within which such a contrast can be understood. Reality is literally all-embracing, and this is brought out clearly by a structural analysis of the concept.

Such a structural analysis provides all the resources needed for a clarification of true negative propositions, including negative existentials. If the world is not in the state S-ly, this is for the simple reason that it would be arranged differently if it was S-ly. S-ly (unless it is contradictory) represents in this case an unrealised possibility, and the idea of 'unrealised possibilities' is a necessary built-in feature of a system capable of 'talking about itself', such as the one of which we are part.

In short, negative propositions, including negative existentials, must be seen in a wider context of structural conditions that together define what I have called 'the world'. They are part of the self-monitoring and self-correcting mechanism that helps to keep the structural unity of the 'field' in being. It follows that if fiction can be 'talked about', it can be talked about only as a feature of the real.

It is the real that we aim at and try to understand. And aiming at the real means at the same time aiming at the truth. Truth, I have argued, is the fulfilment of the demands that form the structure of a truth-claim. These demands reflect the structure of reality. A truth-claim aims at reality; it aims at revealing how things are, and sometimes it miscarries. But the possibility of a failure does not affect the structure of its demands, and this structure never changes.

Index

293